Enjoying the Closeness of God

Enjoying the Closeness of God

Know the Pleasure of Being His Friend

Roger C. Palms

World Wide Publications
A ministry of the Billy Graham Evangelistic Association
1303 Hennepin Ave., Minneapolis, Minnesota 55403

Enjoying the Closeness of God

© 1989 by Roger C. Palms

Chapters 1, 2, 3, 4, 10, 11, 12, 15, 16, 17, 18, and 23 originally published as *The Pleasure of His Company* (Wheaton, Illinois: Tyndale House Publishers, 1982), © 1982 Roger C. Palms.

Chapters 5, 6, 7, 8, 9, 13, 14, 19, 20, 21, 22, and 24 originally published as *Living Under the Smile of God* (Wheaton, Illinois: Tyndale House Publishers, 1984) © 1984 Roger C. Palms.

World Wide Publications is the publishing ministry of the Billy Graham Evangelistic Association.

Unless otherwise indicated, Scripture quotations are taken from The Holy Bible, New International Version. Copyright © 1973, 1978, 1984 International Bible Society. Used by permission of Zondervan Bible Publishers.

Scripture quotations marked KJV are taken from the Authorized King James Version of the Bible.

Scripture quotations marked TLB are taken from The Living Bible, © 1971 Tyndale House Publishers. Used by permission.

Scripture quotations marked NASB are taken by permission from the New American Standard Bible, © 1960, 1962, 1963, 1968, 1971, 1972, 1973, 1975, 1977, The Lockman Foundation, La Habra, California.

Library of Congress Catalog Card Number: 89–050481

ISBN: 0–89066–171–5

Printed in the United States of America

Contents

■ ■ ■

Preface

Why struggle day in, day out, missing a friendship that was meant to be so special? If you have been grasping for meaning in your life and wondering why you haven't found what you really want—*then please stop what you are doing!* It is time to turn around.

Commitment, discipline, understanding, holiness, and trust are the ingredients of a rewarding life based on the deepest of all relationships—your friendship with God. God wants you to have that. The only question is, do you want it too!

Come, discover what it means to enjoy the closeness of God. Know the pleasure of being his friend.

1

Sand Castles Don't Last

■ ■ ■

One afternoon in Paris I tried to absorb with my senses the Cathedral of Notre Dame, that beautiful Gothic structure built in the Middle Ages. There was so much to enjoy aesthetically: the altar appointments, the smell of candles, the feel of old polished wood, the great rose windows, the awesome grandeur of the organ sounding through that massive building. . . . It could have been a memorable and serene experience.

It turned out to be memorable, but it wasn't serene. In front of me, darting quickly here and there with cameras rapidly clicking, were dozens of tourists scurrying through the cathedral. They had only a few minutes before returning to their waiting tour buses for a fast drive to some other historic spot where they would click their cameras some more. Pushing past other people, they raced first to one side, then to the other, frantically taking pictures. Then they were gone, only to be replaced by another busload of tourists doing the same thing.

I had made no other plans for that afternoon. Meditation in that historic place, quiet prayer, and the enjoyment of the beauty were what I had wanted. But I couldn't shut out the confusion around me.

Finally I left. On the way out I walked behind an American couple. The man had a checklist in his hand. As they stepped into the sunlight, the man asked his wife, "Was that the Cathedral of Notre Dame?" She answered that it was. With that confirmation, he took out his pencil, ticked off that item on his tour list, and they hurried away. They will probably tell their friends that they have seen Notre Dame; perhaps they'll show slides and rave about how much they enjoyed their visit. Unhappily, they didn't really see it at all.

People seem desperate to experience, yet they really don't experience anything. They go through the act of looking but rarely know the joy of seeing.

It is as if we are on an ocean beach called Earth. We are frantic. We build castles—or at least we think we do. But what we are really doing is just throwing up sand piles as fast as we can before the next big wave comes in. And that wave is coming. We can't run from it; there's no escaping it. We will stay on the beach building our castles higher, bigger, more elaborate. We won't enjoy them. There will be no time for that. The wave is coming.

There have been other waves; tides have risen and ebbed. This is our time. Our little shovels flash in the sun as we dig in the midst of other frenzied diggers, each trying to heap more sand before the end. Never mind the next person's castle; never mind the next person at all. Just build. Dig, dig, dig. Keep an eye on the wave . . . a few more seconds. It's coming—grab one more bit of sand.

Look at those fistfuls of sand. What is that sand that runs through fingers, that won't pack down, won't hold? *Things,* maybe; that's always the start of the grabbing. *Pleasure,* usually; that's the drive. Grabbing things and pleasures, tangible and sensual, is our attempt to get more of what has always given us security. But they don't any longer.

We Want Something and We Want It Now

We know that our old systems are in crisis, and no one seems to have new or better answers. Each of us thinks, "I've got to look out for me and mine. And the only way I know is the familiar way. I've got to go for what has always worked. I'll reach for more of what I know."

The social confusion, the sex exploitation, the deterioration of family and home, and the end of cultural stability are all exploding around us. We do all we know to do. Afraid to be left behind, we grasp for even more. And the deterioration quickens.

Logic would tell us that if the end is coming, there is no need to grab for things and pleasures, because they're temporary. But we aren't logical. What we face is a deeper fear, a fear based on emptiness. And that hideous emptiness causes us to clutch to ourselves what has always given security and pleasure before.

So we are desperate and don't even know what we are desperate for. We are in a frightening world and do not understand it. We have lost our grip on society, on culture, on family, on stable value systems, and with our fingernails torn, our fingertips bleeding, we feel it all slipping from our grasp. We want. We don't know what it is that we want, but we want something and we want it now. It is a hurting pressure, a feeling that, whatever that something is that we want, it is out of our grasp and we must grab whatever else is close—anything.

What is happening to us? We have done more than just spawn a generation caught in the mindset of self. We have created a human religion that is insatiable in its thirst. We are addicts overdosing on ourselves even though we know there isn't a high in it anymore. Nothing satisfies. So we try harder, push farther, and grasp for still more, for whatever might give some hope that our emptiness will be filled.

Grabbing for Things That Break

People have always built sand castles, and those castles have always crumbled. There have always been those who grabbed for things that break. But now it is like the beginning of the end, like the first moments of a stock market crash, and the scramble is on. And even as the social commentators write about the cultural phenomena of these times, as psychologists give their explanations and theologians theirs, the frustration of wanting and not finding permeates their own thinking so much that it is difficult for any of them to be objective in their analysis: these interpreters of us are on the beach too, grasping their own handfuls of sand.

At first, newspaper advertisements called it "the good life." We were told "to grab for," "you deserve," "like it, charge it." And in our "there-is-no-tomorrow" mentality, that is what we did. The results are easily traced now: over-consumption, depletion of natural resources, physical stress, emotional breakdown, family and marital discord, crime. And sadly, we pretended that we were happy—or soon would be. We pretended that we controlled our madness. We didn't; we don't.

In a test given by a popular magazine on people's "happiness quotient," it was shown that people have crossed the line from trying to make themselves happy to just plain racing to grab for anything that they don't now have. A few years ago, *The New York Times* counted three thousand diet books, two thousand self-improvement books, and at least one thousand sex manuals on the market. Bookstore owners said that people were looking for answers.[1] And when religious leaders started promoting self-help and self-transformation books, we knew that even Christians had crossed a line. Self-help was charted by publishers, simplified by writers, and swallowed up by readers. As Christians, we learned how we could lose weight, enjoy sex, be assertive, or negotiate so that anyone could be a winner. God in his wonder, majesty, and strength was to be *utilized*: to love him was self-loving as we "sensitized" ourselves to his wonder, majesty, and strength. We tried to have God packaged, wrapped, marketed, and consumed.

Boys Who Chase Butterflies

Pathetic? Yes, it is. And with the increase in what were sometimes little more than Christian road shows, the availability of the media to them, and the willingness of churches to be booking agents for any new act that came to town, more and more people started asking for the unusual and exciting rather than the Answer. We found people-exploiters to tell us that life should be a miracle every minute with a continuous feeling of ecstasy and joined the rest of the desperate people building their sand castles on the beach.

Like a dog chasing its own tail, we chased after what was always eluding us. What we wanted was always just out of reach, never quite within our grasp, yet always in sight—the back end of something going away which we thought we must catch before it disappeared.

John Bunyan, the seventeenth-century tinker-turned-preacher, described people like us as boys who chase butterflies:

Behold how eager our little boy
Is for this butterfly, as if all joy,
All profits, honors, and lasting pleasures,
Were wrapt up in her—or the richest treasures
Found in her—
When her all is lighter than a feather. . . .

His running through the nettles, thorns and briars
To gratify his boyish fond desires;
His tumbling over molehills to attain
His end, namely his butterfly to gain,
Plainly shows what hazards some men run
To get what will be lost as soon as won.
Men seem, in choice, than children far more wise
Because they run not after butterflies,
When yet, alas, for what are empty toys
They follow them, and act as beardless boys. 2

It is a frantic chase when we run after butterflies as little boys do. We go first here, then there; we can't rest as long as we see anything that glitters in the sun. We dart along our zigzag courses, trying to catch that elusive pretty thing. But our chasing only tires us.

To one degree or another, the "hurry-up-and-grab, then-run-for-more" people are everywhere, including in the church. Chasing butterflies has become so commonplace that some have even stamped it "approved" by Jesus. He never did approve it. By the measure of Scripture, he never will.

We Want Ours Too!

Originally, the race was run toward happiness. Now the race goes on only for the sake of the race. We should have known that it would be that way because the obvious mark of truly happy people is that they need nothing more, and so many of us act as if we need more of everything. The happy life is a pleasant life, yet our quest for happiness is filled with neuroses.

There are no age limits to this sickness. We have taught our "religion" well. Teenagers scream at their parents, "You've used yours; you've taken the resources. We want ours too before it's all gone." In a newspaper interview a seventeen-year-old boy admitted: "I worry a lot. I'm running at a ninety-mile-an-hour pace. I feel like I've lived nineteen or twenty more years because of that feeling of 'I've got to get to work now.'" An eighteen-year-old high-school boy said, "I want to be comfortable. I just want to be happy and have money to do the things I want to do." And several in a group said, "Give us comfort, and give us the money to buy it with."[3]

One seventeen-year-old said that failure is not having a job that gets you enough money. A high school English teacher commented that in eighteen years of teaching she has never seen students who are so materialistic. Then she added: "The whole nation is going that way."[4] Although he wrote more than half a century ago, A. H. McNeile seems to be talking about us when he speaks of people whose lives are . . .

> like the thinnest of rafts, floating upon an ocean of infinite mystery; and they hate to be asked to look over the edge. They are very busy decking out their raft with everything which can make it feel like a permanent home. . . . They never realize that they are on a raft and not a rock, until one day an illness or an accident or a war flicks them off into the ocean, where they have never learnt to swim.[5]

A Me-Centered Sighing

Even the traditional obedience to societal structure or family, which might have taught us a larger view of ourselves, has disappeared. Any inner hint that true meaning might be found outside ourselves is dismissed or denied. There is no frame of reference or justification for our being, other than to take and use more. We have successfully eliminated all controls; we have shed ourselves of all responsibilities.

This is human religion. Even those who never quote the creed have come to live by it. For it isn't only the secular person who is caught; many who wear the label "Christian" have been snared too. Many who speak of being made alive by God really have no idea how satisfying that life in God can be. They're too busy looking elsewhere to find out.

These professing Christians have tried, along with everyone else, to make some sense of their existence. They have looked for the action, gotten involved, given themselves to causes, traveled inward, entered analysis, meditated, tried health foods—anything that might give them what everyone else seems to be chasing. They have gone sermon-tasting and liturgy-hunting, seeking answers from pulpits and prayer groups like so many door-bangers on a pub crawl. They have joined Christian political groups, partied at Christian night spots, and hastened to seminars for the latest spiritual word from whoever is currently big on the Christian circuit. But all they have discovered is that we can't get what we want that way.

We are, as the rest of humanity is discovering, far more complex than we thought. We are more than a soul to be "sensitized," more than an ego to be stroked, more than a mind to be taught. We are wonderfully put together into a self, and with all of our searching we have not been able to make sense of it all. We still cry out for something.

Our needs become a search and our search becomes a further need, but even that need is undefined and unmet. And in our exhaustive quest, there is no exposure to the true and living God. For just as hardened secularists can't point to God, many experts on religion can't either. They point only to a concept. For God is beyond, outside and separate from us, hidden by the wants we feel within. We are turned inward, and he is not there. We don't know that Omnipotent Other. We have, at best, only a poor sampling of him, filtered through a me-centered sighing that says, "This is what God means to *me*."

We have made Jesus to be *our* Jesus, and we are so accustomed to responding to "our" Jesus that we have forgotten how to respond to the Son of the living God.

His teachings have been taken with the pragmatic view of "helping me," not followed because we must obey and can do nothing less. His words have been diluted by so many diverse therapies that all we know to respond to is a "feel-good" deity, a piece of religious plastic which we label "God."

To reject God out of hand is one thing, but to acknowledge him and then live as if he is neither Lord nor God is a horrible existence. Then all we have left is sand.

Life Can Still Be Found

God is ready to rescue us from ourselves. But what if that out-stretched hand clutching at the sleeve is brushed aside with the scream, "Get your hands off me"? God's Word urges, "Taste and see that the Lord is good" (Psalm 34:8). But do we want to see?

Yet because we can still think, we can still be healed. Life—real life with freedom—can still be found. We can still have friendship with God. We can still have the full life. But it must be a committed and disciplined life on God's terms.

God expects us to be disciplined. It is not the unnatural but rather the natural thing to be. We were created to be disciplined, put on this earth by God at this time and in this place not for personal gain or personal pleasure but for his purpose.

The "I've-only-got-one-try-so-I-will-go-for-it" syndrome, like any other orgy, is a suction into meaninglessness, and the vacuum from it draws in any who come near—even many who once acknowledged the words of Jesus, "You cannot serve both God and Money" (Matthew 6:24).

But we still have ears to hear, if we will. For into this scene comes Jesus saying:

A man's life does not consist in the abundance of his possessions (Luke 12:15).

Do not worry about your life, what you will eat; or about your body, what you will wear. Life is more than food, and the body than clothes (Luke 12:22-23).

Do not set your heart on what you will eat or drink; do not worry about it (Luke 12:29).

But seek his kingdom, and these things will be given to you as well (Luke 12:31).

Sell your possessions and give to the poor. Provide purses for yourselves that will not wear out, a treasure in heaven that will not be exhausted, where no thief comes near and no moth destroys (Luke 12:33).

God is here in our world now. He has been all the time. He calls to scrambling, grasping people like us through the words of

Jesus Christ. He says, "Come unto me."
It is time for us to do what he asks.

2

Winning

■ ■ ■

Life is so ordinary.

And because it is, awakening to a daily practice of the disciplines of God is both exciting and liberating. For any who will seek it, there is a new freedom from those daily urgings that have become tyrants. Discipline is a freedom that comes not from taking or exploiting, but from *not* taking and *not* exploiting. In that freedom we become winners—each day, every day.

C. S. Lewis said:

> A man who gives in to temptation after five minutes simply does not know what it would have been like an hour later. That is why bad people, in one sense, know very little about badness. They have lived a sheltered life by always giving in. We never find out the strength of the evil impulse inside us until we try to fight it.[1]

Jesus was disciplined. He said, "For I have come down from heaven not to do my will but to do the will of him who sent me" (John 6:38).

Read the life of Christ in the New Testament, and as you do, keep asking one question over and over: "Was Jesus Christ happy?" What you discover will put your own happiness into focus. This happiness isn't what most of us think it is, nor is it what most of us have been striving for. It is deeper than that. With that realization and the determination to be like Jesus, we can change; we can take the road away from losing; we can find the winning way. It is God's way.

It starts with self-control. But our self-control is not, as many think, a control "of myself, by myself." Rather it is a matter of taking seriously what we know about ourselves, gathering up all that is "self" and yielding it to the rule of Christ. In this way we open up to the love and control of God. It is like a flower at dawn, touched by the warmth of the sun, opening to those sun rays and giving to the world its beauty, its perfume—being for all to see what it was meant to be. That is liberation; that is fulfillment at its highest. It is opposite to the way of the flesh, opposite to our own self-seeking, and opposite to failure.

In his book, *In the Footprints of the Lamb*, G. Steinberger wrote:

> Self-seeking will attempt only that which seems great, and will expect results only from persons of consequence. Its motto is: "I feel that I am sufficient in myself. Everything must exist for me, otherwise it has no value." But when love awakens in us, self-seeking dies; then the law of the flesh no longer rules, but the law of the spirit.[2]

The disciplined life is a happy life. It is a controlled life. That is hard for many to understand, even those who say, "I am a Christian." For Christians are often the least disciplined, taking for their egos and their immediate needs the very things that stand in the way of enjoying and obeying God. Visit some of the Christian conferences or parachurch programs where Christians gather. Attend a meeting where a well-known Christian is the guest. The Christian jet set—dressed alike, talking alike, smiling alike, looking over the shoulders of the people with whom they are speaking in order to see who else has come into the room—all show how much they suffer from inferiority feelings which no child of God should harbor. Name dropping, each tries to impress the other; each takes what he can from a situation because he has nothing inside, nothing from God. Yet these same people tag what they do with the name of God because they "want to give him all the glory," even while they grab for what they hope will give them more personal, social, or even financial gain. They are boxed in, owned by the need for prestige, because they haven't learned how to let God be their all in all.

One of the Few Frontiers Never Fully Conquered

For too long most of us have thought that self-control was some form of punishment—a kind of masochism. That's not true. To indulge oneself not only destroys the spirit and body of a person, it destroys the sense of adventure and accomplishment that helps a person expand and grow. Self-control is probably one of the few frontiers that has never been fully conquered. For each of us it can become a new, exciting challenge.

I will never know what I can be with God until I try to live with him and for him. I need to know what I can resist, what I can do without, and what I can overcome. To work at this is as much a challenge as climbing Mount Everest or walking on the moon.

There is a real person inside each of us. That person is more than a collection of genes, more than a jumble of experiences to be catalogued, more than a bottle of feelings to be uncorked and poured out. Each one of us is too wonderfully made to be reduced to such insignificance. We are much more than that.

God has made us with a profound complexity; we are mirrors of his image. We don't have to be victims of every whim that comes along. Discipline brings happiness. Discipline brings true fulfillment.

Self-controlled living says, "I will obey; I will follow not man-made attractions but God as he reveals himself in Jesus Christ, the Living Word, and in the Bible, the written Word." That is how happiness comes and that is how happiness stays. That kind of disciplined obedience holds its own rewards.

Yet even this can be twisted. It is shameful, but it happens. With our "instant" Christian mentality, we think that even discipline can be made easy and simple and practical. We search for some gimmick to make obedience fun, some formula we can memorize to help us to be disciplined, some austere, self-denying lifestyle we can put on like a coat. God won't be fooled by instant discipleship techniques or gimmicks. He knows that there can be just as much ego-centeredness in being "spiritual," just as much pride in austerity, and just as much dishonoring of God in what we do not do as there is in what we do. We can boast in our silence and seek one-upmanship over others in our pride as much as pagans can.

The instant-oriented, sensual Christian wants to "taste and see that the Lord is good" *now*, have all of his proffered blessings *now*. He wants the windows of heaven open—today. He wants what God gives more than he wants God.

Remember the often-quoted tithing story about the shovels? It is used to encourage people to give a tenth of their income to the Lord's work. Basically it is a proposition: "You shovel into God's bin, God will shovel into your bin, and God has the larger shovel." In other words, tithing is a sure-fire money-maker. You can't lose. "Give to God and he will give more back to you." But that's not true. More may not come back, nor does it have to come back. God is not in the negotiating business. He can and often will give "a good measure, pressed down, shaken together and running over" (Luke 6:38). But he doesn't have to. It seems to be his loving nature to want to do so, but he does it because of who he is. No one bribes God to put into practice his being God.

The reality is this: If we take on the tithing discipline, we may have to do without. We may not be able to make payments on a new automobile or buy a boat. If we send gifts to missionaries, we may not also have money for entertainment. Tithing is a priorities proposition. It is based on obedience, not on wheeling and dealing with God. If God gives back to us more than we give, then that's his business. It is then his gift, an undeserved one, given for reasons that only he knows.

But It Costs

Any discipline is to be practiced for him simply because he asks us to do it. We agree to it because we don't want to disobey God. We can make no demands of God in return for doing what we are expected to do.

. The good Samaritan did not practice a "service–on–my–terms–if–it–suits–me–and–there–is–benefit–in–it–for–me" religion. The rules by which he lived were clear. He would help the sufferer. It cost him to do it, too—not only his time, but he probably got blood on his good suit. He left a deposit for the man's convalescence, then promised to pay the rest of the bill later. At no time did he ask for a receipt for income tax purposes, or for a *quid pro quo* from the beaten man.

Faithfulness and obedience are based on doing what we must do because we are committed to the One who asks us to do it. That's what we were created for.

We are entitled to true freedom, but entitled because he wants it for us. "It is for freedom that Christ has set us free. Stand firm, then, and do not let yourselves be burdened again by a yoke of slavery" (Galatians 5:1). We are free! But we are free only in Christ. That's the paradox—there is liberty in discipline. We don't have to stay in our prisons of profligacy that we once misread as liberation. He wants us to be free *in his control*. That's real freedom, and we all can have it!

But it costs. We are so easily swept away in spite of our good intentions and resolves. Then we find ourselves down again, asking, "Will it always be like this? Can I never win against the world's control?" People who could be victorious find themselves little more than carbon copies of those who have never even tried to win. Instead of looking toward God, they look around, compare themselves to others, imitate, and end up feeling miserable.

That comparing and wanting is destructive. We should have known all along it would be, because Scripture shows that what is happening around us and to us is not new; it has happened to others.

The Bible gives examples of people who looked around and made the wrong comparisons. And it shows what happened when they did. Cain compared himself with Abel—and killed him (Genesis 4:3-8). Esau compared himself with Jacob, caring nothing about what he had in his birthright—and ended up losing his inheritance (Genesis 25:29-34). Saul compared himself with David— and developed serious mental problems (1 Samuel 18:6-11).

We look at the athletes, the heroes, the superstars, the ones who have it all together or at least pretend that they have, and we try to copy them even though they are probably doing the same thing— copying someone else. We become envious, or, worse, jealous and morose. Finally we become angry with God. We deny how able he is to bless and fulfill and satisfy. And we lose. Because even if we succeed in getting all we want, become the person we envy in others, and say, "I've made it," we haven't made it at all.

Some three hundred years ago, Richard Baxter described this mistake we keep making:

> When we should study God, we study ourselves; when we should mind God, we mind ourselves; when we should love God, we love our carnal selves; when we should trust God, we trust ourselves; when we should honour God, we honour ourselves; and when we should ascribe to God, and admire him, we ascribe

to and admire ourselves: and instead of God we would have all men's eyes and dependence on us, and all men's thanks returned to us, and would gladly be the only men on earth extolled and admired by all. And thus naturally we are our own idols.[3]

Satan loves to have it that way. He works on any one of us—he did it with Jesus. When he began tempting Jesus on the mountain, there was no immediate intervention from the Father. Jesus had to struggle alone for forty days. Week in and week out he waited to be delivered. Deliverance didn't come. He could have taken the easy way, providing his own bread, rationalizing Satan's offer. He could have done that. He knew that it was possible. We do too. But to give in is failure. Jesus did not give in. He trusted the Father. He was obedient. Here, in the Son of God, our Savior, is our only true model.

Another Way, Another Choice

Unfortunately, the pattern we usually see around us is not the pattern of obedience but the pattern of independence and failure. Richard Lovelace states:

Much of the Christian community today is deeply penetrated by worldly patterns of thinking, motivation and behavior, and thus its spiritual life is deadened and its witness rendered ineffectual. Individuals, churches, schools and ministries must become sensitive to the areas of unholy conformity to the world in their behavior if the Spirit of holiness is really to possess them in fullness. But this is an awesome task, requiring an experience of the revelation of God's holiness and the depth of human sin like that which gripped Isaiah, who in his vision of God saw clearly not only his own sin but also the unclean lips of the people among whom he lived. Only this vision will motivate the world—and the church—to appropriate all the dimensions of life available in the fullness of Jesus Christ.[4]

If we miss this appropriation of the fullness of Christ now, we could miss it again and again. We may never break out.

The Spirit of freedom, discipline, obedience, and holiness can possess us if our measure of what is good and desirable is God, instead of what is touted by those who give no heed to his standards. There is an evil around us; it infects society and we are not to be a part of it. To compromise, to bring in the "me" perspective, is idolatry and it destroys.

G. Steinberger said:

> The self-seeking soul is a robber, for he steals from God that which belongs to Him, and takes for himself that which belongs to others. Not only does self-seeking carry on its devilish work out in the world, but also in the gatherings of religious people, in the house of the righteous, even in the hearts of those who desire to follow the unselfish Jesus. It is self-seeking when one desires to appear more pious than others, to pray more beautifully than others, when one always wants to have the advantage for oneself. But the Scriptures say: "Cursed be the deceiver" (Malachi 1:14).[5]

To the world in its darkness there is no choice, no other way to exist. But we who are in Christ do have another way, another choice. We can win. We must win. For to drift on into darkness brings us to failure before our God, and before others who would like to follow him and need help in order to do it. We must not fail those who are still in darkness and want a light by which they too can find their way out. If we are going to be any kind of light to a rebellious, disobedient, and undisciplined world, it will be only as we discipline ourselves under God's commands and allow him through us to demonstrate to the world that true experience of happiness that comes from obedience.

But if we slide farther and farther into the religion of the self, if we create a "friend in Jesus" who on *our terms* is going to fulfill whatever we ask, never mind the plan, the will, the purpose, the design, or even the privilege of Almighty God, then we have denied God. Like the sixteenth-century church people who trotted after John Tetzel when he declared, "As soon as the coin in the coffer rings, the soul from purgatory springs," we trot after our made-up religion. It took the Reformation to turn people to what God wanted. That kind of reformation is due again, for so many still prefer to follow their Tetzels.

Richard Baxter asks:

> If you tell others of the admirable joys of heaven, and yourselves do nothing but drudge for the world, and are as much taken up in striving to be rich, or as quarrelsome with your neighbours in a case of commodity, as any others, who will then believe you, or who will be persuaded by you to seek the everlasting riches?[6]

Yes, who will believe?

A Waking-up

So many who have taken his name have fallen away. They have come to the Light and have claimed the life-changing gifts of God's grace and peace, and then have surrendered them again, diving into the waters of sin, thinking that only in those waters will fulfillment come. Oh, how we cheapen his grace!

And many who claim the name but have not been living for him know that that is true. Winning will start when we come back to where we can hear his voice and determine to obey what he says.

It is like a waking-up, a coming back to life. It is that point where we say, "Enough." It is where we decide that we will follow Christ only and that we will not be bound by any other philosophy or agency or force. It is a renewing of our mind, a decision that we must be free and we will be free. We will move in the direction of the One who owns us, the Lord Jesus Christ. It is a vow we make, a promise that we will accept, whatever sacrifice is necessary in order to be free. For each one of us, it is a decision: "I must have him. I will have him."

The Christian disciple will obey. There is no law or structure to demand it; the disciples' obedience is built on a love that calls them to hear and to do what the Master asks.

Have you told God yet that you love him? Have you told him yet that you are willing to obey him?

What are you waiting for?

As we come closer to that predicted day when "people will be lovers of themselves" (2 Timothy 3:2), each of us has to decide: Even if I am the only one, I will live a life of faithfulness and obedience.

Many will be coming to this late in life. We cannot undo our undisciplined years. We cannot give back what we have already taken, nor rebuild what our rebellion has destroyed. We cannot fully heal what we have hurt. But we can begin again now, and God wants us to. He makes possible the new beginning. He is the giver of our desire for obedience and the rewarder of our attempts at the disciplined life. Obedience to discipline is built on trust, and he does bless those who trust him. Scripture states, "Blessed is the man who makes the Lord his trust" (Psalm 40:4).

When that simple winning choice is made, the forward steps begin. At last each of us can say, "I don't have to be a victim any more. Before God I can live out a holy, obedient, and disciplined life. I can start over. I *will* start over."

3

Starting Over

■ ■ ■

Haven't you had enough?

There is a time for coming back to discipline, self-control, and a life lived on God's terms. Now is that time. We have been through it all—the grasping, the looking, the searching. We have lived as people who try to serve God and mammon, and we know now that it cannot be done. Friendship with God and friendship with that which is not of God just cannot be.

It is time to turn away from the mix of God's Word plus my opinions, God's orders plus my wants, God's love plus my lusts, and turn back to a true commitment. For many, the heresy of these mixtures isn't even obvious. It will become obvious only when the concern to be obedient and the love for the Word become consuming passions. A. W. Tozer urged:

> Come near to the holy men and women of the past and you will soon feel the heat of their desire after God. They mourned for Him, they prayed and wrestled and sought for Him day and night, in season and out, and when they had found Him the finding was all the sweeter for the long seeking. Moses used the fact that he knew God as an argument for knowing Him better. "Now, therefore, I pray thee, if I have found grace in thy sight, show me now thy way, that I may know thee, that I may find grace in thy sight"; and from there he rose to make the daring request, "I beseech thee, show me thy glory." God was frankly pleased by this display of ardor, and the next day called Moses onto the mount, and there in solemn procession made all His glory pass before him.

David's life was a torrent of spiritual desire, and his psalms ring with the cry of the seeker and the glad shout of the finder. Paul confessed the mainspring of his life to be his burning desire after Christ. "That I may know him," was the goal of his heart, and to this he sacrificed everything. "Yea doubtless, and I count all things but loss for the excellency of the knowledge of Christ Jesus my Lord: for whom I have suffered the loss of all things, and do count them but refuse, that I may win Christ."[1]

Perhaps most of the people you know will not turn back; most may keep right on in the same old way. But that shouldn't matter to you. You can't wait to see what the trend will be. You know that you've followed the world long enough. You know the emptiness of trying to find your happiness in ways other than those God offers. You know from experience that those other ways don't work.

Most of us have watched people who have gone to extremes in ways that are not God's ways. We have seen the result of absorbing values that are loose, weak, undisciplined, and unbiblical. Now we can see, even apart from all the scriptural warnings that should have helped us to see sooner, where uncontrolled living goes. We know the misery. We have seen it; many of us have felt it. Now we come to the point where we say, "No more!" With Joshua we say, "Choose . . . this day whom you will serve," and then we stand, even if we are the only ones to do so, and declare, "As for me and my household, we will serve the Lord" (Joshua 24:15).

This is not an easy commitment to make. For some it won't even come from great conviction. It will come from the pain of having gone the other route, the mammon route, and finding nothing there. It will come because at last we will have looked at ourselves and said, "Oh, God, why does so much seem so wrong? What is happening?" And we will know that we have come to the turning point.

We turn back not because God has punished us. He hasn't; he has simply allowed us to dig our own holes and fall into them. As we have fallen, he has allowed it. When we said "no" to his pity and his offer of rescue, he did not force himself upon us. We wanted him to leave us alone, and he did. But he has always been ready to ask again, "Haven't you had enough?"

Any Stick of Wood Can Drift

We know when and if we have reached that time of personal realization: "I'm at a dead end." We know if we are ready to turn fully to God. But even if you think that time has come for you now, be careful of what you agree to before God. Don't come to him just for a warm glow or a feeling of euphoria. Don't come to him for success or miracles. If you do, you won't stay with him. Come to be a disciple.

But you had better be quiet and inconspicuous about it. Don't wear a button declaring that Jesus is now the master of your life. Just let him be Master. Don't call a press conference to tell the world that you are "pro-Jesus." Satan knows your weaknesses. He knows how to trip you. Just follow Jesus. Give an account for your obedience when asked, tell people the Good News, point to Christ, but when you do that, get yourself out of the way. You are entering God's business, and it isn't a game.

But be prepared. You'll still be seduced by the appeals that attempt to connect real living to cosmetic and plastic pleasures. There will still be packaged pretty people generating insecurity in you by pushing you toward something else—whether it's a new lifestyle, a new theology, or a new deodorant. They will still tell you that you don't have to look the way you look; you don't have to dress the way you dress; you needn't drive what you drive; or do without, or exercise self-control, or use the Bible as your guide. You will still be offered ways to live on tomorrow's earnings, to take more and give less. You will still be urged to modify biblical injunctions to suit your pleasure, to justify an easier lifestyle. Expect it to happen.

Conquer it!

Know that this pressure will come. Give it over to God. Any stick of wood can drift downstream, but it takes someone determined and alive to swim upstream. Richard Foster says in *Celebration of Discipline*, "Refuse to be a slave to anything but God."[2] The Apostle Paul said to people greatly influenced by their culture and society, "I urge you, brothers, in view of God's mercy, to offer your bodies as living sacrifices" (Romans 12:1). He is begging us by God's mercy, not our merit, to be "living" perpetual sacrifices, not something transient or occasional. We are to purposefully surrender completely to God. As a living gift, we turn over to God all that we are and all that he put into us—our abilities, our thoughts, our strengths. And as living sacrifices, offered as presents, we are to be holy and acceptable, pure and unblemished, just as the ancient animal sacrifices were.

Gifts From Him

How can this be? Both our holiness and our acceptability are his doing, his act of grace. We will have it if we claim it as an offered gift through the redeeming, transforming transaction at the cross. Jesus Christ paid for our sins and destroyed their consequences. And we receive the gift of gifts from him: his life, eternal life, a post-grave life. In response, this presentation of our bodies—head, heart, hands—is our worship. We owe him this.

We should know, then, that this is what worship is—a presentation of ourselves in whom he delights. Following an order of service in church is worship only if it is a part of that self-presentation. For neither songs nor sermons nor liturgy nor prayer is worship unless it is part of and comes out of that giving of the only present we can give—ourselves, a living sacrifice, holy and acceptable.

We are no longer to be conformed to the world as unrenewed people are. No one who is in Christ Jesus can be the same as one who is not. We who are in Christ are different. We have begun a new process. Do not continue to grow into conformity with the world, the Apostle says, but be transformed. We are to be changed by the renewing of our minds. This is an act that involves the mind; we are transformed by a lasting change as we think it through, weigh it, and say yes. Then we can be—indeed we will be—in the business of proving in our lives the perfect will of God. Day by day we will do this, committed to being proof for all to see of what is the good, perfect, and acceptable will of God.

Is that what you're ready to do?

As a child who has placed his hand in the hand of his father, the Christian walks into new life in Christ knowing that God is in control. We enter with an awareness that God is God. We know we cannot understand God's total will. The Father knows what lies ahead; the Christian is asked to go with him. There is no other way for obedience to be practiced.

This is not blindness on our part; this is coming to grips at last with the reality of knowing who we are and who he is. It is knowing who made us, who owns us, and what we are worth by the purchase of Jesus Christ. A. H. McNeile said, "The only way in which to know ourselves better is to know Christ better, and to be constantly comparing ourselves, not with other people, but, with Him."[3]

We Have Watched Job

Most scholars believe that Job is the oldest book in the Bible. If that is true, then it is interesting that the very first Scripture given to us isn't about blessing. It is about afflictions and pain that became so unbearable that Job's wife told him to curse God and die. Job refused; he cursed the day he was born, he wished he had never lived, but he refused to curse God and die. Job is a testimony to faithfulness no matter what happens in life.

Some me-oriented people, starting from their own perspective rather than God's, look at Job and say, "But Job was blessed later on." That's true, for God is gracious. But during the time of suffering and faithfulness Job didn't know he would ultimately be blessed. He trusted God not because he expected that God would give back more than he took; he trusted because he knew that God was God. In his suffering and misery he believed God.

Job didn't even have what we have to go on; he didn't have the example of a previous Job! He had to face his life without such a biblical example to help him. But because he did, we have his example to help us today. Whatever we face, whatever good or bad comes, we know what faithfulness is—we have watched Job.

The first and only reason for obedience is that God is God. We have no secret agendas as we throw ourselves on the altar as living sacrifices. We don't make demands of God. If we could, he would be too small. He would be our size. But he is the God beyond and above all of us, yet involved totally with us, with an understanding of our todays that is way beyond our own understanding, and with knowledge of tomorrows which are already in his hands.

Look at Joseph. When he was sold as a slave into Egypt, could he have known what God had ordained for the future? There was no way for him to know, yet in his faithfulness he worked at becoming the best man he could be for God. And God honored that. Though others meant Joseph's slavery for evil, God used it for his larger plan. Joseph was faithful to God long before anything good happened in his life. And since he did not know what we know now about the latter part of his life, we have to assume that he would have remained faithful even if he had died without ever knowing God's ultimate purpose or plan for him.

Stephen the evangelist died without realizing his influence on Saul of Tarsus. He didn't demand, "Tell me, God, how my death is a good thing for the Christian church." No, he endured stoning for his faith and died a horrible death. How God used Stephen's death for his glory was determined later. We are blessed today because of Stephen's faithfulness then.

Look at what Moses and his people faced at the hands of Pharaoh. Their suffering was what ultimately brought the people of Israel out of Egypt and produced a great nation, a people from whom would come the Messiah, our Lord Jesus Christ. But did Moses know all that at the time? Did Moses understand Pharaoh's role in his life?

What about the pharaohs in your life? What about the people who make your life difficult now when you try to be obedient to God, the ones who make your commitment to God an excuse to try to crush you even more? You may suffer as a disciplined follower, and you may ask why. But God may not answer you because he doesn't have to answer you. What is happening to you may be for a reason far greater than you could ever imagine. Your trouble with a pharaoh or your wilderness wandering may be the prelude to a great act of God. Your responsibility is to be obedient to what you know and to move through life with God.

Whom Are You Influencing Now?

One night while reading a publication from England, I came upon an article about the Archbishop of Canterbury, the Most Reverend Robert Runcie. I took out a pad of paper and wrote an editorial for *Decision* magazine. In it I said:

What caught my attention was the honesty with which this man of God spoke about his spiritual growth and especially his comment about his days as a student and in military service. He said,

"I was taken more with Christians than Christianity." [4]

That struck me because I've drawn some personal comfort (and actually made excuses for myself) by thinking that people shouldn't look at me, they should ignore me and look at Christ. That's fine to say, but the fact is that people do as Robert Runcie did. They look at Christians, not the Church, not even Christ.

The young man who would become Archbishop liked what he saw, so much so that he was inspired to do more decisive thinking about the Christian faith. When a fellow university student who had been preparing for the ministry was killed in the war, the parents of that young man said, "We have come to terms with our son's death because we know that God likes the buds as well as the full flowers." [5] Today the Archbishop looks back to that young man and his parents and those words as the means God used in motivating him toward his own preparation for the ministry.

As I finished reading the interview, I asked myself, "Does the way I live my life attract people to Jesus Christ? If I were to die soon, would my death lead others to go on in the Faith and perhaps do more than I could ever do for Christ and his Kingdom?"

The influence of one person upon another cannot be lightly dismissed. Maybe "my great work" is to be an influence that God uses to bring someone else to himself, someone who will truly do "great things for God." . . .

What really counts is living without guile or pretense and trusting to God the witness of the life we live. Fifty years ago one faithful young man did. The result of his brief life and the response of his parents to his death caused another young man to embark on a spiritual journey that led . . . to his enthronement as the Archbishop of Canterbury. [6]

Whom are you influencing now by your faithfulness? Conversely, whom may you be influencing away from God by your search for a bargain-counter God? No matter how difficult our path seems, God knows what he is doing when he calls us to obedience and discipline.

"Why me, God?" Better to ask, "Why not me?" Are you better than others of the faith? Are you better than a Moses or a Joseph or a Job or even a John the Baptist? You will consume hours, even years, of creative energy if you spend them worrying about why something is happening to you. When you believe in God, you need not worry. If you believe in the economy of God, you will know that he wastes nothing. He knows what he is doing in your life at every moment. He knows why you are here and what your purpose is, and why he put you on this earth with your gifts and your talents and all that makes you what you are. He knows why you live at this time and in this place, with all that is happening around you. David knew that and said so in Psalm 139. You are no accident. All the buffeting and pulling and tearing that happens is not without meaning. God may not cause some things, but he allows them, and the overall plan that guides a committed life is under his control.

If God Had Made You Different

A. H. McNeile has told us what it is to live by the light and rule of God:

> We are only instruments, implements, tools for the building of God's temple. Some people are like the tools fitted for the delicate and delightful work of carving or painting. They have the joy, by their very touch, of converting and beautifying souls. Some, who are able to start great schemes and engineer important movements, are like the powerful cranes that lift masses of masonry into their places. But others, and probably we amongst them, are to do spade work in digging foundations; or we are to be like the humble trowel that slowly adds brick after brick, or the humble hammer that patiently hits nail after nail, or the humble nail itself, firmly fixed in a sure place, invisible, but doing one little piece of work well. [7]
>
> The musician wants something different from the violin, the cello, the cornet, and every other instrument in the orchestra; and yet each can express quite fully what he wants from that particular instrument. S. Jerome put it in stirring words when he said that Christ wants from us "not impossibilities but perfections."
>
> It is impossible for me to express to God what He wants from you. But His ideal is that I should give to Him perfectly what He wants from me. It will save us endless trouble if we grasp that clearly. It will save us from the feeling that it must be easier for so-and-so to please God than for me. If I only had his chances! If I only had his temperament, or upbringing, his surroundings, his friends, his religious privileges, his sphere of work; or his voice, or command of language, or appearance! He is so rich in natural gifts, and I seem to have almost none; I'm a most dreadfully ordinary person. And perhaps in weak moments you have gone so low as to say, he has heaps of money, and I have very little; how can I do as much for God as he can? Perhaps you have gone even lower still, and said, God will make it up to me hereafter, and give

me things that he won't have!

All this, and many more of the doubts and grumbles that sometimes pass through our minds, come from forgetting the plain, obvious truth that if God had made you different from what you are, He would have wanted something different from you. [8]

No matter how Satan prowls and torments and tortures and hurts us, no matter how we suffer (and we will, because we are a part of a fallen world and part of the decay that leads to the end), as long as we are committed to Christ we are always his. We are to measure our lives against his reality, not against our ideals, which are only fantasies.

Being under the discipline of God, then, is not an easy life, but it is a *real* life. It is a life that redefines the meaning of pleasure. It is a life that will redefine you, your significance in the world, and your purpose on earth.

Haven't you had enough of the indulgent life? Isn't it time to come back to discipline, to a life lived on God's terms?

4

Another Way to Live

Something is happening to someone close to you, but you may not have noticed yet. There is a person less anxious than others, someone with a quiet purpose, who understands the meaning of faithfulness, obedience, control; a person who has discovered a deeper satisfaction than what other people pull out of the shallow gratifications of the immediate. This is a person who is able not to take just because the taking is available. This is a person who does not feel angry when someone else "gets there" first. This person is different, refusing to look at life with the narrow view, the view that says, "I'm entitled to satisfaction and pleasure or anything else that I want—and I will have it." This person is bigger than that, having learned another way to live. Particularly—and contentedly—this is someone who has learned to live a disciplined life and who likes himself because he can.

This is the person who, when suffering, resolves to endure.

This is the one who reads the marriage manuals that advise, "You have a right to divorce and remarriage," and still answers, "No, I don't."

This is the person who, like Joseph in Egypt, will go without companions and emotional support if necessary but still refuses to give way to temptation.

This is the one who, when urged to "claim your rights," can say, "I'll go without."

Are people like this mentally unbalanced? Are they masochists?

Or are these a people who have discovered a stronger, more satisfying support structure for living?

They have! They have found not just a cause or a system. But they have thought through the implications of what Oxford don C. S. Lewis said: "If you are thinking of becoming a Christian, I warn you you are embarking on something which is going to take the whole of you . . ."[1] And they have decided to do it. They have accepted the warning and have gained the results.

These are committed followers of Jesus Christ, and they are off on a different adventure. They are the sheep who have heard his voice and have chosen to obey him. Jesus said, "My sheep . . . follow me" (John 10:27)—and they do. Richard Lovelace describes what they are and what they have: "True spirituality is not a super-human religiosity; it is simply true humanity released from bondage to sin and renewed by the Holy Spirit."[2] That is their secret. But it doesn't have to be a secret. It's available to all of us.

The Holy Person Is a Healthy Person

We too can be a people who understand what it means to belong to Jesus Christ. We too can determine to follow and obey him. Each of us can be a person who has chosen to live out his life enjoying the closeness of God. James H. McConkey explains:

> What we are becomes the measure of what we can do or, rather, what God can do through us. We must be Christ-like in inner life, if we would be Christ-like in outward deed. A holy God needs a holy instrument through which to live His holy life.[3]

Holiness means health. The holy person is a healthy person. The person who is not holy is unwell. It isn't normal to want to be unwell. It is normal to want to be healthy. The friends of God, the obedient ones, the disciplined followers, have found health.

But this obedience is not simply a lifestyle that one adopts, or a set of religious rules to try to obey. It is a response. It is a yes to the One who prefaced his teaching with, "If anyone will come after me . . ."

In churches, in neighborhood groups, by ones and twos, people are sorting out what that means; they are scraping away the corroding barnacles of existentialism and secular humanism which have dragged all of us down for so long. They are chucking the theological adjuncts in favor of dependence on God. And to the best of their ability, prayerfully and devotionally they are becoming people who follow him. The French philosopher Emile Cailliet described it:

> New Testament Christianity lives on, lives on with all the rough hedges of the Apostolic Proclamation, lives on with all the foolishness of its otherworldliness. When the theologians and natural scientists have done their best, or their worst, this fact is still there, staring them in the face.[4]

The life of discipleship is the life of living as a friend of God. It is not immediately an easy road to choose, and many won't choose it. Most people will play along the fringe, trying to get a little of the light and warmth of God without walking with him and abiding in him. There will always be people, peripheral believers, superficial adherents, who take the stumbling-along view that says, "Each of us is free to decide the conditions under which God expects us to obey him." Worse, there will always be those people who simply back out if a promise they made to God seems no longer viable.

But not all will do that. Some have learned.

A male college student recalled: "She came to me right at the time when I didn't think I could take much more—the pressure from my parents, the financial strain, the classwork demands. I needed an out, even a temporary escape. Then I felt her touch on my arm. 'You're really tense,' she said. 'Would you like me to help you relax?' I didn't know her except as another member of the class, but apparently she had been watching me. She saw my need and she made her offer. She meant it; there was genuine kindness in her sympathetic tone. But I couldn't. I said, with appreciation for her thoughtfulness, 'No, thank you,' and I walked away."

He didn't preach at her or criticize. How could he criticize kindness? Neither did he refuse her offer because he had some "better" release for his tensions. He had none. He was alone. There was no one else on the horizon offering him any different kind of help, a help that he would and could accept.

He went without. He said no to the caring that she offered, with nothing to replace it. He endured without a release.

Is he unhealthy? Is he foolish? Doesn't he know that bottled-up feelings and emotional stress can bring greater tension? Maybe.

But so does temporary escape, regardless of the form. He knows that too. The clear word that God gave is still there in front of all of us, and that student had it. "*Never* will I leave you; *never* will I forsake you" (Hebrews 13:5). For that, and that alone, he held on until God's help came.

It is in the everyday events of life when people like that student prove whether or not they will be obedient. Holiness is a behavior as well as a belief. It isn't the difference between "criminal" and "law-abiding." It is the difference between good and best. We practice holiness because of friendship with God. There is no semi-friendship, no occasional fear of the Lord.

Why Should I Be So Virtuous?

I know two men who work for a nonprofit organization. Both travel on expense accounts. One lives as a friend of God; the other does not. Circumstances are the same for both, but their responses to those circumstances are opposite. This is how the difference shows:

"Go ahead and order the steak."

"But I don't eat like this at home; I can't afford it."

"You're not at home; it's going on your expense account."

"No."

"You work hard; you've earned it."

"I'm paid to work hard. I am not paid to exploit."

When those two men started their work, both had strong convictions about the high calling of their vocation. They felt a sense of mission in a worthwhile organization, one that helped people in need. They kept costs down so that the money could be used as the donors expected it to be used. But then they began to notice that others in their group weren't so fussy. After a while it became easier for one of those men to change from a high view of commitment to the rationalization, "You won't be appreciated any more if you don't take." Even worse, he gave in to the charge, "You make the rest of us look bad when we turn in our expenses."

Now that man thinks this way: "Others are looking out for themselves; why should I be so virtuous? The money I don't spend on myself doesn't provide more for those in need, it just provides more for the others in the organization who do look out for themselves." So now he has joined the others. He is spending more on himself too.

But the other man won't bend. He says, "When you see poor people who are willing to give a dollar in order to help someone else, that stays with you. You can't spend that money on yourself." He can't do it, and he won't do it. It means fighting against a trend, and he fights it every day. The other man doesn't have to fight anymore; he has already given in. For him there is no longer a battle. For the disciplined man the battle continues; it probably always will. He isn't even feeling good about it. And he isn't announcing, "You're wrong; I'm right." He just goes on, one day at a time, trying to do what is expected of him by God.

And usually that's all we have to go on as we try to be a friend of God. What others say cannot be the measure of what is ethical, moral, or right, even if it is legal. The view of the majority is not necessarily the view of God.

People Who Have Chosen

I know a woman whose husband has been seducing other women for years. She could get a divorce; she has been encouraged by her friends to do it. But she won't. She's not trying to be a martyr or heroine; she's not trying to bring more pain into her life, some kind of self-inflicted psychological punishment. She made a vow to God: "For better or worse," and she meant that vow. The sacred commitment was not only in the words she spoke but in the promise behind those words. Believing that God heard her when she made that promise, she is going to stand on it and seek God's help to implement that promise whether or not his help comes according to her own timetable, or even to the degree of personal satisfaction that she would like to have.

Her stance is so different from that taken by the rest of our culture that to many people it seems incomprehensible. "How can she do what she is doing?" they exclaim. She hears the arguments: "You are the innocent party." "Don't you want a better life?" "Think of your children." "He's going to bring disease home to you." "If divorce is wrong, it isn't the worst wrong; God forgives." "You aren't getting any younger." "You have a responsibility to yourself." "God is love and wants you to be loved." Then comes that often-used line: "God wants you to be happy."

But she already knows all of those arguments. She has heard them over and over again. She has thought them through and has made up her mind.

Even Christians who accept her view and admit that she is probably correct, or who praise her glowingly, look for some compensation from God to be granted her for her faithfulness. But no reward has come. Life is still miserable for her. So then these fellow Christians too begin to argue with her: "If God expected you to endure such suffering, at least he would have given you some other blessing to reward you."

But she responds, "Why should he?"

And she explains again, "I obey my pledge because I promised that I would obey my pledge. Why should God be expected to give me some great reward for doing what I promised to do in the first place? I said, 'For better or worse.' God was there when I said it, and God hasn't moved away. And no matter how my husband has drifted, or for whatever reason, God is with me now. Would I divorce my husband if instead of losing his head to other women he lost his mind to illness?"

She has kept her vow, even though there are still people coming around to remind her that times have changed, her world has changed, her husband has changed, and she has changed. She remembers what they have chosen to forget: God hasn't changed— and her promise was made to God.

The faithful ones, the vow-keepers, the disciplined people of God, are not some new kind of standard bearers. They are simply people who have chosen to be consistent in the adventure of following Jesus. They aren't trying to be different or strange. They aren't looking for personal suffering. They aren't drawing attention to themselves by saying: "Look at all that I'm doing and all that I'm giving up." They want to enjoy life, the pleasures of home and good health. But whether they have the "good" or the "bad," they will follow Jesus. And they will do it faithfully, wherever that obedience leads. They, like St. Paul, know what it is to be in need as well as what it is to have plenty (Philippians 4:12), and will go without if that is what is required within their commitment to obedience. They will be what their Lord has asked—faithful. And if there is some primary word about being a friend of God, it is that word—*faithful*. Everything else is secondary.

Jesus did not come to this earth in order to call a few selected disciples to a happy three-year vacation from routine. Nor was his mission to make people comfortable. He came to obey his Father. That led to a cross. There was no alternative for our redemption but that cross. If there had been, God would not have sent his Son—it was so costly. But he did send his Son, and Jesus obeyed his Father's will. What if Jesus had chosen the more pleasant way of remaining with his Father? Or, once Incarnate, what if he had decided that the situation had changed or the responsibility was too severe? What if he had said no to the cross?

Are Jesus' disciples to take liberties, playing fast and loose with God the Father in the name of him who would not and could not disobey? Do we say yes or no depending on how we feel in a given situation or moment? Are there no firm orders for the one who claims to be a follower of him who "resolutely set out" (Luke 9:51), who from the beginning knew that he had to do the work of him who sent him (John 9:4)?

Those who choose to follow the Master do so on his terms. It is obedience with no reservation clause added to the contract. There is no back door left ajar so that we can slip out when the mood strikes or feelings change. "You are my friends," Jesus said, "if you do what I command" (John 15:14). We are to be obedient even if we never see "good results" from it. The measure of what is "good" is not ours to make.

Even Through Long Spiritual Winters

There is always the human tendency to look down the road, to ask, "How will all this turn out for me, for the kingdom, or for others?" We try to figure it all out. Even when following means extreme suffering, we tend to look at it for its long-range effect. Dietrich Bonhoeffer, the German pastor killed by the Nazis in 1945, did not look for prison and eventual death, nor, if he saw it coming, did he look for its long-range effect on others. He just obeyed God.

To the question, "What if my obedience doesn't turn out well?" we have to respond, "What if it doesn't?"

"What if I make a mistake?"

Well, what if you do? God wants your obedience. Scripture tells us that "Anyone who trusts in him will never be put to shame"

(Romans 10:11). What comes to us as a result of our trust in God is God's responsibility, not ours. We are not worriers about tomorrow, either for ourselves or for our witness to the kingdom. We do not have to anticipate the plan of God and help him develop it.

People who are being martyred today because they are Christians do not necessarily see their deaths as a witness to Christ—all they see is death coming. There is no last-minute realization, "I am a blessed martyr and thus others will come to Christ." There is no last-minute, glorious, divine intervention to ease the pain of bullets or blade. There is none of that for them. But they are faithful anyway. They have to be because they are his. That's what it is to be a friend of God.

Ultimately, those who say yes to Jesus Christ have to know that they are making a decision, choosing an option to obey, following whether there are great rewards in it or none, whether it is for good or for suffering, life or death. Some summertime believers will do without for a while if God will provide blessings for them in the end. But God may not. And the committed disciples don't question that. They know they must go on even through long spiritual winters.

Any person who has not made this commitment to Jesus Christ will be confused, even angry, at this explanation of true friendship with God. That's to be expected. Such persons won't—indeed can't—understand. "The man without the Spirit does not accept the things that come from the Spirit of God, for they are foolishness to him" (1 Corinthians 2:14). Those people are wrong if they presume obedience is simple self-denial—an ascetic, masochistic way of life. Self-negation is not at all what obedience means. The person who goes without something in order to be noticed, or who becomes a martyr by his own doing, is still seeking a reward—and as Jesus said of the hypocrites who blew their trumpets, "They have received their reward in full" (Matthew 6:2). Those who impose on themselves the ascetic, self-denying life do so on their terms—it is merely a religious facade. It is not real obedience to Jesus. God's call for us to deny ourselves doesn't stop there; it has a purpose, being linked to his call for us to *follow him.*

Jesus said, "If anyone would come after me, he must deny himself and take up his cross and follow me" (Matthew 16:24). That means exactly what Jesus says it means—follow him! It doesn't mean that I decide to live on a smaller income, but I will if *he* decides it for me. It doesn't mean that I surrender my house, but I will if *he* wishes it. It doesn't mean that *I* choose to face a firing squad or the persecution of my neighbors, but I will if that's where *obedience* takes me.

It has to be that way because in coming to him I am purposely and willingly choosing to yield my body as a living sacrifice, "holy and pleasing to God—which is . . . worship" (Romans 12:1). I am no longer my own; I am bought with a price—the price of the Lord Jesus Christ. I am paid for. The Christian is a disciple; more accurately, he is "an instrument for noble purposes, made holy, useful to the Master and prepared to do any good work" (2 Timothy 2:21).

No Cheers From the Crowds

That's what is so different about this adventure called friendship with God. There is neither heroics nor fame to it, no cheers from the crowd; there is no recognition in biographies; no motion pictures are filmed. It is a choice to walk quietly but faithfully beside Jesus even while all around the noise of the market of worldliness attracts, while those who are avoiding Jesus, seeming to live comfortably and well in their unbelief, are smirking and saying under their breath, "What a fool."

But we are not fools; we are discoverers of a new and stirring life. As Thomas Kelly explained:

Deep within us all there is an amazing inner sanctuary of the soul, a holy place, a Divine Center, a speaking Voice, to which we may continuously return. Eternity is at our hearts, pressing upon our time-torn lives, warming us with intimations of an astounding destiny, calling us home unto Itself. Yielding to these persuasions, gladly committing ourselves in body and soul, utterly and completely, to the Light Within, is the beginning of true life. . . . It is a Light Within which illumines the face of God and casts new shadows and new glories upon the face of men. It is a seed stirring to life if we do not choke it. It is the Shekinah of the soul, the Presence in the midst. Here is the Slumbering Christ, stirring to be awakened, to become the soul we clothe in earthly form and action. And He is within us all.[5]

Disciples determine that they must have what God wants for them. Nothing less will do. This means they cannot and will not give in to the temptations that dissipate and hurt and destroy. There is too much at stake. Their very being and welfare—a full life—is at stake. A follower of Jesus has only one life to enjoy on this earth. Why should it be used to run after what can never satisfy? Why should this one life be given to anything less than the wholeness, the purity, the love, and the joy of God?

Why would we want to work so hard for a few years to gain what "moth and rust will corrupt," what "thieves will break through and steal," when we can have so much more that will never corrupt or decay? Why would we not want the eternal investments now and the dividends of those investments forever?

What can this friendship with God fully mean? Do any of us really know what it is to be holy, to be blameless, to be loved? We know a little of it, but there is so much more of it to know—and God calls us to discover it all.

God wants you near him and wants lovingly to guide your life. There is still that one clear certainty in an age when nothing else is certain at all: God wants you to be his friend.

Long ago, God said through Elijah, "How long will you waver between two opinions? If the Lord is God, follow him" (1 Kings 18:21). It is time to heed that call again. If we have forsaken or compromised the disciplines of faithfulness, we have made the wrong choice. It is time to come back, to start over.

Start a life of holy obedience now; start where you are, as you are. Whether or not others do it, start. There is no better time. Tell God you are ready—tell him now. Say your yes to God.

5

I Don't See God Smiling

■ ■ ■

He was four years old when he died. He was a happy boy singing a Sunday school song. The car skidded and crashed. As his mother bent down to him, he said, "Mommy, I'm going to see Jesus now."

Where is God?

A middle-aged woman is bitter. All she has ever wanted from God is to be a wife and mother, to do the domestic things that go with being a housewife.

After high school she took an ordinary, unchallenging job. It was to be only temporary. She really wanted to get married. Through the years she waited, occasionally changing to other "temporary" jobs, always anticipating the day when she'd be able to have a husband, make a home, and build a family.

She was counseled to develop a career, attend college, and plan for her own future. But no. She knew what she wanted.

She talked to God about it—often. "Surely God knows I would be a dedicated wife, a committed mother," she'd say. "Surely I'm better suited than many women who aren't excited about their marriages or their children. Why does God give others what I want? Why doesn't God satisfy me? Why isn't God smiling at me?"

Where is God?

How can we answer the question of the man who, one week before he is to begin his eagerly awaited retirement, learns that he has cancer? What can we say to the mother whose baby is born with a severe physical or mental disorder? What comfort can be given to the father and mother whose student son writes them a note saying, "I can't make it," and slashes his wrists?

These aren't evil people. They haven't rejected God. These are people who look for, even wish for, the smile of God. But they don't see it. These stories can be multiplied; we all know others.

Where is God?

Sometimes when we talk about the smile of God it's only a humorous comment. "God isn't smiling at me," we say.

One morning I was comfortably driving along on the freeway in my Volkswagen when suddenly a tire on a car ahead of me came loose. It bounced back, was knocked down by another car, and before I could stop or swerve I drove up on top of it, pulling the tire along until the car came grinding to a stop with all four wheels of my Volkswagen off the ground.

There I sat, traffic piling up behind me, drivers in the other two lanes laughing at me as they zoomed by. Eventually enough people gathered to lift the car off the tire and I drove on, embarrassed.

When I got home that night, seeking sympathy for my suffering, I told my wife about the embarrassing event. She started laughing. When she finally got enough control of herself to speak, she said, "Why didn't you just sit there? It might have hatched!"

God wasn't smiling at me that day.

That incident was embarrassing, but it wasn't serious. It's when everything crumbles around us that we begin to wonder about God.

The very week that I was writing this, two of my friends lost their sons. Both of these young men were in their early twenties. One had just made a public commitment in a church service: "Lord, I'll go where you want me to go." Within a few days he was gone, home with God.

Is God smiling when people lose their young sons? Afterward, these parents echoed the thought in Romans 8:28, "Yes, I believe that in all things God works for the good of those who love him, who have been called according to his purpose." And by the time of the funerals, friends were saying it too.

That's hard for some people to accept. But when we go through that with a committed Christian, we see something of this dimension that is not make believe. It is real. They know.

Good does come, even in great suffering, to those who live under the smile of God. But some people miss it. Legalists miss it because they have become cold and formal, building their faith on God's revelation as an abstract thing. The teachings of God have become historical, objective, impersonal. They become carved in stone, laws to be obeyed with a strictness that eliminates the joy of life in Christ. The legalist misses the smile of God.

So do the existentialists, but for a different reason. Because they are so caught up with their own experiences, they think God is what they feel God is. They think they have God's truth when all they have are that moment's feelings about God's truth. The sensations of the moment are their teachers, and they cannot build anything stable on them. Feelings change, they fluctuate, and the person who bases faith on them also misses the smile of God.

Even Through the Valley

Many evangelical Christians talk about the smile of God, but don't experience it. That's because, unfortunately, they have been led along a path of rosy belief that makes them think they must always see God smiling. Our God, some are led to believe, would not allow anything bad to happen to us.

But if, in our desire for the smooth life, we persist in this wishful thinking, we will miss the joy of the companionship of the One who will walk with us even through the valley of the shadow of death. We will miss the depth, the height, and the breadth of God.

It is a lie to tell people that good fortune always belongs to those who have faith. It is a lie because we are still in the fallen world and subject to it. We hurt people, heap guilt upon them, contribute to their pain in a cruel way when we insist that any problems in their lives are their own fault, the result of lacking faith. Our faith is in the "man of sorrows, and familiar with suffering" (Isaiah 53:3) who will go through sorrows and grief with us. The Son of God knows, God proved his smile in Jesus Christ.

We turn in faith to God as people ready to receive, as flowers to the sun, as children to their parents—and we don't presume to determine the meaning of the events of our lives, no matter what they are. Meaning for our lives is determined by the thinking of God.

Scripture tells me that God is thinking about me all the time. That's hard to grasp, but it's true. "And when I waken in the morning, you are still thinking of me" (Psalm 139:18, TLB).

God said:

"For I know the plans I have for you," declares the Lord, "plans to prosper you and not to harm you, plans to give you hope and a future. Then you will call upon me and come and pray to me, and I will listen to you. You will seek me and find me when you seek me with all your heart. I will be found by you," declares the Lord, "and will bring you back from captivity" (Jeremiah 29:11-14).

God means that!

Does God have good plans for me? Yes, he does. Are his plans for my good, my welfare? Yes, they are—he says so. Does he want to give me a future and a hope? Yes, he promises that. Can I call upon him? Pray to him? Will he hear me? Yes, he has already promised that. He said he would, and he will never go back on his Word.

But there is a part, something else, that depends upon each of us. Notice: "You will seek me and find me when you seek me with all your heart." All your heart—not part of your heart. When all is involved in the search for God, you will find him. "'I will be found by you,' declares the Lord." There is no question about that.

The trees in the forest are there whether or not I am near the forest. The stars in the sky are there whether my eyes are open or closed. The sun is there whether or not the clouds block its shining. The reality of God's smile has nothing to do with our seeing that smile. God is smiling whether or not I sense that smile.

It was difficult for me to learn that. Not long ago, I experienced slander to the point that it is still painful to think about. I had to go to God and ask him, "Why? Where were you in all of this? Didn't you know what was going on? Couldn't you have stopped it?"

In the months that followed I learned at least three things through that experience. First, I learned that I am not God. I do not stand outside creation. I am within creation and the Fall and I am subject to all of its weaknesses and evil, including the actions of other people.

Second, I learned that my "reputation," the protection of my "good name," can become sin to me if it becomes a point of merit or prestige to be valued in itself. In myself I have no good name. The only good name I have is "Christian," and I cannot worship that. I must worship him whose name I claim. I must live the name "Christian"; I must live a good reputation because I live it in Christ. My reputation is not mine for my own sake; my reputation is that of a "Christ one," to be honored for his sake.

Third, I learned that just as the Master was himself subjected to slander ("They say, 'Here is a glutton and a drunkard, a friend of tax collectors and "sinners"'" [Matthew 11:19]), so I am subject to slander and all that it brings upon a person. This world does cause suffering. I learned that I am not above my Master, and if in a small way I too am momentarily a "man of sorrows, and familiar with suffering" (Isaiah 53:3) when I am neither purity nor goodness as he was, what must he have suffered having known all of God—in purity, goodness, and grace?

There is probably a fourth lesson in all of this. That lesson is this: There will always be slander, hurt, physical disease, emotional stress, and spiritual struggle for us as long as we are on this earth. We're not finished with all of it yet; there will be more. That is a reason to long for heaven. Were this life so good, so blessed, all of the time—though it is good some of the time—we would come to like it too much. We might even come to love it. But there is always a reminder—both in the things that happen to us and in what we see happening to those around us—that we are heading for a better place. This is not an escapist mentality but a reasonable and pleasant anticipation. Heaven will soon be ours.

Francis Schaeffer was right when he said, "When I am dead both to good and bad, I have my face turned towards God."[1]

I did not get these answers from God right at the time I was feeling the pain of that slander; I merely suffered and endured it then. But weeks later these answers came as I thought about our Lord and read about other Christians in church history who were maligned and misunderstood. A wise pastor, with many years of experience, explained to me that I should continue to live my life before the Lord—and trust him, and I have vowed to do that.

A Lesson I Had to Learn

Then God began to deal with me in an even deeper way. So I read further in Schaeffer's *True Spirituality*:

> Every time I see something right in another man, it tends to minimize me, and it makes it easier for me to have a proper creature-creature relationship. But each time I see something wrong in others, it is dangerous, for it can exalt self, and when this

happens, my open fellowship with God falls to the ground. So when I am right, I can be wrong. In the midst of being right, if self is exalted, my fellowship with God can be destroyed.[2]

I thought about my attitude toward people who do bad things, and I thought about forgiveness. The early church practiced the love that Jesus taught. It was a mark of the Christian community. It is true that the injury of another person is no light thing. But forgiveness is even more important. It was a lesson that I had to learn.

I learned something else, the comfort that comes from the awareness that God knows everything that happens to me. It is true that not even a sparrow falls to the ground without God knowing about it.

I am worth far more than a sparrow. I belong to the One who also suffered without cause, he who is the perfect sinless one—a claim I could never make for myself. And I had to ask myself, since Jesus was faithful can I as his follower be less? I know that I cannot live a wholesome life if I harbor anger or resentment. I cannot serve God that way. I will forfeit my privilege to live under the loving smile of God.

Whatever the world brings to us, we are still loved by God, we are still his. And that means far more than a pleasant life, a good reputation, personal worth, private and family success, or even a happy state of mind. And I believe now more than ever that a Christian does live under the smile of God, for in a bad situation I saw how God turned my thoughts toward him, and I learned something deeper about his love as he tenderly taught me something deeper about myself.

Scripture tells us:

Dear friends, do not be surprised at the painful trial you are suffering, as though something strange were happening to you. But rejoice that you participate in the sufferings of Christ, so that you may be overjoyed when His glory is revealed. If you are insulted because of the name of Christ, you are blessed, for the Spirit of glory and of God rests on you. If you suffer, it should not be as a murderer or thief or any other kind of criminal, or even as a meddler. However, if you suffer as a Christian, do not be ashamed, but praise God that you bear that name. For it is time for judgment to begin with the family of God; and if it begins with us, what will the outcome be for those who do not obey the gospel of God? And "If it is hard for the righteous to be saved, what will become of the ungodly and the sinner?" So then, those who suffer according to God's will should commit themselves to their faithful Creator and continue to do good (1 Peter 4:12-19).

But maybe you know deep down inside that you have strayed from God and that is the problem. You don't sense God's smile because you have purposely turned away from him—your back is turned to God. It happens. Remember Uzziah? Those Old Testament individuals such as Uzziah are good for us to study. They are a warning for us not to do the same thing.

Uzziah, the Bible says (2 Chronicles 26), worshiped God steadily—at first. "He sought God." What a beautiful description of a man. "He was greatly helped until he became powerful." But then look what happened: "But after he became powerful, his pride led to his downfall." He became bold with God's gift of power; he tried to usurp the rights that were not his. God struck him with leprosy. And when he died, people didn't say, "There was a man who sought God." Instead they said, "he had leprosy." He had left God, left the strength, and was remembered no more for what he once was. If only he had heeded the warnings and turned back. If only....

Your own sorrow, your own remorse, may be from your blatant rebellion against God, and it tells you God is not smiling. You feel it. What can you do? God himself gives the answer. The Bible says, "Yet the Lord pleads with you still: Ask where the good road is, the godly paths you used to walk in, in the days of long ago. Travel there, and you will find rest for your souls" (Jeremiah 6:16, TLB).

God wants to support you strongly. You don't have to go on frantically looking for God. God is looking for you to support you with his strength. Give your heart back to him.

David, in spite of his evil before God, in spite of taking another man's wife and then killing that man, turned back to God. You are no worse than David. Take the way back that he took. He prayed, "Create in me a pure heart, O God, and renew a steadfast spirit within me" (Psalm 51:10).

That is still the way back. "'God opposes the proud but gives grace to the humble.' Humble yourselves, therefore, under God's mighty hand, that he may lift you up in due time" (1 Peter 5:5-6).

That is now, and always will be, the way to come back and live "under the smile of God."

6

When I Want to Be Honest With God

■ ■ ■

It was two o'clock in the morning. I was asleep in my hotel room when suddenly behind my head came the pounding of rock music over a stereo system that vibrated the wall. It continued for an hour while I lay there angrily fuming as my head started pounding.

The next night it happened again, and the next. I had no choice. If I were going to get a night's sleep, I had to move.

Unless the hotel manager said something, whoever was playing the music night after night probably still doesn't know the headaches he gave me, or the trouble I went through packing and moving. But that experience made me do some serious thinking about myself.

Do I, too, annoy people without even realizing that I am doing it? I know what others do to annoy me, but what about things that I do? Are people quietly fuming because I've irritated them somehow? Can I be sure at the beginning of a day that I will not hurt anybody, and at the close of the day can I know for certain that I didn't? Can I know that wherever I have gone there has come encouragement and a building-up, that I have brought pleasure and peace?

I went to my Bible; I needed a checklist. I needed to find out about me. I learned that "wise men turn away anger" (Proverbs 29:8). If that is true, and God's Word says it is, then the opposite must also be true—that one who doesn't pay attention to the wisdom that comes from God brings anger.

I found the words of Jesus: "The good man brings good things out of the good stored up in his heart, and the evil man brings evil things out of the evil stored up in his heart" (Luke 6:45). My actions, then, are determined by what is in my heart. I don't need to check what I *do* so much as I need to check my heart.

And then I went on to read Ecclesiastes: "For God will bring every deed into judgment" (Ecclesiastes 12:14). He sees everything and he will judge everything. God wants to bring good things out of our hearts because he is the judge of the good. He wants to have a good word for us at the Judgment; he wants to be able to say to us, "Well done, good and faithful servant! . . . Come and share your master's happiness!" (Matthew 25:21).

And I found even more hope in my search of the Word. In Micah I learned that even when I fall and bear the Lord's wrath, "because I have sinned against him . . . He will bring me out into the light" (Micah 7:9). He will because he promised.

I can relax in him; when I slip I can know that he will bring me to the light again. I don't have to live in the fear that I will offend and be condemned for it. God in his love and through his Word has offered the guidelines to keep me from hurting others, even unknowingly.

My rock music neighbor in that hotel helped me to make that discovery. I'm certain God knew that he would. God is a loving Father; he doesn't miss opportunities like that.

Life Isn't Fair

We have all asked, "Why do the wicked prosper?" And we have stood silently with those who know tragedy and pain as they ask, with tears streaming down their faces, "Where is God?" More than once I have found myself saying to people in a counseling situation: "No, life isn't fair. Where did you get the idea that it is?"

Life, in fact, is a tragedy. We should know that. The Bible is quite explicit about man's fall. We are not what God intended us to be nor are we living in the kind of world God intended. We are fallen creatures in a fallen world. We are victims of broken relationships, of a fallen structure where there is disease, decay, anger, hate, war, strife, misery. We live in that world. We are not yet in heaven. Though we have been redeemed and brought close to the

One who gives peace in the midst of struggle and healing in the course of pain, we are still in this world—a painful and tragic world.

But there is nothing wrong with being honest with God about what we are enduring and how we feel about it. It is not wrong for me to feel like pounding my fists against God and saying, "This is not fair!" There is nothing wrong with saying, "Why did you let this happen to me?" No, there is nothing wrong with that if we know to whom we are speaking and can come to the point of saying, as Job did, "Though he slay me, yet will I hope in him" (Job 13:15).

I like Job; he's my kind of person. I like him because he is honest. He respected, trusted, and honored God, but he wasn't afraid to ask "Why?"

His friends, those counselors with easy words, were not evil men. Job admitted that what they taught about sin was true. "Who does not know all these things?" he said (Job 12:3). He didn't dispute it. But he came right back and protested his innocence in all his suffering and his helplessness in not being able to confront God about it. "Oh, how I long to speak directly to the Almighty. I want to talk this over with God himself" (Job 13:3, TLB). Then with true honesty in his pain, he cried out, "Give . . . a little rest, won't you?" (Job 14:6, TLB), and "Don't abandon me" (Job 13:21, TLB). Job was an honest man.

Though we can show our human feelings, and they are not to be denied, God is—and always will be—Lord. God made us; he put into us all that we are. He may stand by while all we count dear is taken away. But we have no argument. God is God.

Yet we are not victims; we are his. It is the lost, the separated ones, those who deny God who must always be uncertain, always feeling like victims of the toss of the coin. That is not the stand for us who believe in God, who have transferred our trust from ourselves to the Lord Jesus Christ.

There is suffering for us and there always will be so long as we live on this earth. God knows that. There is no need to pretend otherwise. It is not somehow more spiritual to lie about our hurts as if God didn't know the truth. Nor do we always have to say in a Pollyanna-ish way that good will come of it. There is sometimes a reward to suffering, but not always.

We try to look for the teaching, the good, the blessing. Sometimes we can find it in the grief of life. But it is not always so. Some events have no reason to them so far as we can see, no teaching value, nothing—just pain. Sometimes suffering isn't rewarding in any way. Sometimes there is no reason for it, no purpose, no apparent good coming from it. All we can do is face it.

But we can still meet God in those times in the same way that we meet him in any other situation or event. He does not desert us in the suffering or the illness, the pain or the mental torture. He is as close as he always was. Rather, in our emptiness, in our suffering, we draw closer to him. We hold on—not for more money, or power, not even a "blessing"—we just hold on to God. That is the only answer for much of what hurts.

We Want to Take God's Hand

Whereas before we may not have felt this desire for him, now in pain we have that need for him, and it is a desperate need. Now we turn to him. Now we want to take God's hand.

The void of the difficult moment clears everything between him and ourselves, and we stand with our empty cup asking for it to be filled. Before, we may have tried to fill that cup ourselves, with our wisdom, our strength, our skills, our abilities. Not now. Now in the pain and the emptiness we admit we have nothing, and we say in our nothingness, "Fill my cup, Lord." And he does. He gives us enough. He brings us through. Then, quietly, we breathe our anguished, "Thank you." We have found him close.

If God can offer so much in our emptiness and pain, what can he offer in our times of plenty?

Haggai knew. Haggai was preparing the people to build the house of God. The people were living in their own paneled houses and thought they had so much. Actually, they didn't have much at all. "You have planted much, but have harvested little. You eat, but never have enough. You drink, but never have your fill. You put on clothes, but are not warm. You earn wages, only to put them in a purse with holes in it" (Haggai 1:6).

We don't have much either, even when we think we do. Maybe in our honesty we need to be aware that we are building our own little temples and are ignoring God. God has a building that he wants to build, a spiritual temple. Maybe honesty requires that we look around at our other temples and admit: "All that I have isn't anything after all," and ask him to build and fill his temple in us. Honesty demands openness—about ourselves, about him, about where we are. Honesty doesn't pretend.

An Awareness of Ourselves

It is the mark of friendship to tell the truth. If you are God's friend, if you walk with him, if you have known him in the good times and were honest with him then, be honest with him in the bad times too. Don't be afraid to say what you feel. That's being honest.

Of course, some won't do that. They avoid God, ignore him; their resentment or anger continues, festering. "God is not God," they say. "He can't be a God of love," they insist. There have always been people like that. Some have even been our teachers. Harold B. Walker comments that the philosopher Jean-Paul Sartre was like that, and his reaction to God was, in reality, a reaction against himself:

> One who reads Sartre's biography is constrained to feel that his existentialism, so devoid of spiritual depth and with scorn for the very idea of God, is primarily the consequence not of rational thought, but of self-hate bottled within him. Hate for himself and for those who nurtured him left him unable to believe that love is anything but phony. Of course, the God who is love is phony too.[1]

Honesty is not only an expression to God about the feelings we have for him, but an awareness of ourselves. We have to admit what we feel and we have to admit what we are. There is sin, there is guilt, and we are loaded with both. Denying this is like denying the diagnosis of cancer—it is still there. Shutting our eyes won't make it go away. David A. Redding said: "Making guilt inadmissible has made it all the more dangerous. Since it is undefined, sin now enjoys a reign of terror. We refuse to believe that there is anything to forgive. We will not recognize an occasion for a Redeemer."[2]

David said in Psalm 119:176: "I have strayed like a lost sheep. Seek your servant." That is what Isaiah was also telling us: "We all, like sheep, have gone astray" (Isaiah 53:6).

Jesus describes us as sheep without a shepherd. David had enough experience as a shepherd to know that sheep get lost easily. David was a smart man; he knew he was like a sheep, prone to wander off. Other people are lost too, but are not smart enough to know it. They are the ones who haven't yet said, "Seek thy servant." We have a need for God to come looking for us.

A Tender Touch

Being honest with God in personal pain or individual despair is not an experience we should go through on our own. We need perspective, we need the help and vision of others. "Is any one of you sick? He should call the elders of the church to pray over him and anoint him with oil in the name of the Lord" (James 5:14).

Paul served God and suffered for God—but not alone. He had support; his letters show it. Josiah Royce pointed out:

> Mystical piety can never either exhaust or express the whole Christian doctrine of life. For the Christian doctrine of life, in its manifoldness, in the intensity and variety of the human interests to which it appeals, is an essentially social doctrine. Private individual devotion can never justly interpret it.
>
> Paul was a mystic; but he was a mystic with a community to furnish the garden where the mystical flowers grew; and where the fruits of the spirit were ripened, and where all the gifts of the spirit found their only worthy expression.[3]

When we speak to God about our feelings, our angers, our hurts, we need the help of Christian friends; we need them to keep us straight lest we are guided only by our own emotions.

We are not, in the light of the holiness of God, ever justified to question him as if we are equals. Job knew that. But we are, in our humanity, allowed to express our honest feelings to him. Still, as we do that, even though we may be corrected by our brethren, we can also look for and expect their empathy. We can look for an arm around the shoulder, a tender touch, an embrace, assurance, the words, "I understand." Their tears blend with ours. We draw from their love; and through it we can know the quality of oneness, the bearing of one another's burdens, for that's what Scripture urges lest those burdens become so heavy they break our backs.

We need the help of other believers, and they need ours. But we don't need their condemnation and they don't need ours either. We have a right to stand before God to be judged; they do too. And we all will be. But only God is God. The wood, hay, and stubble in our lives is his to burn away. We have a right to be corrected by loving brethren and sometimes the right to correct them, but we don't have to take the cynical judgment of people who are quick to see our sins but not their own, the sliver in our eye but not the railroad tie in theirs.

Often I meet people who are truly done in—not so much by their sin, though that is overwhelming, but by the destructive accusations of another Christian. We cannot judge others because we have not been there with them. We cannot because we are not allowed to. "Do not judge, or you too will be judged" (Matthew 7:1). We can only be silent and care, counsel as asked, and gently correct when needed—not out of our superiority but out of an awareness of our own sin.

When one is crying out to God we can stand with him, hold him, help him, and let him cry. He is a friend of God; God will hear his friend. Maybe he is a wayward friend, but his anger, his anguish, his tears, his cries, are the reality of a soul wanting God again—and that's good.

What Are You Doing Here?

But honesty does not always mean anger with God. Sometimes honesty brings us to the confession that we doubt him. Who has not at least once in his life doubted God? We can have one glorious experience after another, experiences of God answering prayer, experiences with his guidance, experiences even with his comfort; yet, because we are so human, the next time we go to prayer we doubt that he will answer.

Everyone has been through that, or will sometime. But in the story of the prophet Elijah, we have a great example of our own humanity in action and how to handle it. Look at this man of God. In chapter 18 of 1 Kings, he experienced the power of prayer as he called upon God before the prophets of Baal, and fire from heaven came down on the water-soaked sacrifice and consumed it. The Baal worshippers had to declare, "The Lord—he is God!" (1 Kings

18:39). Right then Elijah had dramatic evidence of God answering prayer.

And later, in quiet faith, Elijah could see a great rainstorm coming—even when there were no clouds in the sky. He knew what God could do. He was confident, and God brought the rain.

Yet on another day this same Elijah, now depressed and uncertain, stood on the mountain with his mantle covering his face, seeking visible evidence of the presence of God passing by.

God said to him: "What are you doing here, Elijah?" In other words, "Where is your faith, man? What are you doing, hiding in this cave with your scarf over your face?" This was the Elijah who, having seen the power of God, having experienced dramatic answers to prayer, was still scared by the threat of Jezebel. She had sent a messenger to Elijah telling him that he was going to die. And in 1 Kings 19, Elijah's humanity shows. He was afraid and ran for his life. Crawling under a juniper tree, he cried out to God.

God met Elijah that day, but not in the wind, not in the earthquake, not in the fire, but in a still, small voice.

This was the mighty man of God, scared by the verbal threats of Jezebel. He couldn't handle the threat. This is the man who had seen more of God's strength than most human beings have ever seen. But this day God had to send an angel to help him. Elijah had to experience the drama of an angel giving him cakes baked on a hot stone and a drink of water to believe in the help of God.

Experience told Elijah he could trust God; reason told him he could trust God. But his human frailties made him afraid. His doubts still won out.

We are like that; we know we are. And, like the father of the boy whom Jesus healed, we can only say, "Lord, I do believe; help me overcome my unbelief!" (Mark 9:24). No matter the number of experiences we have had with the power of God, we may still doubt again. Knowing that gives us an honesty when we turn to God on our knees and say, "Oh, God, help me!"

That's honesty, and that's good.

7

Praying When Prayer Doesn't Seem to Work

■ ■ ■

One Saturday in Houston, Texas, I toured the National Aeronautics and Space Administration (NASA) headquarters. It was the week that the second space shuttle, Columbia, was launched. I left the main tourist attractions and, escorted by a project engineer, climbed into the simulator, the practice unit of Columbia. It was an exact duplicate of the one that went into space.

As I sat in the commander's seat, I tried to imagine what it must be like to be in space. But even as I pretended, I knew that in reality, "I'm on the ground." I will probably never get off the ground in a spacecraft. I can only guess what it might be like in space. I am earthbound; that is my reference point.

But others know what it is like not to have Earth as a reference point. Once in space, astronauts think about a particular focus. They have to be strapped in somewhere, or they float adrift. They wear suction cups on their feet to enable them to stand. These suction cups release with a twist of the foot, then hold firm again with the proper placement. Astronauts need to be attached somewhere in order to work. If they aren't, they can't even push a switch on a computer, for in trying to push switches they push themselves backward. That's a problem with weightlessness.

And when they sleep, it doesn't matter whether they sleep on the "top" of the bunk or on the opposite side of it, the "bottom" of the bunk, or even sleep standing up. There is no "top" or "bottom," no "up" or "down" in space. They shut their eyes and their inner reference tells them that they are lying down. Since there is no weight, it doesn't matter which way they are facing when they sleep—up, down, or sideways. Sleep comes because their minds decide for them which way is up and which way is down.

We are in a weightless world too. There are no fixed reference points, no "up" or "down," no right way or wrong way. The only reference we have is in the mind of each person—we decide our reference point. We decide to what we will be tied; we determine each step we take. Without a reference point we aren't able to function. We can't accomplish anything.

In a society without fixed points we have to decide to make our own or we will be adrift and every action will be negated by a counterthrust.

People have to be committed to something, and only those who determine that they will be, who have a reference point, will ever touch the world in a meaningful way. The Christian, with reference to the Rock and obedience to the high calling of God in Christ Jesus, has a reason for commitment.

God's Word says: "You will keep in perfect peace him whose mind is steadfast, because he trusts in you" (Isaiah 26:3). We are urged to be "transformed by the renewing of [our] mind. Then [we] will be able to test and approve what God's will is—his good, pleasing and perfect will" (Romans 12:2). We are told, "Let this mind be in you, which was also in Christ Jesus" (Philippians 2:5, KJV).

Astronauts train their minds and fix a reference point; it is the only way they can live in their weightless environment. Christians do that too, all the time, in this "weightless" environment in which we live. For there are no fixed social values for us anymore, and if we function like the rest of society we too will drift. With no fixed position, no matter what we do, no matter what we try to touch in life, it will push us as much as we try to push against it. We will be useless.

Our Reference Point

In our daily existence only obedience to the guidance that God gives will keep us going; only commitment to him will keep us from floating. We will walk only when we clamp down on him— he alone is firm; he is unchanging. We stand or move in what is fixed—God—and we know that if we move from that point of reference we will start to drift again.

With God, your reference point spiritually is always relational, not existential. Check this again and again, not for the sake of having sensations or voices coming to you from the outside but simply to know how you are doing. That is what prayer is, a relational conversation with our reference point. God is our focus, and because he is, we can act.

Prayer isn't something that "delivers." Prayer isn't a computer, a button we push. Prayer is a relationship with God. Prayer is listening; prayer is talking. Prayer is moving along in the confidence that God is guiding whether or not we happen to be aware of where we are at the moment. What we are certain of is that no matter where we are, he is there too.

Babies cry when they don't see their mother. She has to show herself and say, "Here I am. Mommy's right here," and then the baby is at peace. As children grow older, they still need mother, but it's enough to know that mother is in the next room. They know to whom they belong. And though some think they "grow up" and don't need to be looked after or need God, they are only kidding themselves. Their inability to cope is proof enough of their need for God. Our maturity in praying is a constant renewing of our reference contact. God is there, near us, whether or not we always see evidence of him.

God isn't always saying to us, "Here I am." He doesn't have to. We don't keep track of him; he is keeping track of us. Thomas à Kempis said:

> My son, trust not the emotion of the moment; for whatsoever it may be, it will soon give place to another. As long as thou livest in this world, thou art subject to change, even against thy will. Thus thou art now glad, now sad . . . now diligent, now listless; now grave, now light-hearted. But he that is wise and well-instructed in the things of the spirit standeth above these changing emotions. He is not swayed by personal feelings, nor doth he study from which quarter the wind of instability bloweth; but only that his whole mind and intention are directed to the right and wished-for end. Thus will he be able to remain steadfast and unshaken in the midst of many changes; for that his singleness of purpose is directed unceasingly to Me.[1]

Satan would like to have us measure God's concern for us only by what God shows in a tangible way. If he can get a person to think about measurable results, visible answers, physical gifts, then the moment we don't see them he can hint, then suggest, then boldly declare, "Prayer doesn't work." He will have been successful in the oldest deception. He will have changed our reference point.

God is our reference point because we have determined that, for us, he will live in our hearts; we will be his person—heart, soul, mind, and strength. That's a trust act. This is "up," we say—and we rest in that. How do we know it is "up"? Because the One who lives in us knows. We are concentrating on him, deriving our balance, our focus, our direction, our ability to act from him.

Not My Ability

God should be our focus, not the act of praying. Prayer doesn't have to "work." God answers prayer because he is God, not because we have to see answers. Don't get confused about that. Too many people teach that prayer is a form of magic, and their belief comes very close to the occult. Satan is subtle; he knows what he is doing when he turns people from God who *is* to prayer as something that works.

The efficacy of prayer does not depend upon my ability as "pray-er" or on the intensity of my praying. It does depend upon my trust. But even my trust, my faith, is not strictly my own doing. "It is the gift of God—not by works, so that no one can boast" (Ephesians 2:8-9). Faith is the work of the Holy Spirit. The efficacy of my prayer is based on my desire to have the Divine Intercessor be my intercessor. "There is one God and one mediator between God and men, the man Christ Jesus" (1 Timothy 2:5). We have Jesus standing in the place of prayer on our behalf. He is the one who understands us, our circumstances, our world, and who knows how to intercede for us because he knows us and he knows the Father.

We cannot go along on our feelings, or by what we think we know, or what we have conjectured in our own minds. For then we will have made for ourselves a god who is no bigger than we are. The Son knows the Father, and he is our High Priest, our Intercessor, our Go-between, the One who has entered the Holy of

Holies on our behalf.

The question, therefore, is not, "Does prayer work for me?" but rather, "Is my relationship to God the Son as it ought to be?" Am I concentrating on that work of obedience that places me under the command and control of the Savior? Through his lordship, he is interceding on my behalf. God answers prayer for my sake because it is first of all for Jesus' sake. I am his and he lives in me. He cares about that which is his own, and I am his own. I know it on the basis of his promise and finished work.

On My Behalf

Dietrich Bonhoeffer talks about God being aware of the Son, Christ Jesus. My Intercessor is neither overwhelmed by nor limited by my limitations or by that which overwhelms me. God hears me praying because God hears his Son praying. And if indeed the relationship is as it should be, a vine-and-branches relationship, then we can cling to and live in the freedom of John 15:7: "If you remain in me and my words remain in you, ask whatever you wish, and it will be given you."

Prayer "works" because we can daily abide in the One who is the Intercessor, the One who is the High Priest, the One who is Lord. We are his, not because we think so or feel so, but because it *is* so on the basis of his great redemptive transaction for us. Through the cross and the resurrection, he is there on my behalf.

And even if disaster comes, realize that he has you; thank him for his leading because he is leading you even if you can't see it immediately.

We pray, and we may think no answer comes. But we keep on going in trust because he doesn't have to give us every answer. He is God; that is enough. He repeats in his Word that he is near. That's what we believe in—his promise, not our definition of results. When we are dealing with the omnipotent God, the word "result" is a puny word. God is much, much bigger than just what we want. God is big enough to want for us what he wants. He comes to us in his timing, with his acts, by his will. Our act is the faith act.

J. Oswald Sanders said:

For our encouragement, we should remember that the walls of Jericho did not fall until the Israelites had circled them a full thirteen times and then shouted the shout of faith (Joshua 6:1-20). We may have circled our prayer-Jericho the full thirteen times, and yet the answer has not come. Why? Could it be that God is waiting to hear the shout of faith? Perhaps that is the reason the forbidding walls are still intact. He delights to see us step out in faith upon His naked promise.[2]

Prayer time is a very personal time because God is personal. We are his son or daughter—that's the ultimate in an intimate relationship. "You received the Spirit of sonship. And by him we cry, 'Abba, Father'" (Romans 8:15).

Dangers in Not Discerning

We should be aware that what we know about prayer individually does not always apply corporately. I meet people who are so desperate for answers to prayer that they take their needs to a prayer fellowship—maybe a small group, maybe their church. And that is usually a good thing to do. That's biblical. All of us have had great times of prayer support when brothers and sisters in Christ have loved us and prayed for us, times when we have been able to bare our soul to them. There is nothing more helpful than to be supported, cared for, and loved in the difficult times of our lives. It is then that we know we are functioning in a supportive way.

But just as individuals can sometimes take their eyes off Christ and put them on circumstances, events, sensations, or the act of praying itself, so people can look to fellowship groups when they ought to be looking at Christ. The fellowship may be immature, or worse, all may be victims of the same teaching. Instead of finding deeper spiritual insights in a group, some persons may find bad teaching, even allowing the group rather than Jesus to be their priest.

There are dangers in not discerning when a group is misguided or when the group becomes a spiritual substitute for God. And it is evident from many experiences that a fellowship group may not be able to handle prayer needs because its own focus is off—it too is adrift and weightless. It is part of the problem.

Not everyone, even in a group, has the heart relationship

needed for prayer ministry. Some believe in prayer as a belief in prayer, not as a belief in the prayer-answering God. Others want to hear prayer needs, comfort and affirm, but they don't pray. "I'm thinking about you," they say. Still others are too insecure even to handle the prayer needs on a human caring or affirming level.

In a prayer fellowship, sometimes what could be a time for compassion and help turns instead into a time of destruction for the person or people involved.

I thought about this when I read an article by a pastor who insisted that people ought to share all their needs with others in the church so that the church could pray intelligently. Indeed, he said, the more severe the problem the more necessary to tell it to the church. He could be right—in theory—but in the real church, the human church, his advice could create chaos and great pain.

One evening a pastor met with his deacons about the serious misconduct of one of the church members. Most of the deacons sat quietly and listened; one wept. But one deacon let everyone know that he had "seen it coming," was not surprised by what happened, and was obviously eager for the meeting to end so that he could get out of the room and spread the news of the sin committed by his brother in Christ. The repair work on the damage he did took years.

People in Process

What does a Christian who truly wants to pray with other believers do about discussing delicate situations in the church? We read articles which tell us that the church body has a right to know, that we are all members one of another, that the ear can't ignore the eye, that if there is a pain in the toe certainly it is felt elsewhere in the body. We know from Scripture that believers are one, that they must bear one another's burdens. We know that Christians are to care for each other, that there should be no secrets among us.

We know all of that about the body, but the body is rarely what it ought to be. Christians are still people in process; they are not all mature. The simplistic teaching that declares, "Tell all for the good of the church," ignores the hurt caused to the individual whose sins are broadcast because some in the congregation can't handle what they hear. Emotionally unstable church members can't be allowed to play fast and loose with the lives and emotions of other people. We are told by some that privacy violates the community, the essence of the church. But that is wrong. It doesn't violate the community any more than I violate a five-year-old member of the family by not telling him all that I tell a fifteen-year-old. The five-year-old isn't old enough to handle it.

One day our daughter, then a little girl, began to talk about an event in a parishioner's life which she should not have known about. "Where did you hear that?" her mother asked. And she told. It seems our pastor had shared private confidences of a parishioner at his dining room table. His children, hearing all of this, proceeded to tell their friends. The children didn't know any better; the pastor should have.

Parishioners, like children, do not all mature at the same pace. A pastor has to know who is able to handle information and who is not; he may even have to help the parishioner who is in pain and wants to share his burden to understand that. For example, wanting help I might be willing, even eager, to share my deep needs with the whole church. But not everyone can handle my needs, and the pastor or another mature believer may have to explain that fact to me lest I create a greater problem for myself by expecting some to take on more information than they can spiritually and emotionally handle. If we don't protect Christians from their own willingness to implicitly trust the body, they may end up hating the body, hating prayer, and hating God.

Maturity means that we understand the body and know what stress the body can take. We don't overload certain parts of it with problems it cannot handle. This calls for judgment, and no one is better equipped than a pastor or elder to know where the weaknesses are because they know the congregation. And if spiritual leaders have had psychological training, they also know any weakness in themselves. At least they should know, and if they don't, it's up to others in the church to tell them. A pastor should know if he has a weakness for saying to his ministerial colleagues: "Well, I was praying with one of my members the other day, the president of the bank; he has a mistress. This is what I said to him. . . ."

He should recognize this weakness if he tends to illustrate his sermons with, "I was counseling someone in our church who has a problem with alcohol." Because if he does, a large portion of the congregation will mentally resolve, "I will never tell him anything." He should know that he must not only keep a confidence himself but recognize in the body others who can also keep a confidence so that there is a prayer support group in the church that people can trust.

God Understands the Details

Mature Christians are quite happy to pray for someone even if they don't know all the details. They know that God understands the details. Mature parishioners will pray for the pastor and his counseling without knowing who the pastor is counseling or what it is about. The mature church member will know that when told something it is for prayer and not for gossip. And the immature, as they grow, will learn from the mature, until they too will be able to take on larger responsibilities of concern.

But as much as we work to develop the ideal congregation, we must know that we will always have some weaker parts. That's the nature of the church—it is a fellowship of less-than-whole people.

To assume that any are born into the kingdom full grown is to assume too much. It is to risk injury to members of the body. It opens the door to anger about prayer and the charges that "prayer doesn't work." Spiritual toddlers need help. That's not an insult, it's a fact. As they mature, they will walk, run, and not fall down as much. Then they too will be able to teach other young ones to walk. Until then, we can't expect them to be spiritual adults—particularly about real prayer.

When the focus is right, the reference is right, the obedience is right, and the relationship is right, we will no longer have to wonder, "Does prayer work?" or ask, "What if prayer doesn't work?" For we will no longer be looking at prayer, we will be looking at God. And just as the astronauts work in space, each with reference to the same point, the church with Christ as the reference will be a place not of drifting souls but of firmly attached functioning people who can live and act.

In a weightless, drifting society we can pray because we know the One who answers prayer—and we know his directions are right.

8

When I Am Pressured to
Do What Is Wrong

■ ■ ■

The life of a Christian is like the flight of a spaceship. His new birth
is the ignition of the rocket. He begins slowly, but it's a start. And
as he gains momentum, moving higher and higher, some of the
once-important support systems drop away. The craft needs to be
free to move. The rocket thrusters, the hooked-up launch equipment, is needed on the ground for lift off but not needed when the
craft truly flies. For Christians in their new life that is true also.
There is much of the pre-launch life that they don't need anymore.
They are out and away and moving. They are set free to fly just as
they were designed to do.

For the non-Christians that is not so. They too are designed to
fly, but they choose to stay on the ground. They like the hookups,
the support systems, the security of lots of fuel, the constant main-
tenance of their needs. They see the small world of activity around
them as the real world, and the people running here and there to
add this or adjust that as the reason for their existence. This is their
universe. It is their world and they understand it. There are people
ready to analyze their problems, people to fuel their large capacity
to consume, experts to repair some physical breakdown—everything they need—focusing on them. They are the center of all
activity. But they don't fly; they don't even get off the ground.
They don't go anywhere.

Yet from their base they may be quick to sneer at the little
spacecraft that is launched and flying. It is small and it appears to
be alone. The heavy, consuming crafts on the ground call to the

spacecraft above, "Real life is here. Real life is what is happening around me." They can't and won't believe the spaceship which says: "I started there too; I know where you are. This is better—this is what we were designed for!"

The Christian soars in the orbit of God. Unbelievers call from their launch pad and insist that their base living is real living. And for them it is, because all they have ever known is their base activity. They have never flown. For them, this is the real world and they assume that because we are not part of their base-locked mentality, we do not understand where they are. We are "out in space somewhere," out of touch with the real aspects of life. They cannot grasp the fact that we were once there on the ground too, and have been launched into something better. Now we are flying in a new dimension but they can't believe it. How could they? They can't conceive of another dimension, especially one without all of the familiar activity around them. And they can't conceive of our freedom from the weight of all that once held us down too. They don't understand because their "big" world isn't big at all. It isn't that they see more; it's that they see less. They are unable to see the bigger world beyond their own immediate sphere. They are, as someone once put it, "as a maggot in a piece of cheese, who, because he lives there and it is his food, thinks that that is all there is to the universe because it is his universe."

Should I Be Flying Too?

Those who stay on the ground aren't happy about those of us who fly. They look at their own design and wonder, "Is there more? Should I be flying too?" But being the center of their world, where the servicing is so good, they don't really want to fly. Still there is that invitation, that reminder every time we fly by, that those soaring free of earth's gravity do have something, a larger panorama than those on the ground can see. Yet they stay where they are.

And still convincing themselves that they are where the best is, the base-bound try to entice the flying ones down to them. Occasionally they succeed and "prove" that they are right—for a spacecraft away from space, lying on the ground, is a helpless thing. It has neither flight nor ground support. The base-living persons need only one such example to prove their theory about themselves and their life. But can they entice one down? Can they convince these flying-free ones that it is so much better where they are? Since they don't want to fly themselves, can they find some flying ones to join them on the ground? If they can, they will not be so uncomfortable. There will be one less to relay descriptions of the awesome view that is reserved for fliers.

Christians are made to fly with God. If you're flying, don't be caught by those who pressure you to come down and become one with them. Nehemiah asked: "Why should the work stop while I leave it and go down to you?" (Nehemiah 6:3). The Christian can also ask: "Why should I stay on the launchpad? Why shouldn't I soar into space? Why shouldn't I be free? That's what I was made for! Why should I be entangled with all of the things that hold the unlaunched rocket in place?"

Christians will always be pressured by those who don't want believers telling them that there is another way to live. Those on the ground don't want to know that there is a better "view" and that they are missing it. They want to stay below and focus on themselves. But they would be a lot more comfortable about it if believers would join them.

Whether it be a little or a lot, don't compromise with those on the ground, the unlaunched ones, even for a minute.

There has been in every era of history pressure to compromise, to engage in sin, to worship mankind instead of God as the center of everything. This has always been and always will be because of people's gullible buying into the lie of the snake. "For God knows that when you eat of it your eyes will be opened, and you will be like God, knowing good and evil" (Genesis 3:5).

Slogans Are Easy

This pressure from Satan has reared its head in every generation, and the tendency for Christian reaction is the same in each generation too. And so also is the need to classify or label all the sins and evil around us. It is so easy to do because it doesn't require much thought just to label and react.

Classifications are simple; we like slogans because they're easy to work with. Every politician knows that. Every advertiser knows that. We like to lump everything together in order to get a handle on it. But when we use labels, we ignore the fine distinctions between various points of view.

In evangelical circles our current label for all this evil is "secular humanism." People's sufficiency unto themselves *does* turn them from much of what is moral, decent, and kind. Human beings in their fallenness aren't just separate; the correct word for that which is the opposite to "holy" is "profane." Profanity is the lifestyle of trying to live apart from God. Mankind apart from God becomes the personification of a swear word. Profane persons become the opposite to the good of God. In saying no to God, they put themselves up as their own god; that's *profane* humanism—to be assessed, avoided, fought against, and judged.

But we should not attack to the point of hurting the humanist as a person. Many humanists believe what they believe because they are searching. If they try to pull down the Christian it is because they are miserable in their search. We must realize that, perverted as it may be, humanity is still the beautiful creation of God, the reflection of the divine nature of the true and living God.

We Can Help the Humanist

Honest humanism, because it begins with mankind (for that's the only place people can start in their quest, even in a quest for something larger than themselves), is searching humanism. Therefore honest humanism doesn't have to end with mankind; we can help the humanists look. We can help them in their searching. We can help them question their own beliefs, because if they do, their conclusions will lead beyond themselves. God is truth, God is holy, God is beautiful. Any steps in seeking those attributes of God bring a person toward God; they open that person to God. For if we help others touch truth, beauty, and love, they will see for themselves that there must be a larger source of beauty, truth, and love than they have ever known before, one certainly larger than themselves.

We must provide opportunities for humanists to find the well from which the living waters are drawn. Even humanistic scholarship will bring people to God if it is indeed *honest* scholarship—a seeking after truth and wisdom—because God alone is absolute truth and absolute wisdom.

It is becoming more and more obvious that it is the true thinkers, the honest men and women, who are turning in believing faith to God. It is the little minds, the people who haven't gone far enough, the ones with but a little learning, who have yet to sense the reality of God. That's why we hurt them if we throw labels at them. They don't have to search any further when we react like that. Their little bits of truth satisfy. We actually isolate them and interrupt them from the pursuit of real truth. We hurt rather than help if we do not allow them to pursue their thinking to logical conclusions.

Enlarge Their View

Why do we react? After all, they cannot hurt God or dethrone him. God does not need a defense. We need instead to get close to them, help them go on, encourage them, lead their thinking. Honest humanism may be their first step. If they explore the streams of life, perhaps they will come to the source of life; certainly they will more likely do that if we take them further in their thinking. We need to have more to do, not less, with the narrowness of secular humanism. We need to work constantly to enlarge their view. We need to know where they are, why they are there, and lovingly help them take the next steps.

But that doesn't mean compromise or even toleration of the actions of unredeemed persons. It means caring for and helping them, not turning them off or insulting them. It doesn't mean wallowing in person-centered worship with them, gorging on human lust with them, or worshiping their gods with them. We are first and foremost bound to God himself; there is to be no compromise with that. But if we are secure in God, the temptations won't hurt us. It isn't temptation that is our downfall anyway, it's the giving in to temptation. Don't insist that the world stop tempting with its secular humanism. Instead, go deeper and deeper into the biblical truth of God and obey him. This will bring far more to light because the Holy Spirit is in us working. We mustn't forget where we are or what we have. We are salt and light. It will be known.

Show the better way, the higher truth. Don't insist that people must stop practicing "secular humanism"; they have nothing else to practice. Rather, show them God's truth, the attractive life in Christ. If secular humanism is having its day, it may be because many who claim the name "Christian" have in fact become "Christian humanists." They don't want secular humanism to reign unchecked, but they don't want the absolute rule of Christ in their lives either.

Sören Kierkegaard, the nineteenth-century Danish philosopher, wrote about the Christian's purity of heart. The pure heart is a heart that is bound to God. God is pure, and the heart tied to that purity is pure. We are tied to him, connected with him, one with him; we are—consider the vine and the branches—attached to him. The question is never how pure should I try to be, rather the question is how closely attached to Absolute Purity—God—do I want to be? James 4:8 encourages us to draw near to God. That's our work, drawing near to him, and thus to draw near to his purity. If we are near, the purity will be there in us. But ours cannot be a drawing near to God in words only, it must be a drawing near in deed and in fact. It comes in our daily lives through the practice of the presence of God. It comes from the transformed mind. The desire for God is as the deer panting for the streams of water (Psalm 42:1). A thirsty soul and a pure heart are what God wants. Stay close to God, seek his presence in all of this life, be closer to him than to anything or anyone else.

I Have Another Perspective

H. C. G. Moule said:

> The Christian's aim is bound, absolutely bound, to be nothing less than this: "Let the words of my lips, and the meditation of my heart, be always acceptable in thy sight, O Lord, my Rock and my Redeemer" (Psalm 19:14). We are absolutely bound to put quite aside all secret purposes of moral compromise; all tolerance of besetting sin, for the sad reason that it is besetting. With open face we behold the glory of the Lord, and ask to be changed (2 Corinthians 3:18) at any cost, all round the circle of life, into the same image. We cannot possibly rest short of a daily, hourly, continuous walk with God, in Christ, by the grace of the Holy Ghost.[1]

When I am urged to do the unclean thing, the impure thing, when immorality or illegal behavior or selfish grasping is put before me, I can't blame those who tempt me with all that. They don't know any better. Still, I don't have to be a part of it.

I can work for better television, seek the end of pornography, commit myself to the care of the poor, the elderly, the disenfranchised, the dispossessed. But I can't criticize those who cause these problems; they probably don't know any better.

Because I have another perspective, because I know what life can be, because I know what we were designed to be, I need to live an example of that life to the fullest, not only for its life-giving renewal hour by hour for my sake but for the example it gives to encourage a struggler who needs to find this life too. For those reasons I will not, I cannot, compromise.

Dietrich Bonhoeffer said, "So the Christian lives from the times of God, and not from his own idea of life. He does not say that he lives in constant temptation and constant testing, but ... prays that God may not let the time of temptation come over him."[2]

Scripture is clear to those of us who are determined that we will be governed by it. First Thessalonians 4:7 states: "For God did not call us to be impure, but to live a holy life."

Impurity Is Not Our Calling

God does not want us to live in impurity; he did not create us for that. He created us for holiness, for his sanctification. It isn't that he calls us to develop our own sanctification; that is not something we can achieve. He does it in us. The sanctifying One is the Lord Jesus Christ. We are already in him, and he works out in us that sanctification. Therefore, because we belong to the sanctifying One and he is sanctifying us, we don't engage in impurity. We can't do it, not because it does anything to God, for God is not touched by us, but rather for what it does to us. God knows what impurity does to us and it breaks his heart. He loves us too much for it not to break his heart.

People are confused, of course, by teachings such as these, for they think of impurity as something from which to abstain on their own strength, and of sanctification as something to achieve. We are being sanctified; if we are in Christ, that's what he is doing in us. We are clean, whole, complete, justified, and since that is so we do not practice impurity. We are in Christ and he is pure; therefore, it is contrary to what we are in Christ to be impure. We cannot practice what we are not. That does not mean that we will not fall into impurity, trip into it, or wander into it when we take our eyes off the True Light—it happens regularly. We are not freed from the flesh yet, we aren't in heaven yet; we will stray. But we will not *live* in impurity. That is not our calling. Our calling is to live out what we are as justified and sanctified ones in Christ Jesus.

Jesus said, "If anyone would come after me, he must deny himself and take up his cross daily and follow me" (Luke 9:23). Self-denial is more than self-control. It is the ability, purposely and decidedly, to say no to self. It is a willingness to turn our backs on something and to turn our faces toward something. It is not just controlling or regulating by laws what is corrupting, destroying, or hurting us; it is a purposeful turning away from these. We do it for God's sake and for our own sake.

That's the way we face down what tempts and corrupts. And at the same time we lead others out from it, showing them a better way, encouraging them to look at what is better, and not letting them go. We hold on and help but we don't get dragged down with them. A person who joins another in a ditch can't pull him out.

Mankind Is Not Getting Better

Don't be trapped into believing that all is right in this world. There are those who will try to teach you that and sometimes even use Scripture to do so.

It was Gottfried Leibnitz, writing in the seventeenth century, who spoke of a world that was good, a world of truth and joy, a world that had in it the essence of perfection. What then of sin and pain and struggle and suffering, you ask? Well, he tried to explain suffering by saying it is similar to the grain of wheat falling to the ground and dying so that it can produce more. It is what Jesus spoke about. In fact, Leibnitz taught that such pain contributes to man's good. For as man suffers and feels pain, fruit comes. It leads him on to an even greater perfection.

Leibnitz's observation is true enough in one sense, for many people become stronger because of suffering. But that is only an explanation for what *happens* to man, not for what man *is*. In fact, the world is not more perfect for all of its pain. Nor are people. Mankind is not getting better, nor will we, for we are part of fallen creation. We are not living as Adam did before the fall. We are not in communion with God. And even when redeemed and given life and wholeness in the centrality of Jesus Christ, the decay and the corruption that attacks us from every side is still there, surrounding every individual. People will use drugs, alcohol, sex, the deadening effect of a television set, or even the busyness of everyday life as devices to distract them from reality. This world is painful. For some the threshold of pain is higher than for others, but the pain is still there. And we do not get better for it. Leibnitz was wrong.

A Reminder of Another Way

God offers himself in the midst of an anti-God, painfully fallen environment. It is peace amid turmoil, rest in confusion. In despair, he is the reason for being. And fallen humanity senses it. If people were content in their own private separation from God, why would they not rest in their separateness? Why do they work so hard to bring others down to themselves? Because others who are not like them are a threat, a reminder of another way, another world, another life. And they know it.

Our standing firm as believers in the true God is a beacon light; it is salt. To compromise, to become one with the world—whether it's in our cheating, our divorcing, our aborting human lives, our lying, our conniving—is to say to the world, "Your suspicions are wrong. There is no better life than what you have. We are only pretending about what we have; we are faking it. Your inner longings for God are all misunderstood." We tell people that there is nothing better than what they have, and in doing so we leave them without hope. For even though they attack, tempt, urge us to compromise, they are always wondering deep down inside if perhaps we are right and they are wrong. They must be shown light, for only when they see a light can they hope to have that light too.

There is a better life, a better view, one free of the compromising controls of the corruption around us. We can enjoy, indeed revel in, the "more" of God, and say to those missing it: "It's here; launch out, be free, come to the living God and live—fly!" The hope that we offer, the better life we seek for others, is the life which amid the tragic offerings of the confused and the lost is in friendship with God.

God is your defense, he is your armor; he is your righteousness too, in all the temptations that come. Hear again the words of Bonhoeffer:

> From heaven the Lord gives to the defenseless the heavenly armor before which, though men's eyes do not see it, Satan flees. *He* clothes us with the armor of God, *he* gives into our hand the shield of faith, *he* sets upon our brow the helmet of salvation, *he* gives us the sword of the spirit in the right hand. It is the garment of Christ, the robe of his victory, that he puts upon his struggling community.[3]

And again, this man who faced the world and died said:

> He who loses courage because of the suddenness and the awfulness of temptation, has forgotten the main point, namely that he will quite certainly withstand the temptation because God will not let it go beyond that which he is able to endure. There are temptations by which we are particularly frightened because we are so often wrecked upon them. When they are suddenly there again, we so often give ourselves up for lost from the beginning. But we must look at these temptations in the greatest peace and composure for they can be conquered, and they are conquered, so certain is it that God is faithful. Temptation must find us in humility and in certainty of victory.[4]

Know this: You wouldn't have to face any temptation if you had already given in. If you were already the devil's possession, he wouldn't have to work so hard on you. But you are "someone"—and if the snake invaded the garden of purity once, he will do it again and again. He has so much to lose if he doesn't. Remember the One who said, "Take heart! I have overcome the world" (John 16:33). That's his word for you.

Take heart! That's for the soaring one. Enjoy the view of your Christian life. It's what you were designed for. Don't ever compromise it or give it up. You are set free to fly.

9

Becoming Free
■ ■ ■

Augustine was a brilliant, faithful Christian born in the fourth century. To him the Christian church owes much, for he followed God's Word faithfully and taught the church during the onslaught of the heresies of Manichaeism, Donatism, and Pelagianism. He was a man of God, but he didn't start out that way. As a young man, Augustine lived for his lusts. At sixteen he was living with his mistress, having already enjoyed the lascivious pleasures of Carthage. At age thirty-one, then a teacher at the University of Milan, he was sitting thoughtfully one day in a Milan garden when he picked up the Scriptures and read, "Let us behave decently, as in the daytime, not in orgies and drunkenness, not in sexual immorality and debauchery, not in dissension and jealousy. Rather, clothe yourselves with the Lord Jesus Christ" (Romans 13:13-14). He met Christ Jesus—and claimed him as Lord.

On Easter Sunday, at thirty-three years of age, Augustine was baptized into the Christian church. His experience with Christ was liberating. He had been confined in his sin; he was set free in Jesus Christ.

That is difficult for people to understand. They think the opposite. They see lasciviousness as liberating and the putting on of the Lord Jesus Christ as confining. Even some Christians, followers of Christ, still wonder if it is that way. This man Augustine, who studied rhetoric, mathematics, and philosophy throughout his life, said, "Believe in order that you may understand." When he wrote the twenty-two books entitled *The City of God,* he wrote of what he understood—the battle between two cities: the city founded by Satan and all of his wickedness, and the other city, the city of God. He wrote of slavery to Satan versus freedom in Christ. He knew the difference between the two.

In the book *Why I Am Not a Christian,* Bertrand Russell also talked about freedom. To him freedom meant standing on our own two feet, looking squarely at the world, and making the best we can of life. He said that believing in God is not a worthy belief of a free man. Was Bertrand Russell free? Was he more liberated for having denied the existence of God than he would have been if he had admitted to it? Are we weaker for believing in the God of the universe and for willfully, purposely following him as our Master and King?

Or is it, rather, the *believers* who know true freedom, because they know the Source of life? Can one be free who is apart from God? How can any human being, subject to the forces of nature, living under the laws of creation, ignore the Creator, the Source and the Reason behind our existence? Some think they can; we know that to be in balance they can't.

It used to be that there were many "free thinkers" like Russell. There aren't so many anymore. The few who choose to be are mostly of Russell's vintage. Having read a little bit, they have accepted his teachings. But there aren't very many. We have come too far and learned too much. We've discovered the holes in his thought.

I read Russell's book *Why I Am Not a Christian* more than twenty-five years ago. Recently I read it again. I found that though twenty-five years ago I disagreed with him on the basis of my own experience with God, I now disagree with him also through just plain thinking. Russell started with premises which eliminate, step by step, what he called the reasons for belief in God. But the reasons he criticized are the reasons of nonrational religionists. As a rationalist he had an answer for them. As a Christian I do too. But Russell did not have an answer for Christians because he saw Christians simply as people governed by fear.

But anyone who knows true Christianity knows that Jesus Christ takes away our fear. The Scripture is as true a description as it is a promise: "You did not receive a spirit that makes you a slave again to fear, but you received the Spirit of sonship. And by him we cry, '*Abba,* Father'" (Romans 8:15).

Russell took the fear of bondage and attributed it to Christians—then knocked Christians for that weakness. His conclusions are the only conclusions that he could have come to, because his premise was faulty to begin with.

Russell thought he was liberated. He wasn't. No person can be when his only source of thought, action, or belief is himself. He was confined by his own limitations—and those limitations included all the confinement of sin.

Their Step of Faith

Francis Schaeffer taught that God *is*, whether or not we believe in him. God's existence does not depend on our belief in God. Ludwig Wittgenstein, the Austrian philosopher, taught that skepticism is senseless because it is built on doubt about a question: He states that if any question can be phrased at all then it can also be answered. But we cannot phrase a question about God. We cannot question the Infinite because our finite minds cannot grasp him. We can accept God, we can reject God, but we cannot question God. Only God can answer for God. He is beyond our proving. Therefore, skepticism about God becomes nonsense.

There are people who are skeptics, but they have no basis for it except that they want to be skeptical. That is their step of faith. The Christian chooses a faith step too. Abraham Kuyper said:

> Verily Christ and He alone has disclosed to us the eternal love of God, which was, from the beginning, the moving principle of this world-order. Above all, Christ has strengthened in us the ability to walk in this world-order with a firm, unfaltering step. [1]

And in our faith steps we are secure. Why? Because in a firm way God enters into the life built on faith. Faith is an act of trust. Trust yields security, and God in turn liberates the life committed in faith and trust. Liberty is by security made.

Kierkegaard suggested that God can have nothing to do with an insecure person. That's a startling thought. He was referring to the child of God, the person who is in Christ Jesus. Kierkegaard was right. We are God's. That is not a wishful state; it is a secure state. What matters is not whether I am secure in "my faith" (for "my faith" is not secure), but am I secure in *God* by faith?

What does God think of me? Am I pleasing him? Am I faithful to him? Do I measure up to his standards? These are the important questions because they are already built on a conviction—the conviction that God is. That is the basis for courage, freedom, boldness in life. If we are insecure it is because we are not looking at God as the One to whom we belong; we are looking rather at ourselves or at other people.

Christians are "enslaved" to the One beyond themselves, the One not limited by their limitations. He is the One who came into this creation and made plain, "If the Son sets you free, you will be free indeed" (John 8:36).

Why So Insecure?

How can we become strong, free, and courageous? What does it mean to be liberated? How are we to cope with and handle life? The answer comes from knowing a simple truth, that God is "for me." And on this basis we step out, we act, we venture, we live. The person who doesn't have that basis of freedom cannot reach the goal of liberation. He'll always be heading in the direction of further confinement.

I am free; Jesus set me free. Why should I reduce the full meaning of that truth by comparing myself with other Christians? Am I supposed to be as successful as they are? As talented? As skilled? If God has made me, called me, and placed me where I am for his reason, if I am his child, adopted, loved, redeemed, chosen, blest, then why am I—why are you—so insecure?

There is only one reason for insecurity: We are not looking at the Person who *is* our security; we are looking at someone or something else. Sometimes we are even looking for evidence of God's security—and missing the security. That's why so many of us are not as free as we could be.

Not many years ago, if we talked about obeying the Scriptures, participating in a Bible study, living by the Word of God, we were looked at askance by those who were not believers. Those who called themselves Bible-believing Christians tended to see a clear distinction between the world's view of God and the view of God as God explained it in Scripture.

Those called "liberals," who accepted society's views, were

intolerant of any stand or view other than their own. It was a joke for years that the least liberal people were those who labeled themselves liberals. Opposing them were fundamentalists, who were known for a narrow view, particularly of Scripture, but unlike the liberals, admitted to and even boasted of their narrow stand.

Today many fundamentalist Christians, once critical of those liberals who mixed together Christianity and a lot of secular, even pagan, culture, are doing the same with their own "fundamental" beliefs.

"How inconsistent, how immoral, how weak, how pagan!" fundamentalists used to say. "They have made their own religion. It certainly isn't Christian." But how many evangelical or fundamental Christians are doing exactly the same thing? There are Bible studies in almost every neighborhood, on college campuses (not only in every dormitory but often on every floor of every dormitory). There are Bible studies in factories, offices, and in government buildings. It's good that people are "into" the Word, but judging from their manner of life they are also into the world. The distinction between the Word of God and the teaching of society around them is no longer clear. In some cases, the Bible is being squeezed into the mold of the world.

Recently, I picked up a book on sex and marriage written by an attorney. In his introduction he stated that the book was written for New Testament Christians, and those who did not accept the teachings of Jesus Christ as authoritative would have difficulty understanding the spiritual concepts presented. I started reading the book. Inside, the author explained how the Bible is misunderstood when it talks about premarital sex being sin, how it is up to the individual to make that decision, how there are times when premarital sex is appropriate and correct. And all that he wrote he backed by Scripture—even giving some Greek texts and using references to well-known commentaries. He was unbiblical, yet his beliefs, he said, were based "on the Bible."

Blind Spots

One day I had a conversation with two lesbian women who assured me that they were born-again evangelical Christians who believed that the Bible is the inspired Word of God. Yet when I turned to specific passages of Scripture about their relationship, they absolutely did not understand them. It wasn't that they were purposely trying to avoid those verses, it was just that they saw no relationship between the Scriptures—what they believed—and their behavior, which the Scripture condemns. At first I thought they were dodging the clear teachings of Scripture. But then I realized that they were not purposely disobedient, they were blind. No matter how I tried to show them the meaning of those passages, the application of the words escaped them. They couldn't see.

Later I said to some Christians, "Those two women weren't pretending, they honestly did not see. Are there also blind spots in my life? I too believe the Bible, but are there passages that I am not seeing because they relate specifically to me?"

I thought about that when I met a family that now only worships privately together; they want no fellowship with other Christians. They want to follow the Bible, they say, and in the churches there are too many inconsistent Christians. So the father leads their family worship every Sunday. They sing, they pray, they study the Bible together, sincerely wanting to follow Christ. But, I keep wondering, who corrects them? I asked them, "How do you know when you are true to Scripture and when you are not?" The answer: "The Holy Spirit teaches us." They are correct in that the Holy Spirit who inspired the writing of the Word certainly inspires the reading of the Word, but he uses the body of believers too.

In the physical body the hands, the eyes, the nose, all work together. The body doesn't know its environment only by the signals in the feet or the nose. Isn't the spiritual body the same?

Several college students in a Bible study group asked me, "What can we do about one or two people in our group who want to dominate the Bible study and tell us what the Bible says because 'the Holy Spirit has revealed that truth' to them? How do we argue with them?" They had a problem, and it faces us all.

Even as we joyfully boast about the number of evangelical Christians who are engaged in Bible study, we are recognizing also a rapid falling away from biblical morality, ethics, and truth. Teaching in the evangelical community is becoming a cacophony of sound. It's like an orchestra without a leader, each musician playing his or her own tune because the conductor is out of the room. There is no harmony, there is no orchestration, and, as a result, the musicians are unable to accomplish what they are supposed to do. They are not free to be musicians; they are unable to learn new arrangements. They can't do what they were meant to do.

People are searching the Scripture, but many are searching for what they want to find. The Bible warns, "Do not let this Book of the Law depart from your mouth; meditate on it day and night, so that you may be careful to do everything written in it. Then you will be prosperous and successful" (Joshua 1:8). Meditate on the Word, yes! But why? "To do everything that is written in it." That's our way to freedom. Our role is not to make our own way prosperous; that's God's role. Our job is not to work toward success; that's God's aim. Our task is to make sure that God's Word is in our hearts, that we meditate on his truth, that it becomes our food, our nourishment, our guide. God takes care of the rest.

The Discipline of the Free

Jesus said, "You diligently study the Scriptures because you think that by them you possess eternal life. These are the Scriptures that testify about me, yet you refuse to come to me to have life" (John 5:39-40).

We search the Scripture, then gather in with it all that is around us and call all the accumulation of it "inspired." We no longer present a clear, distinct message to our world. We are no longer biblical. The Bible says: "All Scripture is God breathed and is useful for teaching, rebuking, correcting and training" (2 Timothy 3:16). That means the Bible is to instruct me so I can be complete and perfect. That's what God wants, but that's not what Satan wants, and Satan seems to be getting his way.

C. Roy Angell, in his book, *Iron Shoes*, said:

Not only is there "power in the blood" to cleanse us from sin, but there is power in the Son of God to break the bonds of Satan and set us free. Through the counsel room of every minister limps a continual stream of men and women who are handcuffed by some habit, some appetite, some sin that has made them prisoners, has hung chains too heavy to carry over their necks. They need to know that Christ, God's Son, can lift them up, make them straight, and break the bonds of Satan.[2]

And many of those "handcuffed" people claim salvation but

haven't pursued obedience to its proper end—their freedom. We are to be servants; then we will be free. We are to follow him; then we will be bold to live. Only surrender will put us in the hands of Christ. He gives a certain message: "If the Son sets you free, you will be free indeed" (John 8:36).

An editorial in the now defunct *Watchman-Examiner* stated:

> Only if we accept the discipline of the free shall we be free indeed. He that persists in sin shall become the slave of sin. The lukewarm will worship the antichrist. The soft free are putty in the tyrant's power. They get that way by imagining he is not so bad after all.[3]

What People Worship

I know a Christian who spends most of his waking time thinking about his investments ("How can I get the best return on my money?"), or what he buys ("I got a really good deal"), or on food ("The cooking in that restaurant is outstanding"). These are first in his thinking. He is a slave to those passions but doesn't know it. He justifies his thinking with words like "stewardship." He says, "I want to be a good steward with the money God gives me," and there is nothing wrong with that. Or, "I have to eat," and that is true too. But the emphasis controls him. It is his primary emphasis, his life, and each year it becomes more and more important to him.

A friend said to me: "You can tell what people worship by what they talk about." And he's right. I hear Christians talk about the value of their stocks. I hear Christians talk about their boats, their cottages—not just occasionally, as one does about anything in life, but all of the time. Because it's what they are thinking about all of the time. We talk about what we are interested in. Nothing else is important. Scripture, and the obedience called for in Scripture, the obedience which truly liberates, is pushed aside. Even our responsibility to others in obedience to Christ is governed by convenience to ourselves or "what's in it for me."

Try something: Explain to some Christians that maybe God didn't make a mistake when he put the natural resources such as minerals or good soil in the world. Maybe there is enough for everyone on earth but maybe God didn't intend that a few people in a few regions use it all while others go without. Try to explain that we ought to be using less. The reaction is sometimes outright anger. "I am not responsible for the rest of the world. I'm not even responsible for the poor in this country; that's what I pay taxes for." Or, "Who is going to take care of me if I don't look out for myself?" Or, "I'm a Christian; I have a right to all the things I want and need. I'm a child of the King; I ought to be able to live as the King's child." And when everything is all used up, well, they have an answer for that too. "Jesus is going to come and take us all home before there is ever any pain or suffering for us." They have it all worked out. Someone once parodied, "I'll build a sweet little nest, shut out the distressed, and let the rest of the world go by."

What does all this mean? Simply that we are not free. We are owned by all that we have made important. If God was important, then we would be obeying him and following him.

We are not able to cope and handle life knowing that God is for us because in reality we have made our own gods. We are enslaved by our wants, our lusts, our passion to satisfy ourselves.

Am I for God?

As a magazine editor, I find increasingly that manuscripts coming in contain various roots of heresy. An author might be 98 percent faithful to Scripture and may have a zeal and enthusiasm for God that is commendable. But there is error too, usually the kind of error that makes God what man wants God to be or adds something to go alongside faith or takes away from the deity of Jesus Christ.

Those authors don't even realize what they have done because they are reflecting a Christian culture that doesn't recognize its assimilations from pagan culture. They have no teaching that gives them a balanced biblical theology, nor a Christology that is sound, nor a knowledge of church history that exposes problem teachings of the past. Nor is there even a willingness to note these problems. Never mind the heresies of church history, never mind that we flirt with them again, never mind that so many are claiming to belong to Christ who really belong to themselves, never mind that Christians are dissipating their lives and calling what they do "of God."

These are captured people who want the assurance that "God is for me," without asking, "Am I for God?" The communion with God is gone; they are owned by other values, and that entrapment has taken away their liberty to be free in Christ. A. Kuyper, in his book *Calvinism,* said: "Only he who personally stands before God on his own account, and enjoys an uninterrupted communion with God, can properly display the glorious wings of liberty."[4]

Where are those who are yielded to the Scripture on the basis of what the Scripture says, not what people want it to say? Where are the Christians who will subject themselves to the whole counsel of God? Where are those who will read church history and theology to see what other people have wrestled with in the past? Where are the theologians of the day who can help us learn that we can't baptize culture and call it Christian? Where are the books that teach us something more than the faith of pleasure, that do more than tell us what we are entitled to, that we ought to have a happy life, a pleasant sex experience, the best stocks—all in the name of Jesus?

Where is our freedom? We have managed this far, many of us, because life has been fairly comfortable. But what will happen when the crunch comes? When persecution comes to us and we find that we are not snatched away? When we, like many Christians in the world, are martyrs too? Where will we be when the dissipation of the present age catches up with us? Already we are beginning to see the signs of failure in those who have been living without disciplinary controls. And how will we function if we choose enslavement on an even grander scale?

Only when we can be trusted to read the Word on our knees will we be free. Then God will be with us on *his* terms. He will be able to trust us with his power; he will be our God; we will be his people.

When Peter came out of prison, the angel said, "Go, stand in the temple courts . . . and tell the people the full message of this new life" (Acts 5:20). He was to speak all of it, not part of it. He was released from prison for a reason. We are released from prison too. We are released from our own fancies about God and from the prisons of our own wants and desires. We are free and we have the liberty of declaring by our lives, our actions, as well as our words the whole counsel of God—not only in the church but in the marketplace as well.

Secular life was all around Peter, but he told the people about the Christ-life, the eternal life, the whole message of God. So we are called to declare that message in the marketplace, in the temple, wherever we are. That's why we were let out of the prison of Satan's bindings. We are to stand as declarers of the whole counsel of God in word and deed, proving by our lives the gospel of true freedom.

We're released from prison to do what we're told to do. Whether it results in our success or our death, faithfulness is the key to freedom. Faithfulness is the way to live every day.

10

At Last!
I Can Say No

■ ■ ■

Hans Rookmaaker, the Dutch writer on art history and a disciplined Calvinist, felt deep pain when he learned that a friend had left his wife to live with another woman. Rookmaaker was shocked that this man believed he could do it as a Christian because "the gospel gives me freedom." Said Rookmaaker: "I told him that—unless things drastically change—he is not seen anymore as a Christian by me. I want to remain friends, but not within the Christian group."[1]

Someone may say, "That's cruel! We have to live in this world, and the world is not ideal. There are temptations and struggles; none of us is perfect. Who has a right to judge another?" The answer is, God has that right. Isaiah said, "Woe to those who call evil good and good evil, who put darkness for light and light for darkness, who put bitter for sweet and sweet for bitter" (Isaiah 5:20).

God knows our world. In Jesus Christ he entered the world and was tempted in all points as we, yet without sin. He is the one who said, "Take up your cross and follow me." It is not an easy weight, that cross. He never promised that it would be an easy cross to bear or a pretty one to display or one that would bring excitement or pleasure.

We don't have to bear the cross if we don't want to. We can refuse, or worse, say that we will take up the cross knowing full well that we won't. We can be like the son who said to his father, "Yes, I will go into the vineyard," but didn't. We can say that, but we will answer for that kind of lying. We can filter the commands of God through our own system of wants and desires and "needs" if we want to, but we will stand before him and give an account for what we have done. All these things will be "uncovered and laid bare before the eyes of him to whom we must give account" (Hebrews 4:13).

He knows where we are and what we face. He knows where he has placed us. He knows also that we don't have to slip and slide and fall. The mud pits of this world do not have to be entered. We can say no.

An easing of the commandments a little here, the acceptance of something less than the best there, is of our own making; we slide by our own choice. The giving in to personal desires is not his doing, it is ours.

Good for Us to See

In the fourth and fifth centuries in Egypt there were religious people who recognized the dangers of the self-indulgent life. They did something about it. They became monks. We can learn something valuable from them and from the whole monastic movement.

Some may criticize those ancient monks for their theological weaknesses such as not fully understanding salvation by faith in Christ alone. But we can't, by finding fault with their theology, simply dismiss the life they exemplified and taught, for their works of discipline grew out of a desire to separate themselves from a world that knew nothing of the word "no." They did what they did for a reason. They had their sights on God. Their teachings were not for everybody then, and they won't be for everybody now. But their example is good for us to see.

It is written of Abba Dioscorus of Namisias:

> Every year he made one particular resolution: not to meet anyone for a year, or not to speak, or not to taste cooked food, or not to eat any fruit.... This was his system in everything. He made himself master of one thing, and then started on another, and so on each year.[2]

"Why?" some will ask. "To what end is all this?" ask others. But think about it. The man didn't have to do it; he did it for his own gain, and he did it for spiritual reasons too. When a person fights temptation, even innocent ones such as desiring a piece of cooked meat, he discovers that he has within him the ability to resist something far bigger. And before anyone discounts the value of the monks' desire for obedience to the disciplined life, before anyone scoffs, let that person ask, "Will I also scoff at Scripture?" For even if we refuse to learn from these monks, there are still the words of Jesus:

> Be careful, or your hearts will be weighed down with dissipation, drunkenness and the anxieties of life, and that day will close on you unexpectedly like a trap. For it will come upon all those who live on the face of the whole earth. Be always on the watch, and pray that you may be able to escape all that is about to happen, and that you may be able to stand before the Son of Man (Luke 21:34-36).

Jesus told his disciples, "Whoever loses his life for me will find it. What good will it be for a man if he gains the whole world, yet forfeits his soul? Or what can a man give in exchange for his soul?" (Matthew 16:25-26).

Abba Cyrus of Alexandria said:

> If you are not tempted, you have no hope: if you are not tempted, it is because you are used to sinning. The man who does not fight sin at the stage of temptation, sins in his body. And the man who sins in his body has no trouble from temptation.[3]

What a far distance many of us are from Abba Evagrius who said, "Cut out of your heart the desire for many things, and so prevent the mind being disturbed, and the quiet wasted."[4]

There is health in this "cutting-out" process. It is the discipline of not having, not grasping, not seeking personal pleasure, but rather holding to and loving God for who he is in himself. There is true worship in that because it is a worship that centers on him, not self. It is a worship that God honors.

Yet too many of us simply allow ourselves to do what gives us pleasure; we have no controls, we leak out at the edges. Such an undisciplined life leads to all kinds of spiritual distress, and then we wonder why this distress has come. For many, even praying is undisciplined and hollow. I am still surprised, even though I've experienced it often, to meet Christian people, even pastors and church workers, who do not have a regular, disciplined time alone with God. When temptation comes, or problems emerge, they wonder what is wrong. They don't understand why they are so weak.

His Terms, Not Ours

Many ignore the day-by-day meeting with God because, caught up as they are in the quest for spiritual thrills, they expect pleasure even from this prayer time too. And if pleasure with God (by their own definition of it) doesn't come, they stop having their time of personal worship.

For the sake of our pleasure, God has to titillate our senses to prove to us that he is near. If he doesn't, we go looking for something else. We have to hear voices, or have prickly feelings, or feel a warm glow. To many people that is all God is good for. As a result, for some people even the Christian life is an unhappy life because it is centered on the person who is taking, not on the holy God himself.

The riches of the Spirit-filled life don't just drop from heaven. God meets us in the discipline of daily obedience, and in it we are blessed in him. He meets us on his terms, not ours. His coming and his giving are his. If our human weakness has demanded certain experiences and signs, it is time for us to realize that if God were ruled by our spiritual lust he would be no God, he would be only the creation of our inner urgings. Scripture tells us: "We have this treasure in jars of clay to show that this all-surpassing power is from God and not from us" (2 Corinthians 4:7).

In those early monasteries the younger monks watched and learned from the older ones. Even people who never entered the full monastic orders came to spend a year or two with these brothers—not just to secure their salvation, as many of us have tended to assume, but to learn what the Apostle Paul taught, to work out their salvation with fear and trembling. (See Philippians 2:12.)

We had better be learners of obedience and discipline too. Speaking in Scripture, Wisdom says, "Blessed is the man who listens to me, watching daily at my doors, waiting at my doorway. For whoever finds me finds life and receives favor from the Lord. But whoever fails to find me harms himself" (Proverbs 8:34-36).

The old monastics were stable. They were part of the church, giving their lives to it. They were under its umbrella. Today's "monastics" are too. These Christians do not spend their time sniffing the wind for the latest theological fad to chase, or for the teachings of a celebrity to follow. They do not shop around for a more exciting preacher or for the vicarious thrills that come from hearing about the former sinful life of the newest Christian super-star. They are not spiritual gadflies, unwilling to make a commit-ment unless there is some personal enjoyment or recognition in it. Theirs is not a cafeteria religion, sampling a little of this and a little of that, taking whatever appeals to the spiritual palate at the moment. These are not sideshow frequenters who tour the Chris-tian midway, listening to this barker or that one calling to "come see what we have here."

The "new monastics" (and this is a good term to apply to disci-plined believers) are willing to do today what those monastics did in the context of their earlier centuries. For although time and events change, the basic commitment of the believer is the same.

No Other Way to Go

Disciplined believers labor for the fellowship. They pray, they teach, they love, they nurture. They have a purpose in their devo-tion and they practice it day in and day out. They go without, not out of spiritual pride but because they do not have spiritual pride. They want to yield to God.

Discipline is not just following rules, nor is it even copying the early monks; it is existing in and for the One who owns us. We practice discipline neither for self-conceit nor to brag about it, but for him. We obey God because it is the moral and right thing to do.

Committed, disciplined Christians trust God and go on with him every day no matter what the circumstances of their lives. They do so because they must. They know from experience and reason that there is no other way to go. The One who said, "Never will I leave you; never will I forsake you" (Hebrews 13:5), has always kept his word. We can live within the security of that assur-ance.

Those early disciplined monastics did the difficult thing and did it for God. They lived in a world that lacked discipline, and we do too. They were proof to themselves that a person can serve God first. They worked at it—they learned to say no.

They knew something that William Law also knew. In his book, *A Serious Call to a Devout and Holy Life*, he said, "If religion commands us to live wholly unto God, and to do all to His glory, it is because every other way is living wholly against ourselves, and will end in our own shame and confusion of face."[5]

We have moved a long way from that; we have moved too far. It is time to find again what the monastics had. We must come not to a form of monasticism that is nonevangelical and ingrown, shut off from the world with only occasional excursions out to it, but rather a monasticism in which we are shut in with Christ and at the same time shut in with the world.

Is this contrary to reality? Is this a movement against ourselves? No, it isn't. We are not living against ourselves when we follow him. It is "ourselves" that interests him. All that we have read and heard about "me" and "my pleasures" and "my development" and "myself" is what God wants for me too. But he is the giver, the Source, not I. He alone knows the "me" part of myself.

We are false to true self when we seek for ourselves and are not yielded to the One who alone can provide what we need and want. James McConkey said:

> To walk in the Spirit—not to walk in the flesh—is the whole secret of the believer's life of power, privilege and peace. But for the believer to walk in the Spirit, the first essential is his absolute yielding to God of all control and direction of his life.[6]

Try something. Find the command of God that is hardest for you to obey. Then commit your obedience to God and practice living that commandment as if that commandment were no longer being broken by you. You will find that when we give something to God and practice it, we do succeed. He takes away the desire to renege on our promise.

There are thousands of Christians who have experienced deliverance from something that has kept them from a life of obedience because they finally identified their need, took upon themselves the obligation of praying about it, and then did what they promised God they would do. God has reinforced their promise with results. Followers of Jesus do not practice obedience to become someone, but they practice obedience because they *are* someone—God's person. And they intend to leave behind anything and everything that keeps them from being fit representatives of all that is holy.

The Happiest State of All

There is liberty in saying no because it moves us out of the narrow inlet blocked by debris into the great open ocean of the yesses of God. "Yes" turns us from the shallow, from the weak, the restrictive, to the deep, the strong, the liberating—to the resources of the Omnipotent God. He is the One who has a dream for us. He is the One who puts everything together in a magnificent yes. And for us, to be there with him in his great yes, is the happiest state of all! Richard Foster (*The Celebration of Discipline*) is right, and he answers the millions who do not know what they are rejecting when he says, "When one's inner spirit is set free from all that holds it down, that can hardly be described as dull drudgery."[7]

What in fact holds us down is what the unknowing world calls "liberty." That liberty is no liberty at all. Speak of liberty and freedom and excitement to the one who has practiced sexual promiscuity and is enslaved by it. He doesn't have liberty at all. A student newspaper on the campus of Cambridge University in England printed this story:

> Two girl students at Cambridge University bet on who could go to bed with the most men in five days.
> The staggering score for the blue-stocking sex orgy was 98-62. Another brainy bird at the revered seat of learning boasted that she would have sex with every man in her college . . . all 400 of them. [8]

Are they free?

Speak of liberty and joy and freedom to one infected by a venereal disease.

Speak of liberty to the mother who had her child murdered in the womb and now has to live with that thought until the day she dies.

Talk of liberty to one who is so controlled by the need to succeed, to have power, prestige, or riches that he is unable to give his heart, his life, his resources, or his skills to anything else. He may as well be in prison.

Cry "liberty" to the one who has no self-control, who is unable to withstand anything, who is pleasure-oriented, who has missed his calling, whose gifts lie untouched, whose love is strapped and unexpressed, whose power is gone.

Tell these people that they are free. To do that is to whistle in the dark, for we know that it is not true. Worse, they know it too.

Thomas Merton said, "In Christ there is no conflict and no anguish, no dissension and no shadow of division, no change, no sorrow. . . . In Him we find both liberty and security."[9]

It is never too late to say no. The freedom offered in Christ is that we can say no, and when we say it there comes the opposite resounding yes. And out of that yes God builds a life more beautiful, more complete, more satisfying than anything that we could ever create for ourselves. He wants that for each of us.

For more than ten years, first on an eastern campus and then in the midwest, I ministered to university students. We would meet regularly to pray for each other, "How can I pray for you to be the obedient man or woman God wants you to be? What are the blocks that need to be eliminated, and what are the changes that need to be made?" And as we prayed specifically for obedience and holiness and faith, I could see God take those young lives and develop them.

I see how he has honored those times of serious prayer. Wherever I go now, I meet these students with whom I once prayed or who prayed for me, and I see what God is doing in their lives. I compare them to others who missed that time of praying because they were not willing to let God have them—to be all that God wanted them to be—and I see the difference.

A. H. McNeile said: "A man's soul grows, if it is growing, like his body, with a slow imperceptible motion, as a result of everything that he does, every breath that he breathes, and everything that he eats and drinks."[10] God offers this to us. He is our life; he is our gain.

11

My Life, My Gain

■ ■ ■

We have to be honest. Each of us will ask the question, "What's in this for me?"

We'll ask because we are selfish. It is human to be so. It would be a lie to deny that.

One evening in March 1955, I sat in the home of a certified public accountant. We were not discussing money. He was talking to me about Jesus Christ. Through the Scriptures he showed me what salvation means. It was the first time that anyone had ever done that for me.

I listened, but I argued too. I was a college freshman—fairly smart, I thought—and having argued religion before with my friends and having read a little about religion, I had my own beliefs about it.

I had usually done quite well in the past with the argument: "That's fine for you. *I* don't need it." Or, when people really got pushy: "Religion is a weak man's crutch." And then there was the one I used that usually made religious people fold: "I'm as good as any of those hypocrites in the church."

But this man didn't argue with me or react defensively to my rehearsed lines. He simply opened his Bible, placed it on a coffee table in front of us, and pointed to what it said. He responded to my remarks with, "Look what the Bible says." And as he did this, he was wise enough not to flip from book to book or try to impress me with all that he had learned. He stayed in one book, Paul's letter to the Romans, and always he let me read it for myself. That night I became a Christian. Since then I've never doubted the power that is in the Word of God.

My CPA friend started with Romans 3:23: "For all have sinned, and come short of the glory of God" (KJV). It's good that he did because I had no real trouble with that verse. There was no difficulty in my mind about believing that all people are sinful; I could see that by observing people around me and by looking at myself. I learned later how defensive some Christians become about "sin," even just the word, as if they have to explain or justify biblical statements about it. They don't. Most of the people I knew who did not believe in Christ had no problem believing in sin. Most honest people admit that if there is a God, they don't measure up to his standards. What sustains them, and particularly what keeps them from coming to Christ, is not unbelief about sin but their belief that "I'm not as bad as the next person."

I could accept Romans 3:23. It was a straight-out statement and I agreed with it. I suppose all who look squarely at themselves will admit that "all have sinned." The ones who won't acknowledge sin are dodging publicly what they know to be true. But they admit it, most of them, in the privacy of their own minds.

Then my CPA friend turned a few pages in his Bible to Romans 6:23, and that's when I began to argue. The verse states, "For the wages of sin is death; but the gift of God is eternal life through Jesus Christ our Lord" (Romans 6:23, KJV). I did what most people do when they see that Scripture; I trotted out the argument, "How can a just God condemn anybody to hell? How can God, if he is a God of love, not take everybody to heaven?" Having used that argument or some variation of it before, I knew that it usually made Christians stutter. This time it didn't work.

"Read it again," he said. When I had, he asked me, "What are wages?" Well, that's not hard to answer when you have a job, and I did. I punched a time clock, rolled up my sleeves, and worked. So he asked me, "When you receive your paycheck every two weeks, is that a gift?" The answer was so obvious it was silly. Of course the paycheck was not a gift; I earned the money! "Then," he said, "you would never say that when your employer gives you your paycheck he is giving you a gift."

"Right," I agreed.

He emphasized, "The wages of sin is death. Sinners are working too; they are working at their sin and they will earn their wages. They work for it, they earn it, and they will receive it. It is their own doing. God does not condemn them to hell. They choose to work toward it. They can work a little or they can work a lot, but their 'time card' doesn't have God's name on it, nor do they receive God's wages. They receive the wages they are working for."

I had nothing to say. My friend went on. "But," he pointed out, and stressed that something opposite usually follows the "but" in Scripture, "the gift of God is eternal life through Jesus Christ our Lord."

"Now," he asked, "what are you doing to earn that gift?"

I answered, "If you earn a gift, it's not a gift. The only way to receive a gift is to simply put out your hand and take it."

"Well," he said, "God is offering you a gift. Why don't you take it?"

Then I argued some more, but this time not from my "logic" but from my emotions. "This is too simple. There has to be a catch," I said. So he repeated the verse again.

I thought a long time about that, and I'm not sure if it was a head response or a feeling response, but I knew that the Bible made sense. Then he turned to another passage in the same book. This time it was Romans 10:9-10: "If thou shalt confess with thy mouth the Lord Jesus, and shalt believe in thine heart that God hath raised him from the dead, thou shalt be saved. For with the heart man believeth unto righteousness; and with the mouth confession is made unto salvation" (KJV).

"Anyone can say he believes," I argued. "Is that all you want me to do? Okay," I said sarcastically, "I believe."

He wasn't offended.

"There's more, isn't there? It says, 'Believe in your heart that God hath raised him from the dead.' The sacrifice of Jesus is not only that he died," he said. "The work of Jesus not only involved his death but his resurrection. He overcame the power of death. The life that he offers now, eternal life, is a resurrected life, a life after the grave. That's what he offers you—not life that is only a before-death life but life forever from this point on—eternal life."

I believed that, but believing it didn't mean that I was ready to confess that I believed it and I sneered about those people who readily confess Jesus. "I've seen those 'Christians,'" I said.

But Scripture won because Scripture is clear and is truth. A response to God is in both the believing and the confessing, not just one or the other. A person believes and confesses—and so he or she is saved. I knew I had to do *something*.

Then he put the question to me: "If you want that gift of life, what is stopping you from receiving it now?"

I admitted that there was nothing stopping me except my own fear of the unknown. I knew where I was; I didn't know where believing in Jesus would take me.

He prayed for me then, and I said yes to Christ. It was so simple and unemotional that the only reason I remember it is that I knew then and know now that I did indeed receive new life that night. It was a "birth day." All my living dates from that night.

Then he showed me one more passage of Scripture, Romans 8:1: "There is therefore now no condemnation to them which are in Christ Jesus" (KJV). None! No longer condemned—that meant me! And although it took days, maybe weeks, for that to settle into my awareness, those words "no condemnation" set me free.

I Didn't Know Enough Then

Most of what I had done that Thursday night, March 10, 1955, was not fully clear to me then. The act of transferring my trust from myself to Jesus Christ was probably not an act of devotion. I can't even say that I received Jesus as my Savior because I loved him. Later, as I came to understand more fully what he did for me in the incarnation, the crucifixion, the resurrection, I came to love him very much. But not then. I didn't know enough then. Rather, I responded to Christ that night because his atonement made sense to me. I did not want to be separated from God for all eternity—I did not want to be lost by my own choice. I wanted heaven; I did not want hell. And I am quite certain that there is no other way to explain my initial response to Jesus other than "selfishness." I wanted God on my side. I wanted to belong to him. For me it was a "selfish" act.

Now, years later, I can exclaim, as James McConkey does, "Jesus: Savior! How much the word means! He has saved us from the guilt of sin. He is saving us from the power of sin. He will save us from the presence of sin."[1]

I have learned that God is at work in me, "to will and to act according to his good purpose" (Philippians 2:13). Those words are true. I can and do live in peace knowing that he is thinking of me constantly (see Psalm 139:17-18, TLB). I rejoice in the gifts he chooses to use, knowing that I am fearfully and wonderfully made (Psalm 139:14). But I could not say all of that on that March night in 1955. My entrance into life in Christ was based on rebirth; the gains of my new life came later.

There is nothing wrong with starting like that. "What's in this for me?" is a legitimate question. "How is this going to help me?"

It is not wrong to be selfish like that. Selfishness is the starting point. Selfishness made me want redemption. Because God made me for himself, he desires me. I needed to know that.

It was for eternal life, and to have a reason for living now, that I came to him. Adoration came later.

It was for my life and my gain that God asked me to surrender to him. James McConkey says, "And what is this act of surrender? It is a yielding of the life to God to do and suffer *all* His will in *all* things and at *all* times, because we have, once for all, settled that it is the best thing for us."[2] To yield to Christ was the best thing for me to do.

Jesus Christ is for me. He has declared me to be priceless in value—he has proved it. Christ is the measure of my worth, for he is the price paid for me. Sometimes when I try to help someone to see the value God places on a human soul, I'll ask that question: "What has he paid for you?" The answer, of course, is that he paid Jesus. And my reply: "Then, when you can tell me what Jesus Christ is worth to God the Father, I'll tell you what you are worth to God the Father because the price he paid for your redemption is his Son Jesus Christ."

I am of value to God; I am adopted into his family (Romans 8:14-17). I see that and I do not deny it. He has given me life. He has redeemed my soul. He wants me to have the gains of this soul-redeemed life. He does not want me to exhaust my energies trying to become something on my own terms, for my sights are not as high as his. Rather, he is shaping my life and using my life as he cares to, as I surrender it to him for his fulfillment and completion.

And in my "selfishness" I want to be all that he designed me to be, all that he saved me to be. In developing the gifts he has placed in me, how foolish if I only follow after others, trying to be like them, a carbon copy of someone else, and miss the fulfillment that he has for me. I come to the recognition that I am an original because he made me so.

It Is All the Same With Him

In this Christ-original life, I don't fret nearly as much as I used to about what comes or what doesn't come, or worry about the days left to me. I have adequate time to become what he wants me to be, enough time to live. If I die at an early age, that is no loss. There is no incomplete work, assuming that my day-by-day desire has been to seek him, to serve him, and to allow him to work his will in me. If my time is not mine, and it isn't, then there is no such thing as "early" death or "unfinished" work. What matters is that I keep on going with him, either now in the body or then in spirit. No matter which, I continue with him, in his plan, under his control, moving either through time or into eternity. It is all the same with him—and me. If I am taken in the midst of my days of productive work or witness, that is no loss—that is gain. He is God. I'll worship him now in faith and later face to face.

When a friend died in an automobile crash, I was in Stockholm, Sweden, and did not immediately hear the news. A few days after his death, my wife, Andrea, joined me in London. We were going on to Keswick together. Wisely, she waited until we had left Heathrow Airport and were on a bus before she leaned over to tell me the news of his death. Then she let me handle the shock while she looked out the window.

I said what I suppose everybody else said at that time: "Why?" "Why, God, when he was doing so much for you and his most fruitful days still seemed to be ahead. Why?" There was no explanation then and there isn't an explanation now, except that it was God's time, and he was a man who was always serving on God's time.

Our work is never our work; it is his, and we are to be faithful with the days that we have, just as Jesus himself was faithful, though his earthly work was, by human definition, never "finished." More people were sick who could have been healed, more were hungry who could have been fed, more were confused who could have been taught. But his time of incarnation was finished at his death. His redemptive work was in his dying, in his resurrection; and it continues now through the work of the Holy Spirit in his church.

The follower of Jesus belongs to an eternal plan. It is God's work that we do and God's greater life that we live, whether it is here with him today or home with him tomorrow. "You are not your own; you were bought at a price" (1 Corinthians 6:19-20).

The Apostle Paul declared, "I have been crucified with Christ and I no longer live, but Christ lives in me. The life I live in the body, I live by faith in the Son of God, who loved me and gave himself for me" (Galatians 2:20).

Then Everything Fits Together

In this life we don't have to waste our time fretting about where we fit in. God knows where we fit in. Nor are we to worry about the value of various segments of our time; God knows that too. He did not make me to be like someone else or to follow someone else's pattern. I am uniquely, fearfully, and wonderfully made; known before I was born. And that is the most liberating knowledge that anyone can have.

We are not in the process of expanding our consciousness to be like him, as some teach. But because we are in him and he is abiding in us, we *do* expand. We expand because he is expanding us. It is our fitting nature to be in him, and for his life to be in us. We are misfits if this is not so. Three times in John 15:4 we read the word *abide*. "Abide in me, and I in you. As the branch cannot bear fruit of itself, except it abide in the vine; no more can ye, except ye abide in me" (John 15:4, KJV).

That's what life in Christ is all about—abiding. It is not the fruit-producing that matters, it is the abiding. The producing comes from the vine; the branches are only the fruit bearers. To be an abiding branch is to be a faithful branch. The fruit will come. And the fruit that is borne, whether it be large fruit or small, abundant or not so abundant, is his doing. Our role is to be attached to the vine, to fit into our place—to abide.

Union with him, that's what counts. Out of that union comes the gain. It is gain as he designs it and causes it, and a gain that we can enjoy because the enjoyment is part of the belonging. The security of it, the peace of it, and the results of it are for us.

Struggle is no longer there when we abide. For no longer are we somehow trying to lift ourselves toward him, or trying to be perfect in him, or attempting somehow to hold down our independent wills for him; we do not practice our own style of obedience. Obedience is a coming together with him in confidence and trust. This eliminates tension, anxiety, and, in fact, eliminates all the torment that grips so many "unattached" people.

To struggle always in tension with God, to be up and down endlessly like a teeter-totter—never going anywhere yet always being in motion—is such a foolish waste of existence. Trying to please him and yet at the same time trying to please self is just the opposite of what he wants and blesses. No wonder so many people go through new crises in their twenties and thirties and forties. Every change in life is traumatic when people go through it on their own.

We are not to be always trying to fit everything together with God as if we could by our poor effort cement a relationship with the Eternal. God wants us to belong to him; then everything fits together. Then each event in life begins to have purpose.

It's not important to understand fully God's purposes. The Father knows. And in Jesus Christ we know the Father. We don't always have to convince ourselves that all is well or that we are successful, or use any of the other so-called measures that others use; God has told us that he is in control, and he is. The good that God determines is going to be worked out whether or not we understand it (Romans 8:28). He will be God. Where we are going in relationship to him is a decision we do not have to make or even know. Never is it "what will I do?" in order to be in God's will, in order to receive the gains in life that come from him. Rather, the question is, "What will my relationship be with God?"

God alone defines life for us because he is life. Our duty is not to perform a spiritual balancing act, to fit God into our lives or our lives into God. Ours is not an attempt to find wholeness and purpose within the confusion of life. Our responsibility is to be in him.

This is the will of God for us. In this he is glorified; in this we live out our praise.

Thomas Kelly, in his *Testament of Devotion*, said, "He is the center and source of action, not the end-point of thought."[3] God is not someone we try to find; he is the very Center of our being and we act within that Center. Again, it was Kelly who said, "The strong man must become the little child, not understanding but trusting the Father."[4]

"They have found the secret of the Nazarene, and, not content to assent to it intellectually, they have committed themselves to it in action, and walk in newness of life in the vast fellowship of unceasing prayer."[5]

"Yes, I am his," is not something we say with our fingers crossed. It is a walk, a stepping-out in the awareness that we are his for him to watch and develop in a life that is meaningful, whether or not it is "successful" by human standards.

Whether life is rewarding in human terms means nothing; "rewarding" as a measure of life is nonsense. For in ever deeper ways with God we are brought into an exciting frontier of spiritual life that moves forward with a sense of wholeness and with an anticipation (not wishful thinking but secure awareness), that even more is coming in the future because every day we are growing in him and in our capacity to enjoy him.

He Knows How He Wants to Use This Life

God has me! That's an affirmation based on reality: the reality of his promise, the reality of his character, the reality of his action, the reality of his own reputation. Therefore, whereas we can never have happiness or security so long as we are struggling to belong to him, we can have it quickly by accepting his offers. So long as we are always trying to have some kind of oneness with him, a struggle from our part toward God, we will not find that fulfillment. Nor will it come until we admit that we are building on man's efforts and stop doing it. He wants that oneness with us; we must yield ourselves to it.

This doesn't mean we should abandon reason. Nor does it mean we should meekly surrender because we are tired and can no longer battle. Nor are we asked to deny the Scripture "continue to work out your salvation with fear and trembling" (Philippians 2:12), for that verse is based on a relationship that already exists, built on salvation in Christ on his terms, in his way (Philippians 2:13). This is a completing process that God has designed from the beginning. It comes from that divine union. The self is fulfilled by the God who made that self, gave that self, redeemed that self, and now fills that self and uses it.

In my life I have no limits because God who owns me has no limits. If any limits do come in, they are self-imposed. They are imposed by me when I try to determine what God can and cannot do in my life, always measuring him by my own human understanding of God—a measure based on me, the one created; not on him, the Creator. He understands who I am and what he wants to fulfill in me. He knows how he wants to answer my prayers. He knows how he wants to use this life that he has designed.

If he didn't, he never would have designed me and created me in the first place. God had a reason for me, and if I will accept that, then I can begin to live. With A. W. Tozer I can say, "My God, I shall not waste time deploring my weakness or my unfittedness for the work. The responsibility is not mine, but thine. Thou hast said, 'I knew thee—ordained thee—I sanctified thee,' and thou hast also said, 'Thou shalt go to all to whom I shall send thee, and whatsoever I command thee thou shalt speak.' Who am I to argue with thee or to call into question thy sovereign choice? The decision is not mine, but thine. So be it, Lord. Thy will, not mine, be done."[6]

Self-esteem? Yes! He gives self-esteem and will give a better life through that self-esteem. You will begin to discover as he shapes your life that at last you have something more to offer to God and something more to offer other people. Our lives gain because we are offering our lives to him who is life itself. To keep back parts of our lives is not self-control but theft. As we keep, we lose; as we give, we gain. Jesus said that "whoever wants to save his life will lose it, but whoever loses his life for me will find it" (Matthew 16:25). He meant what he said then; he means it now.

I am and have a precious self; God made that self and gave me that self. It is my life. I can rejoice in it because God is so much and, as a result of being his, I have so much.

This is not a state of passive behavior; this is an exciting, active behavior. This is a self-realization by and through his revelation. Unlike people who behave as experimental rats in a laboratory, able to take only so many shocks before they quit and won't struggle any more, we can go on and live and expand no matter what shocks come. God gives us hope for going on and a reason for doing so. This is the opposite to helplessness, the opposite to hopelessness. This is the excitement that there is no end to growth and fulfillment while we are here on earth, and no end when we depart from this life.

Who Is the Greatest Saint in the World?

In Christ I am free to live, free to be flexible, free to move, free to fail, free to succeed. I can confidently know that there are things I will do well and things that I will not be able to do at all. I don't have to try to prove to myself or to others that somehow I can be what I am not. God made me; God owns me.

And as I relax in Christ, I begin to see that there have always been people like me. This reinforces my certainty. I meet people in Scripture—people like Abraham, Moses, Stephen—who did not fully understand themselves or their purpose, but they knew that God understood them. They did not always feel strong or healthy or wise. They wondered at God's commands as sometimes I do. Even the disciple who loved Jesus most didn't always understand everything he did or taught. Realizing this allows me to have moments of depression; it allows me to cry and pound my fists on God's chest. It allows me to be the person I am because I am God's person. I can look to my Creator because I am his. I can look to my Redeemer; I can look ahead to fulfillment and to deliverance. And I can be happy even in my "failures," waiting to see how these too will be used because I am secure in the One who made me and owns me.

I know that there is a tomorrow. I understand with David that my mistakes do not end my usefulness for all time. I know with Peter that even denial is not permanent. I see and know and believe with the Apostle Paul that even "if we are faithless, he will remain faithful, for he cannot disown himself" (2 Timothy 2:13).

It took me a long time to learn that. I have not always understood the dark nights of my crying when God was drawing me away from the things that might control me. I have not always understood when I have resisted him that I was tugging and pulling against God, seeking for myself what was less than his best.

I have not always been able to "count it all joy" with James and see pain as part of the building process. I have not always understood that God is looking at me—always. In depression or the physical disorders brought on by emotional turmoil, I have not always recognized my own anger or my fighting with God.

And when I've run into a dead end, I've not always understood that it was a prelude to a new beginning. I still do not always see this, but I'm learning.

It takes some people a long time to learn that God will not hurt them. Martin Luther knew that. In a letter to a friend he said, "I am sorry to hear that you are still depressed at times. Christ is as near to you as you are to yourself, and he will not harm you, for he shed his blood for you. . . . Believe that he esteems and loves you more than does Dr. Luther or any other Christian."[7]

I've experienced that; I know the love of Christ because I know the love of Christians. Their tears, their embrace, their tenderness, their edification and correction, have been mine. The love of his church is for me a touch of his love, the human channel through which the love of God flows. He has always tried to tell me, "I love you"; I realize that now.

I know that God is seeking to give me more of himself. As Thomas Kelly put it, "He is anxious to swell out our time-nows into an Eternal Now by filling them with a sense of Presence."[8]

I can see him as the active one in my life—regardless of what I call good or bad—I see the gains he wants me to make and how he works those out day by day. I can understand now that saintliness and holiness come from growing in him.

William Law in his *Serious Call to a Devout and Holy Life* said:

> Would you know who is the greatest saint in the world: it is not he who prays most or fasts most; it is not he who gives most alms, or is most eminent for temperance, chastity, or justice; but it is he who is always thankful to God, who wills everything that God willeth, who receives every thing as an instance of God's goodness, and has a heart always ready to praise God for it.[9]

Then he went on to say, "A life thus devoted unto God, looking wholly unto him in all our actions, and doing all things suitably to his glory is so far from being dull and uncomfortable, that it creates new comforts in every thing that we do."[10]

Knowing this is both the fulfillment to life and the doorway to a still greater expansion of my being. To sense the love and the completion and the gain that God builds into life is to live indeed!

If we could only communicate this to others, they could be fulfilled too. How obviously empty, then, would be that secular seeking of God on "my terms in my way." How foolish would be the competition of person with person as if a success measure was all that counted—certainly Christians would no longer do it.

God wants to satisfy, to enlarge, to offer; there is so much more of his grace to be had. When we gain some of it, then we can claim still more, for there are so many more of his promises to claim, so much more of himself to have. And as we do claim him, we will know all the more clearly that we are his friends, no matter what, no matter where. And we will follow him, regardless.

12

Regardless

■ ■ ■

Malcolm Smith tells the story of a man on a business trip who found that his host company's hospitality included a woman for his pleasure. He almost succumbed. Driving her to his hotel, he started struggling with the seventh commandment. He drove her home, went back to his hotel, and fell on his knees crying. Smith wrote:

> He began to force his words out in prayer. "Oh, God, if only I had taken that girl back because I loved You. But I took her back because I was afraid of You. I was just terrified of the consequences. God, I don't love You. I don't know You." He choked on, ashamed and stung at having to have made the statement at all.[1]

Most of us have come to realize that we will always struggle like that; we will always wonder about our commitment to God. In one sense it helps to know that this is the way it will be because then we can say, "Please, God, help me!" And with a determination that is an abandonment to Christ, we can stumble after him with our promise, "I am going to be an imitator of God, regardless" (see Ephesians 5:1).

"I am going to learn Christ, regardless" (see Ephesians 4:20, KJV).

"I will follow him and obey, regardless!"

But if any of us continues to seek only "happiness," as those people who have no Christ, that kind of commitment will never be made. Knowing about Christ and being in Christ are not the same. Knowing about him is not attachment to him. Short of a vine-and-branches relationship, no experience with religion, even with institutionalized Christianity, will keep us from succumbing to the ownership of our environment which is influenced by what is called in the Bible "the spirit who is now at work in those who are disobedient" (Ephesians 2:2).

Some may say, "I will try to be attached to Jesus. I will try to be like him; I will try to obey." They become frustrated, unhappy, and have more problems than ever because they are trying to be something that they are not. Only the branches, because they are attached, can relax and be. They belong. For to be attached to Jesus Christ as the branch is attached to the vine is a natural way to live. There is no effort to it. The branch doesn't "try to hang on" when the storms come. It belongs. Its life is not something it has to work out for itself; it is part of the vine. It doesn't have to struggle to produce "and do great things" for the vine; it just has to be. Its relationship will take care of the fruit-bearing. It has a relationship that is right, natural, and easy.

Half-hearted Obedience Is a Contradiction

But, like the ancient Greeks, too many of us have come to look at faith, life, and holiness as an ideal rather than a practice. We have religion and we have life. And, carefully, we keep them separate. We carry with us through life the very things that cannot be part of true worship: our idols, our other gods.

But when we choose to be abandoned to Christ, to serve him and not mammon, then we will be no longer divided in our thinking, and, most important, we will not want to be. Regardless of any other consideration, we will be obedient to God as best we understand his leading, his teaching, and his purpose for us. We will obey him—regardless.

When I make that promise to him, then no longer can I allow Satan to use my wants to destroy me. Regardless of where a commitment leads I will faithfully obey the One who is above all and in all and through all—not for my sake but for his sake. When I look at my accomplishments, I will do so in the light of who he is, and will even try to see my suffering as he sees it. I will learn to see my development and growth not just in terms of the immediate but in the larger dimension of the eternal. No more will I struggle with temptation just to overcome it, but moving beyond that I will seek to overcome temptation in order to love him and serve him for his sake.

I will picture holiness and focus on it, following him regardless, being good because he owns me. It will be more than acts done; it will be a way of life based on ownership and the living out of that owned life. And, if this commitment seems strange to professing Christians, it only proves how far so many of us have strayed from true obedience and faith.

Others know that half-hearted obedience is a contradiction. For even from Islam, which Christians call less than truth, have come such teachings: "Surrendering one's entire life to the will of Allah is the keystone of the Islamic faith. For the Muslim faithful, Allah is in all things."[2]

"Islam is not a part of life, it is a way of life," said associate professor Iraj Bashiri, an Iranian native who teaches Iranian studies at the University of Minnesota. "It is woven," he said, "into the very fabric of life."[3]

Can it be less so for us who name the name of Jesus Christ?

What Is Stopping You?

We don't know fully, nor can we know, the results of obedience to him or where that obedience may lead; we only know that step by step each day we are to obey God prayerfully—we must do it, regardless. As Dietrich Bonhoeffer explained, "Only Jesus Christ, who bids us follow him, knows the journey's end."[4]

When Jesus called Peter, his first words to that fisherman were, "Come, follow me" (Mark 1:17). And at the end of the Gospels (John 21:22), those were also the last recorded words that Jesus spoke to him—"Follow me."

As disciples, our obedience to Christ lies between those two calls. We begin our Christian life by obeying the command, "Follow me." All life long we hear, "Follow me." And at the end of our life we hear it again, "Follow me"—right on into eternity.

The question to ask is not, "Will such a commitment to follow Jesus regardless really work?" The question is, "Will I make that commitment?"

What is stopping you from making such a commitment now? Is it fear? Think about the fears that rule you, the ones that control your life, the fear that you think must be met on your terms in your way. What fear could possibly be stronger than his power, his blessing, and his love in ownership of you? What fear would control you and keep you from true liberty in Christ?

Is it a fear of the loss of your health? Are you asking, "What if I get sick? What if I can no longer work? What if I lose my eyes or my legs?" Or are you saying, "I need to stay with a company with a good health insurance plan. I can't break away to do what I think God is calling me to do." There are people living like that. Are you one of them? They are fearful, they are owned, they are unable to live free lives in Christ.

Is it the fear of some financial failure? "What if I get too far into debt? What if my house depreciates because of a highway coming through or the construction of a waste treatment plant? What if my stock values plunge? What if I lose my savings through inflation or a strike?"

Is it job security? "Will I be replaced by a younger person, a better educated person, a robot? What if the company folds or they phase out my department? Will I get my vested interest in the pension plan?"

Is it the loss of social position? "What if I can't maintain my club memberships? Will I be elected president of my organization? Will I be able to reciprocate the invitations I receive? What if I stop receiving those invitations? I need important people around me, and others know people who are more important than the ones I know. What if my spouse embarrasses me? What if I can't attain the goals and prominence I've always dreamed about?"

Is it an identity crisis? "I thought by this time in my life I would know who I am. I still don't know where I am going or why I'm here. Why does this have to happen to me? I'm tired of struggling to be something when I don't know who I am. I thought my problems would be solved by now, but the years have only brought different problems."

What's the Worst That Can Happen?

Those fears will own you. You will serve them.

The way to be free is to face those fears and see them for what they are—temptations. Then place those fears against what you have in Christ.

What's the worst thing that can happen to you?

Sickness? Death? You are already dead in Christ, so all is gain. As one Christian put it, that's what we are all getting ready for— the translation, to be with him. Why are we afraid as if we have nothing to look forward to?

You ask, "What if I lose everything I have, my financial security?" Well, what did you have when you came into this world? Most people who fear financial losses are the ones who already have more than most. They are not poor. They fear what will happen to them, when, in fact, if the worst did happen, they would be no worse off than other people in the world.

I remember wrestling with this when I was a seminary student. I wanted to resolve the question, "Am I prepared to go hungry?" I worked as a waiter in the seminary dining hall. It was one of my three jobs. Waiters were allowed to eat the meal they served. But there were more waiters than there were opportunities to work, and a night came when I had no money for food and was not scheduled to wait on tables. I was prepared to go hungry that night and committed my situation to God. Then a few minutes before dinner, a friend called and asked, "Would you be willing to wait tables for me tonight? It's my turn but I have a conflict." I did, and I ate. God could have let me go without, but he chose to arrange for me to eat. I'm ready to go hungry; that day may still come, but so far I've never had to go without a meal. If that comes, or anything else, there will come also the strength of God to match it.

Cameron Thompson, in *The Master Secrets of Prayer*, said, "Rejoice if your needs are great, if they are ever mounting, if they are incredible, if they are impossible! The very trials God puts you through are to enlarge your heart so that He can bless you the more."[5]

We worry about job security. Why? If we do that we are open to doing the unethical, the shady, even if it violates our consciences, in order to hold onto a job. But when we settle in our minds that we are prepared to do any kind of honest work, we are free. Best of all, as free beings, God can move us around as he wishes. Very often people stay with a company for years past the time when they realize they should be elsewhere just because there is security or the promise of a pension there. They are no longer available even to be led to something better. They are caught. People fear losing what in fact owns them. We only have one life, yet so many do nothing more with it than earn money.

Sometimes we put the need for social position or status above serving. Even Christians do that. They cannot do the commonplace or the ordinary; it is "beneath" them. It's even hard sometimes for Christians to ask their brothers and sisters to pray for them, because they think they lose face when they admit that they have such a need for prayer. They feel that they are admitting to a weakness, an inability to "handle it on my own."

It works the other way, too. Sometimes Christians can't handle another Christian's legitimate opportunities. I remember once asking students, who were not impressed one way or the other by anything I did, to pray for a particular responsibility I had in Europe. I couldn't ask the church people to pray because several people had used the time for prayer requests only as a means of announcing their accomplishments. Prayer was a "brag" time. Instead of praying for a real need that I had, they would have seen my request as an announcement of the trip. So I said nothing to them. The students, on the other hand, were secure and free—free enough to pray for my ministry.

Who or what I am to others isn't a primary matter if I know what the Apostle Paul knew: "I have been crucified with Christ and I no longer live, but Christ lives in me. The life I live in the body, I live by faith in the Son of God, who loved me and gave himself for me" (Galatians 2:20). I am his. I cannot know all that this means. I belong to him; that is freeing. I cannot grasp his mind on matters influencing me. I cannot know all that God knows about who I am and what I am to him.

That's What Makes a Whole Human Being

Knowing God, knowing that he is in control of life, and being yielded to that control make a person live in harmony with him; we are one with God. That's what makes a whole human being. We may not recognize that very quickly because there are so many "unwhole" people around. We tend to look for the meaning of life among the majority, but they are not whole. They cannot give us a measure of the meaning of life because they don't have true life.

Dietrich Bonhoeffer explained: "With the loss of the Godlike nature God had given him, man had forfeited the destiny of his being, which was to be like God. In short, man had ceased to be man. He must live without the ability to live."[6] We cannot judge the value of life by measuring against those who have never "passed from death to life" (1 John 3:14). We can only judge the value of life against the true Lifegiver—Jesus Christ.

You've looked at your fears and doubts, the questions that keep you from letting go and living freely with the One who came to give you abundant life. Now look at his Word:

"You will know the truth, and the truth will set you free" (John 8:32).

"I know that everything God does will endure forever; nothing can be added to it and nothing taken from it. God does it so that men will revere him" (Ecclesiastes 3:14).

"For you died, and your life is now hidden with Christ in God" (Colossians 3:3). Those words are God's Word—given to each of us!

Faithfulness brings a life of real peace. It is not self-created; it is God-given. As Scripture describes it, "The peace of God, which transcends all understanding, will guard your hearts and your minds in Christ Jesus" (Philippians 4:7). It is a guarding, preserving, keeping peace. It is a ruling peace: "Let the peace of Christ rule in your hearts, since as members of one body you were called to peace. And be thankful" (Colossians 3:15). And that is a beautiful peace to have.

Joseph had it. I think God put that story about Joseph in the Bible for more than a history lesson. Joseph had his share of troubles. He was sold as a slave, yet God used his slavery to give him a useful life. He was thrown into jail for being morally upright, but God brought him out and gave him authority. Joseph could have lamented that he was taken from his homeland and family. But God used it for good.

Daniel had it. He lived during the reign of three kings. With each of them there was the opportunity to compromise or surrender his faith. In the lions' den, he could have wondered if it pays to be faithful to the living God. Yet there was a calm about Daniel. He knew how to live because he knew God. When Darius warned against praying to God, Daniel prayed anyway. He did what he had always done in his many years of faithful walking with God.

Daniel didn't have to struggle; he just prayed. It was Darius who had to struggle with the results, who had to try to figure out some way to save Daniel from the den of lions. It was Darius who wrestled and fretted and sweated it out and found no escape from his own decree. It was Daniel, not Darius, who was the resting one.

Jesus said, "If anyone would come after me, he must deny himself and take up his cross and follow me" (Mark 8:34). The stress is on the "if." We have to weigh carefully what that "if" means. Then in response to that "if, " we make a choice. But once the weighing of the consequences of that "if" has ended and the choice is made to "come after me," we do not then weigh the value or the desirability of taking up the cross. Having decided to follow, we follow. Nothing less will do.

Wherever That Commitment Leads

There is often misunderstanding about this matter of obeying God to the death. People without Christ see that as some kind of a religious martyr's wish, an attempt to try to please God by self-sacrifice, some kind of merit-earning. It isn't that at all. The unsaved don't understand. When they hear the word "sacrifice," they think this is something that we do in our Christian walk. It is not something that we do in our Christian walk, it is something that may come to us because of our Christian walk. We neither look for it nor avoid it. Our commitment is to Jesus Christ, wherever that commitment leads.

If we try to suffer, to go without for the sake of going without, we are only drawing attention to ourselves. That isn't discipleship.

Dietrich Bonhoeffer said, "Our task is simply to keep on following, looking only to our Leader who goes on before, taking no notice of ourselves or of what we are doing."[7]

The non-Christian—and even some weak Christians—marvel at this. But such obedience is not something extraordinary. It is something that Jesus' followers do. Those who choose *not* to follow Jesus are the "unusual" ones. They have decided against being what God created us all to be—his. They are the extraordinary ones. If indeed we who are followers are "a peculiar people," we are peculiar only to those who are not obedient.

God is building his new community. People are saying yes to Jesus Christ and yes to living the full and well-balanced life regardless of where that leads. But because of this there is opposition too. The number of martyrs around the world is increasing to the point where it is not something that surprises Christians any more. It is a fact of life.

As we begin faithfully to follow the Lord Jesus, we may sometimes walk a stony path. But that doesn't stop us from asking each day, "How can I be faithful to you?"

It is time for each of us to make the decision about whom we will follow. Jesus does not call us to have the faith of some other person, to imitate the obedience of others, or to be disciples like them. He calls each of us to himself: "Follow me!"

That is not to say that in our individual decisions to obey we can ignore other Christians. For the church is a body of believers. I am strengthened by this larger body. When someone else is hurt, I hurt. When someone else is destroyed, something in me is destroyed. But yet, in another sense, I am not destroyed, for Jesus still has me. No matter what happens to me or to others, it still comes to: "What is that to you? You must follow me" (John 21:22).

We are told to take no thought for tomorrow. We are told to look at the lilies of the field and the birds of the air, and we have the example of the children of Israel in the wilderness being fed every day. We must not grab for ourselves, but at the same time we should enjoy what he provides. We must not worship what he gives, but we should worship God who gives it. And because he is meeting our needs today as he said he would, we do not worry about his faithfulness tomorrow.

The chief end of man, as the shorter catechism states it, is to glorify God and enjoy him forever. That means that regardless of what happens to me, I can will to live a life of obedience. That means "Christ in me" is worked out in holiness because in keeping with Galatians 2:20, I am dead; he is alive in me. And he can do no other than to live in me a holy life, for that is what he is—holy.

I wrote in *Decision* magazine:

Holiness means to be God's, no matter what that may come to in our lives; whether we "mount up with wings as eagles" (Isaiah 40:31, KJV), or lose our heads to a madman as did John the Baptist. Holiness is built on a pledge that I am his, a vow that is unbreakable, one in which there are no option clauses. Holiness is obedience without conditions. It is living a life that acknowledges what is true—that God is absolute Lord—a truth that is not to be violated or debated. . . . His working in the world and in our lives is not just for us and for our satisfaction, but for him, his purpose and his plans.

Holiness means following, being ready to know his plan if he chooses to reveal it, even wishing to know his plan but not requiring to know anymore than a child who cannot comprehend all that is happening around him even when his father tries to explain it to him. The child trusts, and hand in hand he and his father go on together; the father knowing the direction, the child content to know that his father knows. It is an act of surrender.

God may not, in the working out of his good plan, give to us what we call benefits or successes or pleasures or joys. He doesn't have to. He is God; and we may never see how our obedience works for good, either now or later because we are not God. He alone knows and comprehends all things. We are his in order to live as his—that is the essence of holiness.

Hudson T. Armerding said, "Let us ask ourselves whether we serve the Lord merely because he blesses us or because he is Lord. And if he is Lord, can we not trust him to do the very best for his glory and for our benefit? Indeed we can." [8]

He is God; we never are and never will be, even when we are with him and like him.[9]

We are called to obey. We are called to serve. That is mature Christianity.

We Have Made Our Pledge

The day before Christmas one year we had a clean-up time at our house. Assignments were given and our teenaged children went to work. They did exactly what they were told to do. "Dust the living room." They did. But no one said to throw away the scraps of things, so they were left there. "Clean the bathroom." They did, but only what was pointed out, nothing more. "Wash the kitchen floor." But no one mentioned specifically the dirty dishes in the sink. By afternoon the dishes were still there.

"Typical teenagers," people say. "They never do anything more than is absolutely required. Then they run for their rooms and put on the stereo headphones so that they can't hear the others working." But look at us. We make the same allowances for ourselves as Christians. We are "teenagers" too, doing exactly what God's law says, but nothing more. We may do enough to keep "peace" because we don't want God to be angry, but never more.

Stick to the letter of the law, we say, and God won't find fault. Like teenagers, we say to God, "But you didn't tell me to do that. I would have done it if you had told me to."

There should come a time when we outgrow the teen years as believers and disciples. Is God waiting for that time in your life? When did you last "pick up the dishcloth" for Christ, not because he commanded you but because you love him?

Jesus Christ is Lord. We have made our pledge to him, and there are no qualifications or escape clauses to that pledge. For the one who is a Christian there can be no more filtering his commands through our preferences or trying to see how little we can do as his children. Instead there is the living-out of a sincere yes in faithfulness. This is a holy privilege.

What does this mean for each of us? James McConkey said, "Consecration, then, does not confer ownership; it presumes it. It is not *in order to be* His, but *because we are* His, that we yield up our lives. It is *purchase* that gives *title; delivery* simply gives *possession.*"[10]

You are a person made in the image of God. You were designed for God. You were purchased by him. To say, "I will be his regardless," is not to quit life or to say I will suffer despite my own feelings. It is to say I am his regardless of what my feelings are, whether good or bad. Philip Doddridge said, "If it is thus that my faith must be exercised, by walking in darkness for days, and months, and years to come, how long soever they may seem, how long soever they may be, I will submit."[11]

To say I will submit regardless is not weakness; it is not fatalism. It is a grasp at last of the reality of whose people we are. It is saying, "I understand me in the context of you." It is agreeing with God in everything: to be willing not to demand that God limit himself to being no more than I am but rather to move into the fullness of the God who knows all about his creation, his world, his universe, his time, his history, his children—to say, "Regardless, I will be his."

There is a stimulus to this kind of living and it comes from a willingness to be dead to ourselves and alive in Christ so that our joy comes not from difficulty being absent but from true life being present. As realists, we understand that only as we face who we are and what we are can we begin to enjoy and live and be satisfied in the fullness and power of God. Then, in obedience, we can walk in his perfect will for us, regardless. We can do it because in Christ we are indeed "new creations." We are able to say with Philip Doddridge:

> I would not merely consecrate unto thee some of my powers, or some of my possessions; or give thee a certain proportion of my services, or all I am capable of for a limited time; but I would be wholly thine, and thine for ever. . . . I leave, O Lord, to thy management and direction, all I possess, and all I wish; and set every enjoyment and every interest before thee, to be disposed of as thou pleasest.[12]

Will we say that? Will we mean it? Regardless?

What will be the result? At long last God will be free to do what he has always wanted to do in each of our lives. He will have that chance to supply our every need "according to his glorious riches in Christ Jesus" (Philippians 4:19).

God wants to do it.

13

When People
Don't Like Me

■ ■ ■

Satan doesn't bother very much with those who stay away from
God. He does bother those who want to come close to God, because he knows that what the Bible promises is true: "Come near to
God and he will come near to you" (James 4:8). And he doesn't
want God to do that. Often the "higher" we go spiritually—that is,
the closer we draw to God the more we will have to bear what is
unpleasant. Satan will put pressure on us.

Jesus had admirers. There were some who liked what he did.
But in the crunch, those in authority would not accept him. He was
acceptable to most if he didn't go against anybody. But when he
did (and to be faithful to the Father he had to), the pressure from
those who were Satan's followers came down on him.

If you are faithful to Christ, you may be pressured by Satan too.
To obey Christ is to take up a cross and follow him. That cross is an
ugly object, a thing of execution. If you take it up, don't be surprised if people want to crucify you on it.

But Christians who are faithful, who are hated for Christ's
sake, though they are knocked down, don't stay down—they
know that other people's opinions of them don't really matter. For
the Christian, God's opinion counts.

Remember: "For the Lord God is a sun and shield; the Lord be-
stows favor and honor; no good thing does he withhold from those
whose walk is blameless" (Psalm 84:11). And if troubles come,
don't worry about it; you know what is happening—God owns
you; keep going. Hear what Scripture says about you: "The steps

of good men are directed by the Lord. He delights in each step they take" (Psalm 37:23, TLB). Those words are for you.

So are these: "I will lead the blind by ways they have not known, along unfamiliar paths I will guide them; I will turn the darkness into light before them, and make the rough places smooth. These are the things I will do; I will not forsake them" (Isaiah 42:16).

And God also promises, "When you pass through the waters, I will be with you; and when you pass through the rivers, they will not sweep over you. When you walk through the fire, you will not be burned; the flames will not set you ablaze" (Isaiah 43:2).

Watch What Happens

Christians are going to be disliked because they love God, and for another reason too. They are going to be disliked because they care about other people. Watch what happens when Christians try to do something about the destruction of people by gambling, alcohol, or drugs. Watch what happens when Christians try to prevent the pornography that often leads to the abuse of children; or the killing of babies by abortion. Watch what happens when Christians speak out for the poor or against racism or for reduction in armaments or against the consumerism that is the religion of so many.

There is an assumption that Christians don't really understand the real world. I remember several years ago discussing abortion with a Christian counselor who was trying to stop it. She said, "You know, they think we are out of our depth because we are older, not married, or don't have children, and can't understand the situation of an unwanted pregnancy. But when these women have an abortion, feel the trauma of having committed murder, think about suicide, and seek to assuage their mental pain, they don't go to the abortionists for help, they come to us. I wish the abortionists would get some of the 'after' counseling that we get. But they don't, and they teach these women that an abortion has no more lasting impact than having the dentist pull a rotten tooth. Those who encourage abortion don't see what we see. They don't have to counsel the suffering; they believe their own propaganda because they don't see the results. We do, and we fight, and then we are told we don't know the problem. In fact, they are the ones who don't know."

It's always painful to listen to the sneers of unbelievers who want to put down Christians. "You hide behind God," they say. "You don't know reality." "I understand life; you wouldn't understand life. You'd be shocked by some of the things I know about," they boast. "You wouldn't go to the places I go; it would overwhelm you if you knew what life was really all about." They speak as if all Christians are people who sit under church steeples with blinders on.

Yet I watch Christians. It is the Christians, because of the love of Christ, who work and keep on working with these same sneering people when they are too drunk to stand up. It is the Christians who, enduring their abuse and their vomit, try to help them keep from killing themselves by driving them home and putting them to bed. And they do it knowing full well that when those they've helped are near sober again, they are going to say to the Christian, "You can't cope with reality; you have to have your God." The Christians take the abuse and watch them go back to their bottles, all the time yearning for them to come to Christ for new birth.

It is the Christians who work with the drug addicts who tell them that they don't really know about life—when all the time the addicts, with their low tolerance for pain, are killing themselves because they can't face themselves or their life.

It is the Christians who work with prisoners in penitentiaries, caring for inmates who to most of society are forgotten people.

Even as they bind up wounds or cook a meal, perhaps for those who are criticizing their beliefs, Christians know that what they are doing is not for themselves (they already have the assurance of heaven, gained for them not by their works but by the cleansing blood of Christ), but for the weak persons they are helping—and they remain silent. Thomas à Kempis said:

> Do not concern thyself overmuch about who is for thee or against thee; but take care to act so that God will be with thee in everything that thou doest. Keep clean thy conscience, and God will defend thee, for he that receiveth the protection of God, no man's malice shall be able to harm.[1]

God Is With You

When people don't like me, it's my responsibility to be sure that I'm not somehow trying to be disliked. Having watched a particular woman antagonize people, I mentioned to her what she was doing. She angrily denied the very thing that I saw her doing. In fact, she then went on the attack, saying she was not the problem, but all the people around her. She couldn't see how people were standing back from her, afraid to speak to her lest they upset her, or saying, "Don't be upset, I'm only trying to help you." She was always the martyr, but a martyr only by her definition, not other people's.

There are Christians who do unkind things, and when their actions backfire they think they are being persecuted "for righteousness' sake." There are Christians who decide on their own terms what following Jesus means, and then get hurt by it. There are Christians who cheat, who hurt, who break the commandments, and claim the resulting trouble as persecution for "righteousness' sake." They serve their egos and reap the result. They do not care about other people and then assume the response they get for their attitude is because they are "Christians." Jesus was never obnoxious. Jesus didn't do offensive things. Jesus offended precisely because there was nothing offensive about him. If Christians have bad manners, a nasty tongue, a critical attitude, an unloving nature, or disgusting habits, they cannot blame the reaction they get on their Christian walk.

I remember meeting a man who had erected a flashing neon sign on the roof of his house. All night long it flashed "Jesus Saves" on and off. When irate neighbors called the police to complain that they were being kept awake by the flashing light, the man wailed that he was being persecuted for righteousness' sake.

There are times when people don't like us because we are, frankly, not likeable. We need to look at ourselves honestly, ask others about our ways, and make adjustments in our behavior. People who know and care for me can tell me how I act and what I communicate, often better than I can determine for myself. We need the advice of other growing believers if we are going to be healthy, maturing, stretching believers ourselves. No matter what your circumstances or how you are hurt as a Christian, as long as you have examined yourself, counseled with others, and prayed, you can know this: God is with you.

Tucked away in 1 Chronicles 4 is the description of an interesting man named Jabez. His name sounds like the Hebrew "pain" or "hurt." His mother gave him that name because she cried, "I gave birth to him in pain" (v. 9). Think what a burden she put on that child! His name was a description—he was a hurt to her. Children must have mocked him on the street and called him "Hurt." Adults would think of pain when they spoke of him. He could have been destroyed by that name.

But Jabez, by his example, gives us all hope. Scripture says: "Jabez cried out to the God of Israel, 'Oh, that you would bless me and enlarge my territory! Let your hand be with me, and keep me from harm so that I will be free from pain'" (1 Chronicles 4:10). He cried out to God and God undid everything that his mother and other people had done to him. The Scripture says: "And God granted his request."

People may be unkind; God is not. There is cruelty in the world but not in the heart of God. Others may despise; God loves. Others may put down; God builds up. And even this one named "hurt" God saw as honorable.

That little story of Jabez appears in the midst of all the genealogies in 1 Chronicles. It is a passage so many skip over in their reading. Perhaps God tucked it in there because he wanted us to find it and take courage. Jabez did what all of us can do—seek God about the matter.

Messes That Others Put You In

Turn to God to work out for you the messes that others put you in. Believe God as Joseph did, certainly as Daniel had to. They believed. They trusted, and trust is the opposite of worry. Worry will consume you. Worry cripples. Worry about your situation is a denial that God can handle it. No one, no matter what burdens he or she places on you, should cause you to stop trusting God.

Lisa was crying when she told me, "Nobody likes me. I don't belong anywhere: I don't belong at home, I don't belong at school, I don't belong in the youth group at church. Nobody likes me."

Lisa was fifteen, and as she tried to express her feelings her body shook with deep, deep sobbing. As we talked, several things became evident: She could see that her feelings about not being accepted in school and in the church were really based on her not feeling accepted in the first and basic unit of her world—her home.

"Why don't my parents like me? Why won't they accept me?" she cried.

She told how they were always scolding her: "You don't appreciate all that we are doing for you." And when she went to her parents wanting to talk about her thoughts, her worries, some of her bewilderment about life, they pushed her away with, "Oh, we've all been through that," or "You'll get over it." And if she questioned, "Why won't you talk to me?" they would reply, "We talk to you," and then go on with what they really wanted to do or talk about.

The reason Lisa was talking to me about this was that she had dropped hints that people in her church had picked up—hints that she could see no reason to keep on living.

Lisa is a victim. And although I didn't say so in exactly the same words, she is the victim of her parents' inability to hear her. They can't understand why she doesn't appreciate all the things they purchase for her. They can't see that she could possibly have a problem. To them she has all the material things a young girl could want. But Lisa made some discoveries as we talked—not discoveries that I gave her but discoveries she found within herself.

Her parents had grown up in poverty. Both had longed for the things that money can buy. Both had gone without. In their own way they were giving her what they never had, showering on her all of the things that they had wanted. They couldn't understand why she wasn't happy, because those things would have made them happy when they were young.

Her parents had forgotten what they *did* have as children. They didn't have much in the way of material goods, but they did have a family life. Parents and children talked to each other, listened to each other, cared about each other. Today, as adults, in their busyness, they don't give Lisa what she needs more than anything else—a family: parents who love her, encourage her, and give her counsel when she isn't sure which way to go.

The people who mean the most to her, her mom and dad, aren't helping her to see that she is a pretty neat kid. They are pushing her away. From their actions she is picking up signals that are just the opposite to the signals her parents think they are giving—signals of not being liked, or not being accepted.

Lisa is going to have a hard time, but she is learning that her parents probably aren't going to change. They are still going to measure her happiness by their concept of happiness; they'll still be bewildered by her nighttime crying. Now, with help, Lisa is talking to other people. She is finding an older woman in the church who can be her "mother," and a mature couple who can be parents to her. These are people with whom she can talk freely, friends who will tell her whether or not she is making good choices. They will put some fences around her ethical, moral, and spiritual choices. They will give her love.

And maybe, and it's a big maybe, but maybe when she no longer has so great a need from her parents because she is getting love elsewhere, maybe with fewer demands placed upon her, she will be able to give to her parents some of the affection that *they* need. And maybe they will return some of it to her in the way she needs. And maybe the vicious cycle will be broken.

Secure People of God

There are a lot of Lisas in our world, people who are saying, "Nobody likes me." The signals they are getting reinforce what they believe is true.

There was one other word of comfort I could give Lisa. "God likes you; God loves you." On the authority of God's own words about his love, I could tell her something of the deep dimensions of God creating her and knowing her and understanding her and loving what he created. I could show her that God likes what he put into her and likes what he is going to do with her life.

As we talked about the future, we talked about the day to come when she, more than many, will be able to say to another young person, "I know. I understand what you are saying because I have been there." And Lisa is beginning to see that her feelings are not feelings that can be read about in books or taught in classrooms; they have to be experienced. But because they have been experienced, she is going to be a Christian counselor who will teach about the loving nature of God. Someday she'll help many others who are going through what she is going through now.

We may not be liked, truly not liked. That realization can destroy us, or we can build on it and become secure people of God.

In Scripture we read that the Apostle Paul, a saint of God, had real problems with young John Mark. Mark didn't make it as a missionary, and there were flare-ups over it—hard feelings. Perhaps Mark felt sorry for himself or wondered if there would ever be any value to his life. Having been given a chance to do something with one of the greats in the church and having messed up, and having created such tension that there were splits in the missionary society over him, he felt, "Paul doesn't like me." And Paul didn't, at least not then. But whatever it was that God did with John Mark, this young man changed and grew. He wasn't thrown on the refuse heap. God didn't give up on him. We know he didn't because later Paul said, "Get Mark and bring him with you, because he is helpful to me in my ministry" (2 Timothy 4:11).

We need to know that not being liked is not an end; it may even be a beginning. It depends on what we do with it and what we believe about God's redeeming and rescuing help.

Do you lie awake at night worried? Worried because of what somebody said about you or what is going to happen tomorrow? "What might happen if . . . ?" you wonder. Then you get out of bed and get a glass of milk and sit in a chair wide-eyed, or you pace the floor. All around you is quiet; the family is asleep, the night is still. You sense that you are caught in a maze trying to articulate for yourself all of the ramifications of the confusing things that can't be articulated because they are too mixed up.

Wide awake? Do you know what? So is God. He is there. He wasn't asleep even before you got up. He neither slumbers nor sleeps, the Scripture says. And he is watching. "The eyes of the Lord are on the righteous and his ears are attentive to their cry" (Psalm 34:15).

Paul said of Jesus Christ, "He carries out and fulfills all of God's promises, no matter how many of them there are; and we have told everyone how faithful he is, giving glory to his name" (2 Corinthians 1:20, TLB). That can be a description of what Jesus does for each one of us.

Do people dislike you? Who are they? What if they did like you? Would there be a different problem, a much bigger one? Would you have compromised to win their favor?

No one who carries the name "Christian" should be obnoxious. No Christian should be lazy, or destructive, or a bringer of pain. But having forsaken all to follow Christ and being aligned with his Word, taught through the prayerful counsel of other believers, go out and live in the friendship of God. No matter what people outside of Christ say to you or about you, remember what God told Isaiah: "Do not fear, for I am with you; do not be dismayed, for I am your God. I will strengthen you and help you; I will uphold you with my righteous right hand" (Isaiah 41:10).

Did he mean that? Isaiah knew that God meant it, and he believed him. You can too.

14

As God Goes to Work With Me

■ ■ ■

"If you think most young people have goals, you don't know what is going on."

The man who said that to me one afternoon employs dozens of young people, many of them entry-level, first-job people, some in their middle or late twenties.

He was telling me that my picture of young people who want an education and a career is the exception. "Most," he said, "only have short-term goals focusing on the next payday and immediate thoughts of how they will spend their money. A long-term goal is a new car or a trip. Such things as a house, an education, training for a trade, are not part of their thinking."

Then he added, "And I'm talking about Christians. Just because people accept Christ as Savior doesn't mean they have purpose in their lives."

That conversation came about because I had expressed two emotions—my pleasure over a few people who are willing to work and give their best, and my exasperation over a larger number who want to be paid an attractive wage but have neither the commitment nor the discipline to work for it.

My "education" about people, their willingness to work, to sacrifice, to discipline themselves for long-range goals was broadened by that afternoon's conversation. But that education had begun some months before. I was discovering that Christians can be lazy. In fact, when I gently corrected a slothful worker, I was met with the challenge: "What difference does it make? Jesus is going to return soon." My only response was, "When he does return, I'd like to be found working."

Once when we were looking for new staff I found myself asking: "Where are all the people who are willing to work? They want a paycheck but they do not want to work." Eventually we found just the right people—hard-working, committed Christians who sense the calling of God in their work—but it took awhile to find them. There are a lot of people, including Christians, who are only thinking about what they can take from a work situation, not what they can put into it.

Ask any employer if that is true. Most companies have to program additional help into their labor force just to make up for those who tend to be "sick" on Mondays or who take extended coffee breaks, read a newspaper in the stockroom or leave early on Fridays, all at the cost of thousands of lost hours a year. Statistics published by the personnel departments of large corporations show that these "lost" hours raise production costs by as much as 15 percent.

A Servant Attitude

Christians, even though they refer to their vocation as God's calling, will still complain about their jobs, complain about the atmosphere at work, complain about their salaries, become easily fatigued—all while telling others (often on company time) that they have a living, vital relationship with Jesus Christ.

Scripture says that when David was appointed by Saul (1 Samuel 18:5), "Whatever Saul sent him to do, David did it so successfully that Saul gave him a high rank in the army." David did what he was told to do. He wasn't seeking acclaim or people's praise; he did his job. It doesn't take long in any organization to discover who is willing to work, who has a servant attitude, who is committed to the task to perform, and who is not.

There is no difference in attitude toward one's commitment to a calling, a job, a company, an organization, and a commitment to God. For work is a way of expressing our honesty (earning a day's pay for a day's work instead of expecting to be paid for work not done) and faithfulness (going the second mile, doing the extra task instead of doing just enough to be noticed).

Unfortunately—and it is part of a need to "appear" to be faithful—there are Christians who try to fool their employers. They are the ones who cannot work behind the scenes; they must always be near the people in authority to make sure that they and their work are noticed. They work hard when they are being watched, but disappear when the boss is on vacation or out of town on a trip. If another employee needs help, they find excuses not to give it because there will be no personal gain or recognition for them. "Why should I help him?" they say. "That's his job."

As David did his job, he wasn't paying attention to who noticed. But he did it so well that people did notice and started praising him. As a result, Saul turned on him. That can happen. Our job is to be faithful and hard-working even though fellow employees may turn on us. They may not like it when someone does a better job or gets a higher salary for work well done. They want "equal" pay, but cannot or will not discern that, everything else being equal, they are not worth what the hard worker is earning for the simple reason that they do only enough to get by. It is a delicate thing to work hard in order to be faithful to one's calling while knowing all along that other employees who want the same pay and the same praise resent your hard work that earns it, because it shows them up. Living for God as a worker is not easy. David found that out.

We say, "Yes, but there came a day when David was successful and had the recognition and power." That's true, but it was years later. And it is worth noting that it was after he had success and power that he tripped up and sinned so seriously. We desire the bigger job, but if we get it we also run the risk of falling into the larger temptations.

Why Him? Why Not Me?

Maybe God does us a service in keeping us where we are. The faithful Christians are those who work hard and trust God to do the promoting if there is going to be any promoting—because they also trust God to give the ability to handle the temptations and pressures that would accompany the promotion.

Notice something in Scripture about a little-known worker, a hardly noticed man of God. When it was necessary to replace

Judas Iscariot, bringing the number of apostles to twelve again, two men were put forward (Acts 1:23). One was Joseph called Barsabbas, also named Justus. The other was Matthias. When the disciples prayed over those two men, they acknowledged that God knows people's hearts and that he is the one to choose and ordain who should have an office and who should not. They acknowledged that God makes an apostle. The lot fell to Matthias. He was chosen.

But what then became of the "second" choice? And what can we learn from the "winner"? Who were these two men? Who was Joseph called Barsabbas? Did he also follow Jesus with the twelve? What had made him so outstanding that he could be put forward as one of two choices in the first place? And how did he feel when the lot was cast and he lost? When it was stated, "By God's decision, you are not the one," did he sulk? Did he say: "Why is Matthias so special?" Did he remind the other disciples, "We do the same work; I follow the Master too—why him? Why not me?"

Or was he mature enough to recognize that God chooses some for one work and some for another? We assume that he was mature enough to understand that, or he would not have been mature enough to be put forward as one of the two in the first place. He would have seen that the office of apostle was not something to covet, that the ministry of being one of the twelve was not to be sought for purposes of power or prestige or personal gain. He would not, had he been named one of the twelve, been praised in the assemblies of the rich or the powerful. He would not have had special privileges, or been sought after as a banquet speaker, or been asked for his autograph. When he was put forward for the ministry of an apostle, it was a position that would mean suffering and perhaps even a brutal death. Could he have handled that? Ten or twenty years later would he have had whatever was required to remain a faithful teaching apostle? We will never know, for God made the choice. God chose Matthias.

And who was Matthias, this one who was chosen? We don't know because neither Matthias, the one chosen, nor Joseph, the one rejected, was ever mentioned in Scripture again. So even the one who gained the office did not get the acclaim of a Peter or a Matthew, or a James or a John. Was he jealous? And if so, what would he envy? Would he envy Peter's imprisonment? John's exile? James's death?

Matthias was chosen; Joseph was not. Neither was heard from again. We know nothing of their families, their education, their ministries, their ages—just two names.

Follow God's Choice

God chooses us. Some are chosen to have one ministry, some to have another. Some, like Peter, are chosen to be noticed more than others. Some, like Matthias, not to be noticed at all.

We each have a holy calling. In Christ we follow God's choice. We have put ourselves forward to be available for God's choosing. We did that when we committed our lives to Christ. As Christians, we are chosen for ministry. No matter what that ministry is— whether it's physical labor, office management or medical missions—God calls; we obey. He directs; we faithfully work. And we do so for as long as God commands, following him even more than we follow our careers. For all of us know that once God decides how he will use us, he can still bring change to our lives at any moment. Surely Joseph, the one called Barsabbas or Justus, was doing something vocationally before his name was put forward as an apostle. He had years of experience doing something: obeying God, feeding his family. Maybe he went back to his trade. For a brief moment perhaps he wondered if he was going to have a "mid-career change," only to settle back again into the calling that he had before. God wasn't steering him in a new direction after all. But he was willing. God could have chosen him.

Matthias did make that mid-career change. Was he a carpenter? A fisherman? Did he have a business? Whatever he was doing, he left it for the ministry of apostleship. He was ready to be chosen, and God did choose him. Each of us, in fulfilling our daily vocation, needs to be ready for God to make a choice. James made it clear in his epistle that none of us can say, "Tomorrow we can do thus and so"; we do not know what tomorrow brings. Tomorrow is God's and we are God's. Vocationally we must be faithful and ready.

First a Faithful Worker

That's why it is a sin to be lazy, refusing to do what we are hired to do. Matthias, whatever he did before, could not have suddenly become a faithful apostle if he was not first a faithful worker in his regular field of work. God wouldn't have chosen a man who was always looking for ways to get out of work.

Peter was a skilled fisherman. He was not highly educated but he was not unlettered either. He had the full course of synagogue school training, which meant he had language study, history, Bible memorization (for Jewish boys the entire first five books of the Bible were committed to memory), grammar, geography, and mathematics. He knew at least three languages—Hebrew, Aramaic, Greek—and perhaps Latin also. He knew the principles of management as well as the skills of operating a family fishing company—including the bookkeeping, pricing, purchasing, equipment handling and repair, weather, currents, and the habits of various species of fish. All these were part of a highly skilled craft. All these equipped him to be an apostle by God's grace, the senior minister of the first church in Jerusalem, then a missionary.

Peter was ready. You can be too, for whatever work God calls you to do. God knows you. He knows your likes, your dislikes, your skills, your abilities. He knows, because you're no accident. God knew what he was doing when he made you, he knew what he was doing when he gave you the gifts and talents that he has given you in a unique combination unlike anyone else. He knew what he was doing when he called you into your vocation. And, if you're a committed Christian, you can say with confidence that he knew what he was doing when he brought you to himself through Jesus Christ. He paid a price for you, a price that is above every price. You have great worth. Is there then any moment or any circumstance when he will not care for you and help you and lead you?

God knows what he is doing in your life now. God has placed you where you are because he wanted to place you there. He has given you the work that you have because he wanted to. You may think that you just stumbled into what you are doing, but there are no surprises with God. Surely when you started doing what you are doing now, God's mouth didn't drop open in amazement. Surely he didn't exclaim, "I didn't know he was going to do that."

In the overall plan of God, he is directing you and directing those who work with you whether he gives your job to you for a year or for your whole career.

I know a Christian teacher who spent sixteen years in a small town in Michigan's Upper Peninsula, living on low wages, struggling with inadequate equipment, but working there because God led him there. And how he influenced those students' lives—not only at school but on Sundays in a little Sunday school held in his home. He worked there suffering through those cold Michigan winters because God wanted him there, influencing not thousands, but classes of just a few. One of those classes graduated seventeen young people. I know how that teacher influenced the valedictorian of that class; I know how her life was changed. I know how she has gone on to serve Christ. I know, because she is my wife.

We are to pray, obey, and serve. We are to be ready as were the early followers of Jesus to leave all and follow him, to be ready to have a career as a carpenter or as a tax gatherer, or to be ready to follow in a new role because that's what God wants.

This is true for those who stay at home too. There is no less discipline to homemaking, parenting children, doing traditional "at home" ministry than there is working for a paycheck outside the home. In fact, the disciplines are tougher because there are few immediate rewards. One works as a homemaker out of absolute commitment to a higher calling than a paycheck or company fringe benefits. One works because "God has placed me here."

An Example to Follow

When the Apostle Paul began his work for Christ, he was ready to obey. And God took over from there. God used him to change the world. We have our Christian roots in that faithful man. His missionary work produced a body of believers who are our spiritual forefathers.

Paul had a career before he met Christ. But after he met Christ his career was changed. God could do what he did with that man's life because Paul was ready to obey. It wasn't an easy life that Paul led; it certainly wasn't without pain. Whom do you know who has suffered as much as Paul did? Whom do you know who has been beaten as many times, imprisoned as often, been shipwrecked, hungry, so physically ill—whom do you know who is like that?

Yet, to have a vocation as Paul had, with the hand of God upon him, enjoying the closeness of God—we envy him. We see him as an example to follow. The question for each of us is never, "Am I qualified, capable, or willing to be an apostle like Paul?" The question, rather, is "Am I, as Paul was, ready? Am I faithful right now?"

My vocation, my ministry, is to work under God and also to work alongside those whom God has appointed in ways that he has not appointed me. God has the right to use some people one way, others another way. That's his prerogative. God will use whom God will use. We can fight against it, complain about it, scream, kick, call him unfair; or we can relax and fit into the pattern of God.

In 2 Kings 6:1-7 that is what happened. Elisha was God's anointed, and God gave him tremendous power. One day a man lost his axe head in the water. It was a borrowed axe head. He called on Elisha to help him. He didn't assume that he had the power himself, but he knew that God had anointed Elisha with special power. It was God's choice to use Elisha. Elisha, in the power of God, raised the axe head. But notice something. Elisha didn't go in and pull the axe head out of the water after he made it float. The man had to do that himself. Elisha made it float; that was his gift. But the man had to retrieve it. He had to do something too.

That is so in our lives. It is wise to recognize who has a special anointing of God. But we do not envy them, nor covet their gift; we recognize the gift, go to them to use their gift. But we do not expect them to do everything, or to do what we can do ourselves. We respect what God does through them—their abilities, powers, even the miracles that God works through their lives. We ask them for help, trusting that God is giving that help through them. They are only pieces of clay, tools, but God is using them.

God has given you a special gift and others will ask for your help. It is not your gift; God gave it to you and God expects it to be used. And with our separate gifts we work together. That's what the body of believers is all about.

Don't take credit for your gift. Don't assume that the power seen in your life is in yourself. God has his ways that are beyond our understanding. We act, using what he gives for his sake and the sake of others, and every day God goes to work with us. Work with him, work for him, be faithful in your vocation, and you will please God. That may not mean a larger paycheck or more company benefits—for there is no correlation. But it will mean that each night you will be able to go to sleep knowing that you did your best for God, and that if you died in your sleep and never returned to your job you would have left a work well done. And by the time your co-workers know you are gone you will already be standing with your Lord and will have heard the greatest of all commendations, "Well done, good and faithful servant! . . . Come and share your master's happiness" (Matthew 25:21).

15

And God Will

■ ■ ■

If there is a single desperate need that people have right now, it is not the need for more education, it is not the need for more money, it is not the need for greater security—it is the need to lay claim to this: "God will!"

When we look at who God is, when we look at what he gives, when we look at what he says, then we can believe, "God will meet all your needs." For our God delivers on his promises.

"Never will I leave you; never will I forsake you" (Hebrews 13:5)—that's a promise.

"And surely I am with you always, to the very end of the age" (Matthew 28:20)—that's a promise too!

"Trust in the Lord with all your heart and lean not on your own understanding; in all your ways acknowledge him, and he will make your paths straight" (Proverbs 3:5-6)—he will; he says so!

"Commit your way to the Lord; trust in him and he will do this" (Psalm 37:5)—God will!

"You may ask me for anything in my name, and I will do it" (John 14:14)—"I will!" he said.

"Whoever comes to me I will never drive away" (John 6:37)—we have his word on it.

"You will know the truth, and the truth will set you free" (John 8:32)—you will!

"His divine power has given us everything we need for life and godliness through our knowledge of him who called us by his own glory and goodness" (2 Peter 1:3)—he said "everything" and he means it.

"The eternal God is your refuge, and underneath are the ever-lasting arms" (Deuteronomy 33:27)—and that's his promise too.

But don't stop with these few promises; get your own Bible and keep discovering more of his promises thoughtfully and prayer-fully! You will find that God is much involved with you. Can you believe that? God has given his Word, his promise, his commit-ment, and as Emile Cailliet says in his book, *Journey Into Light*, "Indeed God stands behind the Book."[1]

"His Book" is the revelation of himself; he acts on it. "His Book" doesn't lie; God always keeps his word. Only God can rightly speak about himself and properly interpret the holy things that are his. For his ways defy our human speculation. In this world, in spite of our human disorientation, there is a standard that does not change: the Holy Scripture. Scripture is God's statement. He proclaims and he practices what he proclaims.

"Best Friends" With God

When we allow ourselves to accept his word, rejoice in his word, and determine to obey his word, then everything that we do will take on new dimensions of meaning.

That means we can look at our failures and understand them; we can learn from each one. That means we can make decisions in the assurance that God is the over-all ruler of our lives—even if we make what we call a "bad" decision. That means we no longer have to live with questions about what could have been, but are able to experience life with the One who is the God of life and the overseer of the great friendship he has established with us, a friendship far greater than we can comprehend. We can worship him and love him always because God will always be God and he will always care—he promised that! In Jesus Christ, we are "best friends" with God.

And as God's "friend," I can say with excitement, "You are my God," even though I cannot fully comprehend that. I can acknowl-edge, "You have waiting for me far more than I could ever give to myself." For that I can truly thank him.

It is not mere existence that I celebrate, it is life. And I can cele-brate that life whether mine is a life of great accomplishment or a life with no measurable results. It is within the excitement of the life he gives to me, his gift to me, that I worship him and yield myself to him.

Do you deserve this? Are you asking, "How can God be that way?" You could consume hours, even years, on that question, wasting potentially creative energy in pondering yourself and God, his nature and the meaning of all his love for you. But you don't need to understand it. God's love, his will, and his direction are not conditional on whether or not you understand it or on what you think about it; it is conditional on him, the ever steady omnipotent One, and on your response in faith to him.

"Well, then," you may be asking, "is this the ultimate, the highest goal? Am I to seek God's will so that I can attain more of what I want?" No! Some try to do that. They think, "Since God wants me to be fulfilled and happy, I'll claim God." They go through believing-type motions and then wonder, "Why am I not fulfilled? Is this all there is to the so-called expanded life?" They are not surrendering to God; they are merely trying to use God, and God will not be used.

To have God is to enjoy him; that's completion, that's fulfillment, that's happiness. But he is not a magic "happiness giver." In him we have a happy life because happiness is a by-product of the God-centered life. Ours is a happy life, a larger share of life, because we have in us the One who is life and complete happiness.

Jesus Knows Where I Am

Do you want to have that larger share of living? Then know this: God wants you to have it too!

Come away from the notion that this is some kind of self-improvement plan. True discipleship can't be a self-improvement program. Unfortunately, even some Christians misunderstand that. Their "me-and-God" views have been kept alive by the flood of books on the Christian market listing "how to," "you can be," "steps to," and although many of these books have good biblical resource material, and while the intentions of the authors are sincere, there are some negative aspects too. One is the implication that if we do various things that are taught in these books we will somehow live as close to Jesus as the examples given in the books, or be as successful, or as attractive, or will have a no-conflict marriage, or will find ourselves in circumstances like those of the authors. The second implication is that *we* are the faith-generators. We find ourselves saying, "I must have faith," and focus our attention on the program or the steps to faith, and not on Jesus himself. We become people who follow the teachings about Christ when we should be following the teachings of Christ.

Jesus knows where I am. He knows my circumstances. And although good teaching and good examples can be found among other members within the body, my eyes are not to be on the other members only but on the One who knows me, who put me together, who wants me to be conformed to his likeness. I learn through others, but what I learn is about the Lord Jesus Christ himself and how better to live for him. I learn theologically, I learn systematically, I learn doctrinally, and it all comes together in him.

There are frustrated Christians who have been pushed or coaxed into a self-remodeling program that denies the fact that we are not our own. It is by grace that we are saved, it is not of ourselves, and it is by the grace of God and his direction that we become like him. And all of the teaching, all of the books, all of the lectures—though they can give good information—only make sense when they are incorporated into the leading of God for our lives. We must first be committed to our Lord, and be willing to be what he wants us to be. Then the other teachings make sense.

When the Teton Dam in Idaho burst on June 5, 1976, a wall of water swept down the valley tearing out homes and barns, crumpling farm machinery, and tossing heavy equipment everywhere. A few days later, when the water had receded, twisted trees and dead animals were strewn everywhere, and mud and gravel lay several feet thick over everything.

Ten months after that flood I visited a Christian family who lived there. In the flood they lost everything. But when I arrived, they had already rebuilt their house, bought new farm equipment, erected new buildings, and had scraped the gravel deposits off their land. They were ready to plant. Yet all around them were neighbors who had done nothing. Many of these neighbors were religious people who had built up those farms by hard work. But after the dam broke, they were left without hope. What they had built was theirs; now it was gone. Most had not even scraped the thick gravel deposits from their land. They were still dazed. They couldn't function. They stood helpless. What was "theirs" was gone, and they couldn't handle it.

What was the difference? Though the dam break was said to be caused by human error in construction, the Christian family continued to hang on to Romans 8:28, believing that God knew what was happening. Their house and farm belonged to God before the flood, and it was his afterward. They started to rebuild even before the water receded. They had a sense of direction, clinging to the belief that God would use this for good. Now in their home there is a growing house church; they are ministering to other people. When the flood came, those whose religion was based on "God helping me" were devastated. The Christians believed "God owns me" and were able to function. Good or bad times were not critical to their foundation of faith.

Such severe crises don't come to everybody, but if they do come, the self-improved, self-developed "religious" people often have nothing left. A person who has only his or her own version of the empowering God has no power at all.

Relaxed Awareness

During good times, the true disciple and the simply religious person are not too distinguishable. The differences are inside. But when crises come (and sooner or later they usually do) the one embarked on the "foolish adventure" of being totally yielded to Christ has the strength to endure.

Consider Psalm 5:8. David prayed, "Make thy way straight before my face" (KJV). If you are like some people, you probably learned that verse the other way around: "Make my way straight before thy face." That's because those who are religious on their own terms have learned to pray, "Lord, I want what I am doing to be right with you; I want to please you with what I am and where I am going; I seek your blessing on my life." In other words, "Make my way straight before thy face"—be pleased with where I am going. But David prayed the other way. He prayed that God's way would be straight before him so that he could follow it. The focus of the true believer is on God's way—wherever God's way leads, that is the way the committed believer will go.

Discipleship is a coming under the guidance and the control of the Master Engineer, the Craftsman of the Universe, the Divine Potter. At times it means being thrown hard on the Potter's wheel. Sometimes it means being pressed or even pounded under the hand of God. Sometimes it means being firmly held while the wheel turns. That reshaping and remaking goes on and on, according to the Potter's plan. The clay doesn't say, "Please bless the object I'm about to become as I shape my life." The clay is clay; it becomes something according to the Potter's idea of what it should be. The results that come are what the Potter wants.

Christian maturing means a day-by-day following and obedience, a being available, ready. When the Apostle Paul wrote to the Christians at Rome he told them, "I wanted to come to you but was hindered. I had to go in another direction, but I'm going to come to you now on the way to Spain" (see Romans 15:22-24). But he never got to Spain! When he finally saw the Christians at Rome, he was in chains. He came as a prisoner, which was not at all what he had planned. Yet there was no panic in Paul's writing or in his life. In the relaxed awareness that "God owns me," all things did work together for good. He was not a man serving God on his terms or by his own plan; he served God on God's terms, by God's plan. He said elsewhere, "I know what it is to be in need, and I know what it is to have plenty" (Philippians 4:12). He knew he was being led, and he used his prison time to minister, since that's where he was, just as he would have ministered if he were free. He didn't give up. He made his plans for Spain; those plans didn't work out. Yet he wasn't disappointed. His attention was focused on God.

God Is Building a People

For a lot of people, if what happened to Paul happened to them they would be emotionally or spiritually crippled. If life doesn't go the way they plan, they collapse. "But I prayed about it," they say. Paul prayed about Spain, too. "I felt led," they say. Paul did too, or he wouldn't have started out for Spain. But always, Paul was a man of God. He was a follower.

God is building a people for himself, a people willing to obey and follow. Maybe the hardest thing for you to realize right now is that at this moment he is building *you*. We like to say, "Ah, yes, look at what God did to make a John Wesley or a William Booth."

We like to hear about their conversion to Christ and how God led them. Stories of Wesley and Booth are beautiful and true, and we need the encouragement and the inspiration that come from their stories, but there is a point that is often missed. We overlook God's current miracle. The miracle is not only that God did something radical in the lives of the famous. The miracle is that he is working a great change in each of us too.

Insecure Christians are great at trotting out Christians who are successful and famous, almost as if it is some kind of proof that God is powerful. We point to the Christian entertainer as if he is more "proof" of God's power than the Christian factory worker. Or we take a newly converted sensation and tout him as evidence of the "wonderful grace of Jesus." Many of our church conference planners would never have allowed Saul of Tarsus to go off for those silent but important years while God shaped him into Paul the missionary. They would have had him in their pulpits, or pushed him to write a book, long before he was ready. He would have been urged to sign autographs for people who needed to say to their friends, "I know him."

The titillating, the sensational, the vicarious enjoyment of prestige really points to the weakness in our own relationship to God. It shows that we do not know who we are. The confessed sin of a thief or prostitute doesn't need to be savored again and again for those who really know Christ—they don't need celebrity examples to be certain that God is God. The power of God is amply proven in what he is doing right now in our lives.

It Is So Easy to Slip

Our own discipleship must be a daily matter for prayer. We do not point to ourselves in pride or feel that we have arrived, because we know that we can fall any minute; many have. A. H. McNeile warned himself and in doing so warns us:

> Everyone in my home, my office, my place of business, my school, knows that I care about religion. And I do care; I care intensely; I really don't think I *could* betray my Lord. And yet—"the hand of him that betrayeth Me is with Me on the Table; Mine own familiar friend, whom I trusted."[2]

And C. S. Lewis said:

> When we Christians behave badly, or fail to behave well, we are making Christianity unbelievable to the outside world. The wartime posters told us that Careless Talk Costs Lives. It is equally true that Careless Lives Cost Talk. Our careless lives set the outer world talking, and we give them grounds for talking in a way that throws doubt on the truth of Christianity itself. [3]

Like Peter, I slip back and I surge forward. I might be a failure in some areas, a success in others, but always I must trust that God has me, and I must not stray from him. It is so easy to slip.

The temptation to slip can even creep up on those who are mature in the faith and have a strong witness. When people come to appreciate how God is using a particular man or a woman, they pray for him or her. That is the right thing to do. If we see that God is working through a person, we bring our neighbors and friends under his ministry so more people are blessed and fed. Again, we should do that. But Satan gets in there too and will try to tell the prayed-for Christian leader that the gifts and power evidenced in his life are his own. If the Christian leader ever starts to take credit for what God is doing through him, or if he forgets that what God is doing is in answer to the prayers of the faithful, he can fall, bringing great shame to the Christian church and dishonor to the name he bears. That person may still go on being an instrument in the hand of God, because God is still answering the prayers of others, choosing to use him in spite of himself. But someday, however long it takes, he will answer for his straying and for trying to steal God's glory. God warned, "I will not yield my glory to another" (Isaiah 48:11). God will be God; he may use an "unjust prophet" for a while, but someday that will end. We must never forget that.

The adventure of following Jesus Christ on his terms and for his glory means that it really isn't important whether we have ten talents or one so long as God can use for himself the talents he gives. They are his gift, to be used for his sake. It is blasphemy to take any credit for what he is doing in us or with us.

Moses had an intimate relationship with God, but he didn't try to take credit for his usefulness nor brag about his power—he knew that it wasn't his own.

Moses could argue with God (Exodus 5:22-23), and God with him; they were that close. But in Moses God knew he had a man who wasn't self-seeking. That's the kind of person God looks for today too.

When it comes time to lead people out of the wilderness, God doesn't call an egotistical Pharisee to do it. He calls one who recognizes the cloud and pillar of fire for what they are—God's leading—and one who is willing to put one foot in front of the other and follow because God said to do so. God has never changed his standards.

We have our human standards for who is "great," but they don't impress God. We have our measure for those who are "more useful" than others, but God doesn't measure that way. Paul, a man God used, made it clear that some may plant and some may water, but it is always God who gives the increase. A farmer doesn't spend all of his time harvesting. There is a time for harvest, but only because there was first the planting, and because God gave the increase.

Without Knowing It

I remember as a new Christian that I tried to witness to another student at Wayne State University. I wasn't happy about what I said to him. I felt that I hadn't said things correctly. It wasn't a polished presentation of the gospel, and I was only able to tell him a little bit about the Good News. I did not lead him to faith in Christ.

But God was in it, and perhaps in order to teach me he showed me something special about that witness. A few days after that conversation, another student said to me, "Do you know Tom came to Christ yesterday?" There were five or six of us sitting together when he said that, and together we rejoiced over the news. In particular, we expressed our gratitude for the man who introduced Tom to Christ. But then somebody said, "I spoke to Tom a couple of weeks ago, and this is what I said." Then somebody else added that he too had spoken to Tom about Christ.

As we talked and compared notes, we began to see what had happened. Each of us, without knowing about the others, had witnessed to Tom. None of us had felt that we had been successful or even complete in our witness. Yet as we checked what each had said and the time when we said it, we found that God had led Tom to each of us, and each one in sequence had picked up where the other had left off. Without knowing it, each of us had given Tom one more piece of the gospel message, the next step, until finally the last man led him into the kingdom.

Who was the soul-winner? None of us! It was the Holy Spirit's doing. Sometimes I may be allowed to do the harvesting, sometimes I may do the planting; most of the time my job is to help dig out the weeds or carry the water. We do what has to be done, directed by the One who owns the field. But we will do our job successfully only to the degree that we keep our eyes on the Master and do as we're told.

Get close to God. Listen to him. Let his Word become a part of you, and watch what he does with your life. Then no matter what happens, wherever you go, whatever you do, the deep-down peace that comes with obedience will be yours. During your lifetime you will have the joy of seeing Jesus use you.

We have the guidance of our Namesake—we are Christ-ones—because we live in God's will. In God's will I no longer need to be dominated by fear. In God's will I can practice my true humanity without trying to be superspiritual. In God's will I am free to be me, for I am alive. And in God's will there is pleasure even in doing ordinary things because God is in the ordinary just as much as he is in the spectacular. As Francis of Assisi learned, the mundane can be enjoyed. We can happily do without in Jesus' name.

To be in God's will doesn't mean that we have all things going smoothly. In fact, it is neither biblical nor true that those who have little trouble are blessed and those who have much trouble are not. Jesus made that clear; he talked about the rich man and Lazarus and the crumbs from the table. How foolish to think that someone who struggles with cancer or poverty or unexciting work is less of a saint. God is the Sanctifier. He is the King, and the King gives the orders. We are to follow those orders. We are in his army whether we carry the flag or clean the garbage cans. Be sure that you are in his will where he wants you. Be sure daily that you have sought that place of faithfulness. Jesus said, "You are my friends if you do what I command" (John 15:14). Be sure that you are his friend.

By God's will I can function according to his greatness, not according to my thoughts about a given situation. In him I may cry in my own pain, but will also cry when I see the suffering of others. In God's will I will not be always judging my gift or his use of it, whether I have been given something large or small, whether that gift is for myself or to offer to a person who is hurting a cup of cold water, a word of encouragement, or a piece of bread. By God's will I am here to give. In the church, which is a hospital, I may not be the surgeon but I may be an orderly. And as an orderly for Jesus, I have something to do for this sick world.

Richard Baxter in 1650 said that too:

> The church on earth is a mere hospital. Which way ever we go, we hear complaining, and into what corner soever we cast our eyes, we behold objects of pity and grief.... Who weeps not when all these bleed? As now our friends' distresses are our distresses, so then our friends' deliverance will be part of our own deliverance.... How much more comfortable to see them perfected, than now to see them wounded, weak, sick and afflicted?... Our day of rest will free both them and us from all this. [4]

But until that day of rest comes, we will—we must—minister in Jesus' name out of the wealth of all that he has given to us. It may be tough, but God is tough too.

Give Away the Love He Has Given

John Haggai once stated, "If our path had been smooth, we might have depended upon our own surefootedness. Perhaps God roughened the path so we would take hold of His hand. If the weather had been mild, we might have loitered along the beach."[5]

To be his is to understand that we can work for Christ and rest in Christ, for both activities are ours in him. A Marine wading ashore during an invasion does not do it so that he will have a place to lie down and get a suntan; he does it to conquer. But later, at another time or in another situation, he can just as faithfully take that rest and get a tan. In Christ there is a time for the Christian to do both.

Living in God's will means we can know that he is in charge when we are hard at work, and have the peace of knowing that he is also in charge when we are playing golf or are in bed with the flu. In hard work or soft rest we can enjoy him. We can live every day by God's will and God's leading.

I can enjoy him when I am working to help people or when I ignore the clamoring multitude, as Jesus sometimes did, to go aside and pray. For in both, Jesus was obedient. There is no guilt associated with such obedience. We can say with Philip Doddridge:

> Thou reignest, and I rejoice in it, as it is indeed a matter of universal joy. I believe thy universal providence and care; and I firmly believe thy wise, holy, and kind interposition in every thing which relates to me, and to the circumstances of my abode in this thy world. [6]

And in his *Testament of Devotion*, Thomas Kelly said:

> Walk and talk and work and laugh with your friends. But behind the scenes, keep up the life of simple prayer and inward worship. Keep it up throughout the day. Let inward prayer be your last act before you fall asleep and the first act when you awake. And in time you will find as did Brother Lawrence, that "those who have the gale of the Holy Spirit go forward even in sleep." [7]

So much depends on our willingness to trust and follow. Don't ever measure the meaning of a day by the content of that day. No matter what, God is God. The Bible states, "He who watches over Israel will neither slumber nor sleep" (Psalm 121:4). And if you want to see how obedience and design come together, read the scope of history in Acts 7, then ask yourself, "Do I want my time in history to be the same?"

Scripture assures that God is "thinking about me constantly! ... And when I waken in the morning, you are still thinking of me!" (Psalm 139:17-18, TLB). E. M. Bounds in *Power Through Prayer* said, "God can work wonders if he can get a suitable man. Men can work wonders if they can get God to lead them." [8] Thus being in God's will is the greatest work that I can do even if sometimes it is doing nothing. I can honor him as much in trusting rest as in great works. For trust is what causes us to treat him as he is—God. And our God is great!

Cameron Thompson said:

> We need to ask according to His greatness and not according to the feebleness of our desires. One who asked an incredible boon of Napoleon had it immediately granted because, said Napoleon, "He honored me by the magnitude of his request." [9]

Trust him, ask of him, seek from him, look to him, enjoy him, serve him with obedience knowing that he will provide. Claim his promises knowing that he will provide. He is our God; we are his people. God is for us. He is on our side.

How much larger this kind of living is than the smaller belief that if I do "my" part, God will do *his* part, as if we live by some kind of divine trade-off. His will is bigger than just giving to me. His will for me—and for all of us—is for his honor and for his kingdom.

Let us long to be in him and in his will and to be his people. That for now and always is the very best there is.

16

Able to Be Trusted

■ ■ ■

In 1917, A H. McNeile wrote:

> It has been said that "humility is the truth about ourselves." And
> the truth about ourselves is just what we find it so hard to see.
> Ask God with all your might to enable you to say, "One thing I
> know, that whereas I was blind, now I see." Now I see why I
> could not overcome that temptation; I thought I was safe enough
> without constant watching; I thought I could get along all right
> without daily self-examination; I thought I could get forgiveness
> although I had not really and sincerely confessed my sins; I
> thought I could grow in grace without growing in prayerful-
> ness. [1]

If I am God's person, if I live my life in him and find my satisfaction in him, can God trust me? Can I be trusted as a person who
is wholly his, trusted as an ambassador, trusted as a witness to
Jesus Christ, trusted as a friend of God?

I am not removed from the corruption of this world. I am not
suspended in a cocoon-type state of artificial holiness. I am not
"holier than thou," but I can live a holy life in this world with all of
its pain and sordidness and misery. And you can too.

All of us, in our honest times, have to say truthfully, "I am not
what I ought to be." And we might be tempted to be forever worried about that. But we can't, not if we understand forgiveness—
the meaning of forgotten sin. Instead, each of us has to go on in
confidence in the promise, "If we confess our sins, he is faithful and
just and will forgive us our sins and purify us from all unrighteous-

ness" (1 John 1:9), and live out what we are—forgiven ones, always keeping short accounts with God, always remembering what we might have been without both the liberation and the restraints of the love and law of God.

Do people know that God owns me? Do they know that in my attempts to practice the presence of God I am not trying to show off to them or to impress them? Do they know that what I want for myself and for them is the greatest good, God's best?

We are not safe from failure so long as our feet are in this clay called "the world." We will always be tempted; sometimes we will fall down. Yet can we be trusted because God knows that we want to obey him and because people sense that Christ can have his way in our lives?

Am I Moral?

Not long ago someone said to me, "You are one of the most moral men I know." At first that statement stunned me. Then the seriousness of it almost destroyed me. What an "awful" thing for someone to say. I went home and told Andrea what this person said. Without looking up from the stove where she was stirring something she said, "Well, you are a moral man," and went on with her cooking. That frightened me still more. It is not that I prefer to be immoral; I don't. But I fear being thought of as moral because of the dangers it can bring. I have great weaknesses, temptations; it would take only a second to slip. In my praying I keep facing that. Am I moral in my views about the people around me? Am I moral in my treatment of persons of another culture or race? Am I moral in my attitude toward material things and my consumption of them; the way I handle money or food or resources? Am I moral in my political stand? Am I moral toward my children and their values? Am I moral toward my family, including my larger Christian family? Am I moral in my behavior toward my wife and the life God has given her to live? Am I moral in my thinking and in my dreaming and in my planning? Am I moral in my worship? Can I be trusted, morally, with the name "Christian"?

Not long after I was called a "moral" man, I was requested by my staff to write an article on holiness. I knew that I could write it journalistically. I knew, too, that I could write it biblically and practically. But could I handle the subject personally? Did I have the right to put my thoughts on paper, to make a declaration, to take a stand before others?

I asked my staff, "What if I slip? What if I write about holiness and tomorrow I fall prey to my own temptations? What if I am not in fact living what I write about?" The people heard me out. Then one of them said pointedly, "Well, then you're defeated already."

And that is correct. For none of us writes, or lives, or acts out of our wholeness. We write, live, and act out of our weakness. It is because we are incomplete that we can seek to be holy and to be trusted. We are obedient not because we have arrived at perfection, for none of us has, but because we haven't, and we cry to God for help. F. P. Harton explained it: "Christian morality is, fundamentally, obedience to the revealed will of an holy God."[2]

C. S. Lewis said:

> Does it not make a great difference whether I am, so to speak, the landlord of my own mind and body, or only a tenant, responsible to the real landlord? If somebody else made me for his own purposes, then I shall have a lot of duties which I should not have if I simply belonged to myself. [3]

Because I have chosen to be called by the name Christian, I have a terrible responsibility to serve him and to be his person.

Others Know Too. They Can Tell.

The moment I say I am a Christian, I am declaring that I am a disciple, a follower: "I have been crucified with Christ" (Galatians 2:20). I am saying that I am not my own, that I am bought with a price. Christ is in me.

To be a Christian is a frightening responsibility; yet how can we ever be trusted if we are always burdened by the problems we might encounter? Harry A. Ironside clarified this for me:

> No one will ever know down here the full results of a life lived wholly for God and a will fully yielded to Him. The effects on all with whom such a surrendered believer associates are incalculable in their peace-giving power. On the other hand, no one can tell until the secret things are revealed in the day of the revelation of Jesus Christ, how much harm a restless, quarrelsome, critical,

fault-finding person can do in the way of disturbing the peace of any group with which such a dissatisfied, selfish soul mingles. We are all either helpers in the things which make for peace or we are assisting in spreading unrest and disturbance, which dishonors the Lord, grieves the Holy Spirit and hinders the work of winning the lost for Jesus Christ. [4]

Can I be trusted? Do people know that in the deepest part of my heart I want to follow Christ? Not that there will be a holy aura emanating from me, but is my desire for Christlikeness something that is noted just as much as one notes that I am a certain weight or height or that I walk a particular way? Is this life in Christ as much a part of me as my likes, my tastes, my way of acting? Is it just as clear as anything else about me that I want to be his?

This is critically important because Christians know inside whether or not they sincerely want to follow Jesus or if they only want to talk about following Jesus. And others know too; they can tell. Sometimes those who talk most noisily about following Jesus do not communicate that they are following him. Can you be trusted to be a follower of Jesus—even when no one is looking?

Do people know that in your time alone with God you struggle too, as they do, that sometimes you argue with God about the worth of your life? Do they know that you are up and down, as they are, not having "made it" but always wanting to be better? You may not win all your battles, but do you long to win them in Christ and for Christ? Do people know that even your failures are your teachers to help you toward a closer walk with God?

Can you be trusted to seek out other people for the Savior? Do people who want to find God know that they can talk to you about him? Do your neighbors know that? They may tease you about it, but do they know that you genuinely love God and long to have them know God too? Are you honest with them about that?

Can you be trusted to tell the truth about God, or do you hedge and sidestep? When was the last time you tried to speak to someone about the Lord Jesus? In one of the early draft papers presented at the Consultation on World Evangelization at Pattaya, Thailand, June 1980, was the statement:

The secular man's deepest need is to discover that he is meant to be a redeemed child of God. He is not a complete, fulfilled human being. Although a season of "temporary euphoria" in the lives of many other secular people around him will convince him that they are "moving up the ladder," have "got their act together," and "have got it made"—time and events inevitably cause them to come down off their "secular high" and face their finitude. The secularized man's felt needs—loneliness, emptiness, fear, guilt, meaninglessness, and a search for peace, love and joy—will only be satisfied when he encounters Jesus Christ and commits himself personally to Him. This encounter transforms a life of frustration, superficiality, despair and ultimate judgment. At this point, his unperceived need for self-esteem will be realized. He can live for God's glory, to know, love and obey Him and to serve his fellowman. [5]

Can You Be Trusted?

We must not pretend that people do not want or need Jesus. They do! One of the most hateful things that a Christian can do is to lie to another about that. Richard Baxter, writing in 1650, said:

Do not daub with men, and hide from them their misery or danger, or any part of it; do not make their sins less than they are, nor speak of them in an extenuating language; do not encourage them in a false hope or faith, no more than you would discourage the sound hopes of the righteous. If you see his case is dangerous, tell him plainly of it.... It is not hovering at a distance in a general discourse that will serve the turn. [6]

Scripture says, "Therefore he is able to save completely those who come to God through him, because he always lives to intercede for them" (Hebrews 7:25). Yet there are pastors and whole congregations who keep their worship and their talk on the horizontal. They say, "Worship is what happens between us because we meet together." People, empty from the pain of life and coming in hope into a church sanctuary, are kept from seeing the One who alone can save, fulfill, and offer them life. Even the Lord's Supper is sometimes relegated to the horizontal—"Because we take it together"—and is not worship in remembrance of him. This is more than a heresy problem, for it is more than doctrinal—it is a hatred toward our fellow men. It is purposely keeping people from the sure Word of love. We want people to love each other, but they won't be able to if we keep them from the Source of true love.

Can you be trusted to tell the truth honestly about God, not out of some sense of being superior, but because you sincerely long for people to know the God of truth and life? Certainly the true longing of your heart cannot be hidden.

Do people know even in your silence how much you love them for what they are now as well as for what they can be in Christ? Do people know that you will help them become God's best as they seek God's will? This does not mean that you will be in church work every moment, because some who are give the least help. It does not mean that you will always be available at every call, for sometimes you must step back in order to help the most. But do people know that you will help them, whether they call in the middle of the night or whether they take you from your fireside and family—do they know that you are available to them? Can you be trusted to go to them as Jesus went?

Can you be trusted never to disclose a confidence? Do people know that when they speak to you it will never be told? We have all been hurt, deeply hurt, by those who have promised to keep a confidence only to broadcast it.

Recently someone did that to me. He not only broke his promise, but when I told him how he had betrayed me, he proceeded to tell others what it was that hurt me and repeated my confidence again to his current audience in order to hurt even more. He is a Christian, one whom God uses in many areas of ministry, but I cannot trust him anymore.

A faithful Christian who can be trusted will still sometimes be mistaken for a betrayer. You have surely had it happen that when you have kept private counsel, as you promised, the confidence has come to light through another party. You cannot convince the confider that you kept your word. You endure the pain of being thought a traitor. But God knows; he will still bring others to you when they need help because he knows you can be trusted.

Years ago Andrea and I agreed that we would trust each other enough to allow a ministry of counseling. That wasn't something that came out of our heads but out of a trust of the heart. We can trust each other because what we have between us is deeper and richer than anything each of us may have with another person. When people talk to me, they know that it will go no farther if they wish it not to. The same is true with Andrea. I remember once asking, quite innocently, what somebody said to her and she replied, "I cannot tell you." I was satisfied with that. Of course she could not tell me. It would have been wrong for her to tell me. It was enough that she told me that the person had a need. Trust means that there is no gossip about the subject even "for prayer."

Can you be trusted to keep a confidence because you are secure in Jesus and don't need the reputation for being "in the know"? Can you weep and cry with an individual without him or her ever telling another about your "effective ministry"? Can you be trusted not to use people for your own ego needs?

Know That It Will Happen

If you have been used for someone's ego satisfaction, you know that one of the most painful things to discover is that somebody is using you. You may be in that kind of situation now. But try to be faithful. Help people in their work and ministry even if you know that they are using you to gain some benefit for themselves, or worse, are putting you out on a limb so that if it is cut off they are safe and you take the fall. Not everyone who is in Christ understands faithfulness. Some think trust is weakness and that weakness is something to be exploited for their own gain. Know that it will happen and remain faithful.

The risk that somebody will use you cannot interfere with your ministry in Christ. You can't be paranoid about people who are "out to use you." The trusting Christian knows there are some who will hurt or destroy, just as one knows that there may be dangers in walking down a street late at night. Don't let that stop you from offering your heart and help to others. Be trusted to love regardless of what people do, because in this world people are hungry to be loved. They may not know how to handle it. They may hurt you, but they need your love.

There is such fear among some Christians who have been so used and hurt that they prefer to keep relationships sterile, even cold. Even in their praying they do not really grapple with the true issues but prefer the "platform" approach to prayer where they stay impersonal, where they do not get involved.

Perhaps they are frightened that if they reach out to touch or love they will be seen as getting too close, too intimate. I have sensed it. I remember once when a young man I was trying to help made a serious commitment of his life to Jesus Christ, I hugged him. It was a major step in his life that God is now honoring, but I knew how he had struggled and wrestled for so many months before he took that step. As we embraced, I saw someone look at me with shock in his eyes and I knew immediately what he was thinking: Here was a man hugging another man. He did not understand.

One Sunday I was preaching in a federal penitentiary where 95 percent of the inmates were black. I tried to explain the love and saving work of Jesus Christ, and invited the men to respond to Christ as their Savior and Lord. I gave an altar call and then waited. No one responded. Minutes passed, and I wondered if I had failed to communicate. Then, to close the meeting, I prayed for the men. When I finished praying and opened my eyes, I saw that one man, a black man, had come to the front. I went to him, took him by the hand, and asked him about his decision. He told me that it was to present his life to Christ. I spoke to him for a minute as the rest of the men sat watching. Then, as I continued to hold his hand, I put my other arm around his shoulder and prayed that God would bless his decision and his life and use him there in the prison. When I opened my eyes and looked up, I found that thirteen more men had come forward. Later, I realized why. They had come not because of the content of the sermon but because they had seen that I truly did want that brother to be saved. I was not just a white man talking at black men, but a man who wanted another man to know Christ. I had to love him with that touch; it is my way. Could I have shown my feelings without that touch? Maybe, and some people can, but I can't—and I think it mattered that day.

The same things happen, as I learned over the years with my students, in ministering to women as well as men. It is a delicate thing, but early in my ministry I found that sometimes it was the touch of a hand or a hug that communicated most.

Sometimes I would walk the campus at night with students, men or women, or even visit them in a private place in the dormitory. It was a caring time. I would come home and tell Andrea that I was with this person or that one, and tell her what happened, without revealing a confidence. I had the security of knowing that Andrea trusted me, and because of that trust I could give myself in love to people in need. That is indeed a beautiful thing. And I've told her so.

Bring Wholeness to People

One weekend a young woman came to us for counseling and she and I spent several hours alone in my study. Andrea had asked ahead of time if the woman wanted to speak to both of us or just to me, and she replied that if Andrea didn't mind she would like to talk to me alone. We talked for a long time together, and she cried and we prayed. She felt so terribly separated from God, so unloved, and I was able to put my arm around her and tell her that I loved her but most of all that God loved her in spite of all that had transpired in her life. Today her feet are on the Solid Rock again and events since have borne out that she has gone on with Christ. Later I said to Andrea, "I could never have done that anywhere else. I could not put my arm around a woman who is crying lest someone read into it. I could not say, 'I love you,' except in our home where you are. But you understand, you trust, and you know that there is only one who has all of my heart and love, and that is you."

Of course we should always be aware of our weaknesses. We should be aware of lust where genuine love should be. We are to bring wholeness to people; therefore, we must never in any way hurt or use a person. Always we are to add one more part to their healing as God gives the opportunity.

Can you be trusted to work for healing? Can you help? Can you work to bring about wholeness in people, families, hurting marriages? Can you be trusted to build up the home? If God puts someone in your care, can he trust you to give what he wants that person to have from you? Are you a channel for his blessing?

Can you be trusted to be honest, to work hard, to give your best no matter what? When our daughter held one of her first jobs, she asked me, "How am I to work with people who tell me that I'm doing too much? When I'm through in one area, I go work in another because that's what I'm paid to do. But they say, 'You make us look bad.'" She has learned early that she will be appreciated more by some people if she cheats her employer.

Can you handle that type of response when it happens to you and still be trusted to be faithful? Will you give your employer an honest hour's work for that hour's wage? Are you responsible enough not to cheat even when you are not being watched? Is it known that you will honor God even in the little things?

How difficult it is to want to give people the liberty to develop and grow, and then see them use that liberty to do the opposite— not work, not develop, not grow. It hurts to see it at the employer-employee level, but how much more it must hurt God to see Christians abusing the liberties they have in their new life in Christ. What a painful thing it is when Christians will do less, not more, or abuse people because of their freedom in Christ.

Give Away the Love He Has Given

Can God trust you to follow him even when some in the church may not fully understand what your obedience means? Can he trust you to do what is right whether or not it comes out well by human standards, that you will do it because you are convinced that he has called you to do so, which is the only reason you need?

Can God trust you to give away the love he has given to you and to do it with abandonment? Can he trust you to hold on to him tightly in temptation and seek the way of escape he provides? Can he trust you to know what you can and cannot do in Christ, and yet trust you not to judge others who have no restraints because they don't have Christ?

Can you be trusted to avoid the appearance of evil for the kingdom's sake and yet not avoid a potentially dangerous situation if it means helping, rescuing, delivering an unbeliever, or strengthening some brother or sister in Christ?

There are biblical rules that we must obey before God. But we can't judge others who do not obey those rules. For example, I do not, when I have control of my circumstances, ever work on Sunday. I may work long hours six days a week, but Sunday is a day of rest. It is the Lord's day. It is for worship, and I need that time of worship. Therefore I will not make others work by shopping in stores or eating in restaurants or even buying gasoline if I can in any way avoid it. And yet I try not to be legalistic about it, for some Christians do it and before God have peace as they do it. I did not even keep my teenaged children from working on Sunday afternoons. In fact, I know that many of those they served are Christians who use Sunday for pleasure and family.

And I have helped my neighbors on Sunday to do things that I would never do for myself. Occasionally that has turned out to be a witness because they know from my lifestyle that I do not do those things for myself on Sunday.

Here is another example: I believe strongly that divorce and remarriage is wrong. I cannot accept it on the basis of Scripture. I believe a vow is a vow, that a union is a union, and that it cannot be broken. And I weep over those who look for escape from marriage on the basis that "God wants me to be happy." I will work for healing and can point to homes today where everything was against that marriage and yet it has held and the couple is growing and deepening in their love for each other and in their faith because they refused to divorce. Yet I can love and care for those who do not hold that view and have gone against what I consider to be the strong will of God. I can love them no less. If anything, I have despised my own failure to help them earlier when perhaps something might have been done. I have prayed for and loved people after they have divorced and later when they have found new partners. But my beliefs are the same about the biblical basis for staying together.

Some will charge, "You condemn in silence." But on two occasions I have performed the weddings of divorced people; they knew my stand but they also knew that I loved them. Some don't understand this "contradiction." It is simply that vows are vows, but healing is important too.

Or another example: I believe in tithing on my gross income not my net income. I believe that tithe money is not mine and can't be spent in any way, not even to pay my taxes. The money is God's and true giving on my part does not even begin until the tithe has first been given to him. I believe that if I hold back any part of the full 10 percent saying, "That belongs to the government," or, "This is mine," it is stealing. The first 10 percent of the gross is his.

And yet I cannot feel self-righteous or condemn those who do not practice that. I must do what I must do before God—that is a rule for me to follow, not a rule for measuring others.

I believe in a daily prayer time alone with God, and that it must be kept faithfully. Yet I know many who cannot and do not keep such a time. It is not mine to judge them, because my responsibility before God is for myself. Other people must do as they honestly will before God. They are his too, and I will not play God. Yet I will help others in all the ways I can if I am asked to help them establish a quiet time. I will try to be trustworthy enough to live out what I say I believe.

We are to be light. We are to be "life offerers." We are to be faithful in proclaiming and practicing the truth that Jesus came to reveal. We must do nothing less than our best for people and for God. And, because we are in him and because we are secure and because we vow to be faithful, we can do our best—for he is in us.

Can you be trusted? Can you really be trusted? Does God know it? Do your friends know it? Do even strangers know it?

I once wrote an article about discipline and received some interesting responses. A few came from those who agreed with me, but some responses were from those who didn't. To them discipline looked like a form of works, not faith. They argued that if I really trusted Christ, if I was really a believer, I would have no rules. F. P. Harton said:

> Self-discipline is greatly assisted by the making and keeping of a wise Rule of Life. To the novice this sounds a very forbidding and complicated thing, but it should be neither. The soul that tries to live without rule never really forms habits of virtue or learns to live the Christian life as it should; for without rule the whole of the conduct of life depends on the whim of the moment, instead of being regulated with regard to the will of God, and the soul never knows for certain what to do next. [7]

It takes faith to be disciplined. Only in faith can we be disciplined or discipline ourselves. Only when we trust God can we be trustworthy before God. James said, "Faith without deeds is dead" (James 2:26).

You can have faith and works together—you can be alive and trustworthy. God wants that for you. Because you are trusted, look at all that you have from God. You have gifts to give away.

17

Love Giver

■ ■ ■

It follows—when I can be trusted, then I can be a love giver. Why? Because I am free by God and for God. "If the Son sets you free, you will be free indeed" (John 8:36). He has freed me from all that once limited me, and I am now liberated to be all that he designed me to be. I belong to the Giving One who gave himself for me and continually gives himself. Because of him I have become a "give away."

When I first moved to West Virginia as a young minister, it took me awhile to become accustomed to mountain ways. One afternoon I went calling with a deacon of the little church I pastored. We drove down a narrow, winding dirt road back into one of the hollows and stopped at a little clearing where a cabin stood. Dogs growled at us as we got out of the car, chickens scattered as we approached the wooden steps to the door. A grizzled man greeted us with a look of suspicion. He had lived all his life in those hills and wasn't used to having townspeople come back that far into the hollows. He was a self-taught, homespun philosopher, an independent type, characteristic of mountain people. Besides scratching out a little garden for his sustenance, he was a gun trader. We had come to talk to him about his need for Jesus Christ.

He had heard the "Christian pitch" before and in his slow drawl kept me, a young, eager preacher, somewhat off balance; I was certainly not in control. After we had talked for about an hour he said, "Preacher, you got a gun?"

I replied, "No, I don't."

"I'm going to give you one," he said, and walked over to the wall where various guns were leaning. He picked up a 16-gauge shotgun, stuck it in my hand, and said gruffly, "Take it."

I started to argue, "But I can't take this gun, this is your livelihood. You trade these. I'll buy a gun for hunting someday, but, no, I can't take this."

"Don't you want that gun?" he accused, and then before I could finish stuttering my refusal, he stomped into the kitchen.

Quickly the deacon with me leaned over and in a commanding whisper said, "Take the gun!" Then, before I could protest, the gun trader stepped back into the room.

But I had caught that deacon's urgency and said, "I'm really pleased that you want me to have the shotgun. I've never received a gift like this before. I don't know how to thank you. You are a very generous man." And then I told him how I looked forward to rabbit hunting season. He didn't smile, but I could tell he was pleased.

As we drove back to town, the deacon said, "Preacher, don't you understand? You want to give him the gospel, but if you did he would be taking something from you. First you have to take something from him. Now, when you see him again, you will be indebted to him and he will listen to you."

I learned something that day about giving. Sometimes the first gift a Christian can give is to take. But that doesn't mean we always have to receive before we give. Most of the time we give ourselves as well as our message without receiving anything—ever.

I Am Special to God

The liberation of obedience, the liberation from materialism, the liberation of discipleship frees me. The things that once kept me hesitant and reserved now no longer matter. People's putdowns, fear that the criticism of my ideas is a criticism of me, fear of one-upmanship by someone are things I need not be afraid of anymore. I was chosen before the creation of the world (Ephesians 1:4). I am special to God. Therefore I can offer myself and I must offer myself as a gift to the body of Christ and to those who do not believe in Christ, even to those who hate him.

Within the church, I am a part of the body. I know there are gifts that God has given to me which he will develop. Those are his gifts, but they are mine to exercise. As I use them I make a present of them to other members of the body. God made me the way I am so that I can give gifts. He crafted me for that, equipped me for that, and indeed expects me to strengthen others in the body with "my" gifts even as others strengthen me with theirs.

We are gift givers to and for one another, not for our sake but for his sake and for the sake of the body. We do it quietly, without attracting attention to ourselves. We stay out of the way. George Laird Hunt says, "The word minister means servant, servant of God, and he serves best who attracts little attention to himself and simply lets his Master work."[1]

Filled by the ever-present Holy Spirit, each member of the body gives himself to other members as God puts them together. And together they perform a ministry as God intended it to be performed. We do not have to measure the effect of that ministry ourselves, although certainly we are aware of the effects. God measures by his standard. We don't have to analyze where each step of obedience is leading, how each gift applies, or be shown personally how we fulfill his role for us, though we are to be wise and worshipful about it when we are shown. We serve and give, and that is a completely satisfying way to live.

There is freedom in this kind of living because we know that he has us in his will. We are participants with God in his purpose and plan even though we may or may not know exactly how we are participating. In that participation, we receive what God is and give what God is. Because we are loved, we love. We are love givers. We are not foolish with it, for love is an active, thoughtful gift—God's gift through us, a strong divine love, not a weak, insipid, human love. We just do as we are—we love and we do it prayerfully. If we don't love that way we will forever be crying over "failures," analyzing "developments" and "delays"—and in looking at the details, miss the larger picture, God's picture.

Being "love givers," we are quiet and we are content. The Word of God is correct: "In quietness and trust is your strength" (Isaiah 30:15). We have time to listen, we have time to pray, we have time to teach, we have time for disciple-making, and we have time to bless and be blessed. Why? Because our time is not our own and our trust is not in ourselves.

We can give ourselves both to believers and to unbelievers, and in giving ourselves be praying that we may bring them to God, which is the finest thing we can do for anyone. William Law said, "There is nothing that makes us love a man so much as praying for him; and when you can once do this sincerely for any man, you have fitted your soul for the performance of every thing that is kind and civil towards him."[2]

Love Frees

We are proclaimers, both by our words and by our actions. What we proclaim, we proclaim with our being and our words—both coming out of the love of God. This is the greatest love and the greatest good. We are, as Jesus was, both the teacher and the content of the teaching.

And, as Jesus who came to the world, we will not limit what we give in his name or what we are by his power only to those who are "our own kind." He came to the world, so we go to the world too.

There was a time when I believed so strongly in separation from unbelievers that it was hard for me to live the love of God before an unbeliever, especially if he was a clergyman who denied the basic tenets of the Christian faith. Then, during a year-long course in clinical counseling, I saw myself mirrored in a fellow student. In this person's negative ways and attitudes I saw myself and I learned about being a love giver. This young clergyman, who was very much like me in his theological stance, was asked, "Do you love that man?" referring to a fellow clergyman who had belittled his fundamentalist beliefs.

"Yes, the Bible tells me to."

"But do you love him?"

"Yes, because Jesus does."

As I listened to him I heard what I was saying. I, too, could "love" because "loving" was what I was supposed to do—which was in fact no love at all. I learned from hearing my colleague mouth phrases without opening his heart in love that my "biblical" love was neither biblical nor love.

Love is love that is inside and comes out. It is not "love if," or "love because," but *love*—it cannot be synthetic. It touches everything we do and every person we encounter. God is love and there is no shortage of his love in me when he has me. And because he has me, I neither generate his love nor conserve my energies in presenting it to others. I am free to be a love giver in whatever state or condition or place I am. This is freedom. Love frees.

Our freedom in Christ is the freedom to follow the dictates of Jesus who himself could serve others or leave them and go alone to pray (Mark 1:35). Jesus, the Divine Son of God, showed both the "what" of the Father's love and the "how" of it.

Jesus had a purpose; it is described for us in the Gospels. We have a purpose too. We are to follow him. Jesus came for a reason; we're here for a reason too—we are love givers.

To be in Christ is to have the same ministry that Jesus referred to when he took the prophet's words and said, "The Spirit of the Lord is on me, because he has anointed me to preach good news to the poor. He has sent me to proclaim freedom for the prisoners and recovery of sight for the blind, to release the oppressed, to proclaim the year of the Lord's favor" (Luke 4:18-19).

To be his is to move easily and quietly within the world and within the church, not straining, not struggling, not trying to become, because we already are in him and our becoming is within that framework of his life.

In ministry, in evangelism, in all of life, we have the time and the love to reach out, for both time and love are God's and are of his giving. He knows best how to utilize each day and each situation so that we can love; we need not worry about "redeeming the time." In him, mine is the freedom to give myself away until I am exhausted—or to go fishing to restore my body and soul.

There is a wholeness to all of this. It is the wholeness of understanding who I am, of coming to love my neighbor as myself, of coming to appreciate the gifts that God has given to me—the gifts that I can give away. It's the discovery of pleasure with myself. I can truly appreciate me because I am loved and appreciated by God. And with that sense of personal value, I have also the awareness that in Christ I have so much to give away. It is given in humility, both to the church and to the world, because I have so much and because none of it is of my own making. George Laird Hunt says:

Humility is not a technique with which the adroit leader wins friends and influences people. It is the essential mark of obedience, the attitude of the person who knows that he is reconciled to God by a deed of God, and that the grace of God equips him for the service he is called to render to the community and the world. [3]

Only One "Audience"

No one gives a cheap gift if he truly means to do something special for somebody. He gives a good gift. That's what the Christian is—a good gift. How foolish it is for Christians, having been saved by grace and knowing the complete work that Jesus did in them to make them righteous, to think that they can then add to that righteousness by their own efforts or settle for less than God supplies. Rather, Christians live and move and have their being in him, the One who fulfills his righteousness within us, the One who sends us into communities as his gifts, bearing the truth, the love, the redeeming plan of God to our Judeas, our Samarias, and to the uttermost parts of our earth.

This is why a Christian can keep a low profile but still get into other people's hearts, winning them to the highest and the best. In Jesus, Christians can change the hardened structures around them. Those who are secure in Jesus do not have identity problems or ego needs. They don't have to be watching to see if the right people are recognizing them and what they are doing. There is only one "audience" for the Christian—the One we love, the Lord himself.

William Law said,"Every good thought that we have, every good action that we do, lays us open to pride, and exposes us to the assaults of vanity and self-satisfaction."[4] A Christian leader, noting the difference between the effective Christians and the noisy, incompetent ones, said, "Did you ever notice how ego and incompetence usually go together?"

We can do so much and be so much if our reason for doing what we do and giving what we give is Jesus. I know a man who realized several years ago that just earning a paycheck wasn't all that God put him on this earth to do. He left an important position to put his efforts into Christian ministry. Ten years later he was nowhere near to earning the salary that he had in this previous position but, as he put it, "My wife and I are nearer the Lord, and we don't lack for anything." He will never make the headlines. No one knows very much about him—except God.

Some years ago in Germany a theologian and pastor named

August Hermann Franke established an orphanage. He didn't intend to start one, but while supporting the beggar children who came to his door he also taught them the Scriptures. Then when he opened his home to one orphan boy, he found that there were other brothers and sisters too. So he took them all. By the time Franke died he had built an orphanage, a primary and secondary school, a hospital, and a home for the aged. His little project of caring for the children at his door had developed into a major work.

As Franke asked others for help in supporting his homes, he learned that it was mostly the poor, not the rich, who gave to help others. The rich kept what they had or gave only a pittance. It was with money from the poor that he helped the orphan children and the aged. It is often that way today, too.

The disciple, not being his own, has everything to give. Because he belongs to the One who gave himself, his nature is giving; it cannot be any other way. He is a Christian. He has the desires of the One who lives in him. Jesus did not clutch or grasp at his place with the Father but left it to give himself for us. We receivers of that gift are givers too. We desire to help others. It is as incongruous to hear someone give a testimony about being in Christ while ignoring others in need as it is for the unsaved to give a testimony about being redeemed. Those who love Jesus care for those for whom Jesus cared:

> "Lord, when did we see you hungry and feed you, or thirsty and give you something to drink? When did we see you a stranger and invite you in, or needing clothes and clothe you? When did we see you sick or in prison and go to visit you?" The King will reply, "I tell you the truth, whatever you did for one of the least of these brothers of mine, you did for me" (Matthew 25:37-40).

When God leads people across our paths, whether for a few minutes or a few days, we give them what they need. We care, minister, and instruct because God has placed them with us and us with them.

Hungry for God

In his book about Justo Gonzalez, Floyd Shacklock tells about a man in Santiago, Chile, who was arrested by the police for being drunk. On the way to the jail, two Christian men asked the police if they would give the man to them to take care of. The police did. The men fed him, cared for him, found him a job, and told him about Jesus. The writer tells us:

> The gospel meant a new life for Munoz. He began to repair shoes and was able to make a simple living for his family. He began to talk to his neighbors about the love of God that was changing his life. Step by step he found himself: sober, employed and industrious; soon he was leading a group of neighbors in worship.
>
> It was not easy to be their leader, for he could not read. He had to memorize the Bible verses that his wife read to him. He explained the verses to his friends in terms of their daily lives and hungers. Before long he became the pastor of a new congregation of seventy members and had 150 children in a Sunday school. He still made his living as a shoemaker. [5]

Are you available to give as those two Christian men gave? People are desperate for care and they are hungry for God. They need a chance to see God in you, and to feel the power and warmth of God from you. You are their window.

Who in the world has access to you? Who knows that you live for God and are available to them? Do you communicate peace or do you communicate busyness? Is there ever time for people who need help to reach you? If not, then maybe there isn't even time for God to reach you either.

Whose life is better because you are here on this earth, because you live where you live and know whom you know and do what you do? What good are you for someone else?

For example, who is reaching out in a personal, genuine way to the international students on the university campus near you? They wonder when they are invited once for dinner, "ministered to," and then dropped, not to be invited again. They don't understand when people say, "How are you?" but imply in walking away that they don't really care or want to know. They don't know what to do with shallow friendships which don't go anywhere. Do you know even one person from another country or culture? Do you love them?

During the Billy Graham Cambridge Mission in 1980, I met a man named Vijay Menon. He came to Christ out of Hinduism, but he had to find Christ on his own; no one helped him. Today, realizing the value of Christian friendship, he has a mission to international people in London where he works as a Class A engineer; and he goes annually to university student missions where he serves on his own time.

With a glow of love, he told me about the students to whom he ministers. He told me where each one of them is spiritually and which step they had taken toward Christ. Each is as special to him as his own family. He is a love giver. He cares.

At Oxford, I spent a Saturday morning having coffee with a student who called himself "an indifferent agnostic." He wanted to talk about Jesus. He was eager to learn what it was that so satisfied me in Christ. Even though he claimed indifference, he pursued this conversation. He needed to know and talk to a Christian. People like him are everywhere.

One afternoon, after talking to two Irish students at Cambridge, I started to leave for another appointment. They ran after me to invite me to their rooms for tea. They wanted to know more about personal faith in Christ. People are searching, and many of us aren't even aware of it because we haven't opened the way for them to express themselves. We haven't even shown cursory interest. We need to help them along on the road to determining that they could have God in their lives too.

We Can Only Trust

Quite a few years ago a Danish schoolteacher came to live with our family. She was in the United States for twenty-four weeks, twelve of them with us, while taking graduate studies in education at Rutgers University. We were far apart spiritually and socially. She believed that her son should live with various women before marriage or else "how would he know whom he wanted to marry?" She challenged us when we spanked one of our children. She never sought our Christ. Were those twelve weeks a waste of our time? Should we have given her a quick plan of salvation and then ignored her if she didn't respond, going after "better pickings"? Since we couldn't point to "success" with her, did we fail God? We did what we felt we should do. We entrusted both our witness and her response to God. For twelve weeks we were the ones to be her "Christians." We could only give what we had. Now we can only trust.

Who is reaching out to the children around you? The ones who need a foster parent or a big brother or sister? There are fewer and fewer two-parent homes now and there is a desperate need for love and for adult role models. Fatherless children need to relate to a man. Motherless children need a "mom" to talk to. Is your home open to these children? You have more than yourself to give; you have the gifts that God has given to you to offer to someone else. If you could love just one: Affirm him, help him, teach him—just one. Even if you never saw the results in your lifetime, you would be praying and you would be loving. God would honor that.

Cameron V. Thompson explains:

> Our prayers should be persistent. God's delays are not denials. Each day brings the answers to our prayers nearer.... At a meeting in a small town in the United States a very old man was converted. Another old man stepped forward and with tears told how fifty years earlier twenty-five young people had made a pledge to pray for this man every day. Said he, "I am the only one still living to see the prayers of fifty years answered." [6]

You may never know what you do when you act in love. It doesn't matter—just reach out in love anyway.

Who is touching the lives of the deserted elderly? The people alone in small inner-city apartments or unvisited in nursing homes? One young couple I know spends every Sunday afternoon visiting people in a retirement home. They choose Sunday because that's when those who have families get their visitors, and the ones without families feel the most lonely. This young couple offers themselves. They are "surrogate children." Each week they listen to the same stories that they heard the week before, look at the same photographs that they have seen many times, but they don't mind because they are love givers—people who give themselves and give their love. Jesus would have them do that.

Who is writing letters for those in hospitals or nursing homes who are too weak to write? I know a woman in her eighties who has given more than 4,000 hours of volunteer work to patients in hospitals. She keeps giving and she is happy. I know another woman who is ten years younger but is miserable because she says, "No one ever does anything for me." There is health in being a love giver. Who can best express the love of Jesus? Not those who have their thoughts on their own personal wants; only the love givers can do it, because their time and life and love are not their own.

And when people start to give in one area, it affects the other areas of their lives too. I have a friend who is a listener. She works as a receptionist in a doctor's office. People come seeking treatment for physical ailments, but while they are waiting to see the doctor some of them talk to her, spilling out their anxieties about family or future. She isn't trying to be a doctor, but she knows that part of their treatment is occurring right there, in the outer office, as she listens. She is a different kind of physician, but she is a physician.

Who is going to the jails and prisons to minister there? When I was a young minister I went every week to a medium security prison in Virginia about sixty miles from my home. I came to know about a dozen inmates quite well. I was allowed to eat lunch with them and talk and listen. At first they all talked about being innocent, about being there through no fault of their own. But then the talk of their innocence passed and they got honest, talking about themselves, their feelings, their fears. Soon I was picking up on biblical subjects one week right where I had left off the week before—the continuity was coming with their feelings of security with me.

One day one of the men opened his heart and soul to Jesus Christ, accepting him as Savior and Lord. Shortly after that I moved to another state and lost contact with those men. But about a year later the inmate who had accepted Christ showed up at my church study, suitcase in hand. I heard a knock on my door, and when I opened the door there he stood. He was out, he said; he had served his full sentence rather than take an early parole because he had nowhere to go to start life again and wanted to leave the state to come to me. I took this ex-convict home and he moved in with us. We found him a job and kept him until he had a little money of his own, then helped him find a small apartment.

That was nearly twenty-five years ago, and I haven't seen him since. As far as I know he still lives in that community. I know that he is married and is involved in a church. He was, as far as I know, the only one who came to Christ from more than a year of visits, but I would have gone to that prison even if there had been none. People need us—as Christians we *have* to give.

I Almost Missed God's Opportunity

But that doesn't mean we are only responders to need; love givers are initiators. They are among the most disciplined people anywhere. The time for giving has to come out of the same twenty-four-hour day that everyone else has, and that time is precious. There are always more people with needs than there is time to give, and we have to decide prayerfully how to give ourselves to the people who have the most urgent needs. And the time given has to be *quality* time—we can't rush from one person to another like a politician shaking hands on the campaign trail. I've learned a lot about giving from watching other people. Sometimes one experience teaches two lessons.

I remember watching a clergyman who measured his effectiveness by the number of calls he made in a day. In the little town where I lived there was a small hospital, and since everyone knew everyone else, several clergy often visited the same patients.

One day, sitting by a patient's bedside, I looked up as this minister rushed breathlessly into the room. He asked the patient, "How are you?" and then, without waiting for an answer, talked about God, read a passage of Scripture, said, "Let's pray," and fled. The patient hadn't had time to respond at all. Later I learned that several patients had requested that this clergyman not be allowed into their rooms; the flurry of his visits caused emotional strain.

So, seeing how he acted and thinking I knew more than he did, I decided to do the opposite—just be quiet—which was also wrong. One day a man I knew was admitted to the hospital suffering injuries from a car crash. He was a hard drinker; his reputation in town was that of a tough-living individual who was unapproachable with the gospel. So no one tried to reach him, including me.

I visited him because his wife asked me to, and I practiced my "I-won't-be-like-that-other-clergyman" routine. I said nothing about Christ. Then, after a few minutes with him, preparing to leave, I said casually, "Well, if there is ever anything I can do for you, let me know," and started to walk out the door. As I reached the door he called out. I turned and saw tears streaming down his face. With a choking voice he said, "Please, I want to be saved."

Had I been like Jesus I would have been sensitive—to listen, to ask, to initiate. I almost missed God's opportunity in that hospital room. I might have gone on for years, never knowing what I'd done, repeating that act again and again. I learned that day that just as we can be overbearing and insensitive, we can also be insensitive in our efforts not to be overbearing.

The French philosopher Emile Cailliet said:

> The man of power, then, is the Christ-like man—shall I say it— the saint. And let there be no mistake about it, the saint is the truly successful man. It is not only that his life naturally issues in an ever faithful, ever watchful obedience. Faithfulness and watchfulness are so natural to him that his obedience never gives the impression of effort, still less of strain. It is visibly God in him who does what he does. [7]

The Better Gift

It is easy to be consumed by people when you are a love giver. If that happens, you can lose your usefulness. In fact, you may start to become irritated because someone is consuming so much of your time; you may even become angry at yourself because you let that person do so. When others are permitted to take from you and drain you, the "love" does them little good. Parents aren't better parents when they give in to every cry of their child. They decide what the child needs and lovingly give their attention to that need. They give because they love the child; they withhold because they love the child. They can't give what is really needed if they are always running to do whatever the child demands. So it is with us as Jesus' love givers.

I have learned that often the same people who keep returning for help may not be helped nor do they always want to be helped. Years ago it dawned on me that I was giving the same few people most of my time, with little result. My willingness to come every time they called was not doing them any favors at all. So I began to hold back. I learned that I had to determine prayerfully their needs for them. Otherwise I became exhausted or, worse, I became angry, even bitter. Those who have needs also need to struggle some on their own. It's the only way they can learn. Sometimes love means letting them alone in their pain. This sounds cruel but it isn't, for we must give, not be used. It sounds as if we "determine" the needs of others. No, at least not at first. At first we give without question. But when we see that all the giving is to the same person or persons, we must judge our giving and their taking. Withholding for a while might be the better gift.

One day a man came to my house for counseling. He didn't know what he wanted and couldn't even express what he felt. I was available to him then and for several succeeding visits, but only within limits or I would have never been available to anybody else. I determined when I would see him next. I didn't let him dictate. And because I would not let him consume my time, he learned to vocalize his needs and to wrestle with some of his problems himself—he had to. It was for him a profitable "withholding."

A caution needs to be given here about the act of caring. Some Christians are so insecure that they must be "needed" by others all the time. There are many exhausted Christians running around, pleased with themselves at how much they are giving to others yet hurting inside at the same time. They are quick to tell everybody how busy they are, how great are the demands upon them. But when others step in to take some of the pressures off them, they become resentful. They are really not givers but takers, needing people to need them. It is a backward offering.

These are the people who resent others who "don't give as much as I do" yet continue to take all they can on themselves, even to the detriment of family and personal health. They have to have that tired, "I'm-serving-Jesus" look. This is very sad because they are serving themselves and calling it "serving Christ," running themselves down physically and emotionally, and bringing no honor to Christ who is their Lord. They are not ministering in Christ and for Christ but for their own satisfaction and their own ego needs. They are not helping others; they are impressing themselves and anyone who might notice "how helpful I am."

Why do we think that God is pleased with us when we are worn out? Usually these exhausted love givers can never be questioned about what they are doing; they see their anxiety as Christian responsibility, and they are very virtuous about it, never understanding that they might trust Christ to use *others* as well.

Don't Force Healing

God knows who we are and what we have to offer because he gave us our gifts. And he gave others their gifts too. We cheat others in the body when we insist on doing everything ourselves. Learn to be content to "change the dressings" so that healing can come. Don't try to force healing so that people can see what a good physician you are. You aren't *the* Physician.

We are to be like an instrument in the musician's hand. We don't try to see how loudly we can play, but play the best we can as he chooses to use us, not all the time, but when it's our turn. We know that we are only one part of the whole orchestra. Those who follow the Conductor are part of a divine symphony. Those who do not, contribute to cacophony.

Love givers always have the problem of personal anxiety. We can't reach enough people. We always see more needs. We feel that there are never enough hours or years. But that's where discipleship comes in. We will always have the weak and the sick and the poor with us. Jesus told us we would. He is our example. He didn't panic about it. He could be content with healing some, feeding some, because his will was to do the Father's will. When people were pressing in around him, he said, "I have others, too." And sometimes he left them. It's not wrong to leave. It isn't wrong to want to be alone. Jesus did it. We need time to pray in order to have something more to give the next time. Christians, of all people, should know that. They have to have love to give love. They have to go to the well.

Jesus responded to people selectively. He called out the blind man and the cripple. He determined their needs and touched them. He gave himself away, but always as the One whose will was to do the will of "him who sent me." And that is our rule too.

If you aren't giving, you're like the Dead Sea—closed up. The true followers of Jesus are love givers whose lives are full and overflowing. They are fresh, flowing streams, the conduits of Jesus Christ who is himself the Well of Living Water.

And having found the way to give without struggle or anxiety, the Christian disciples—the friends of God—find that being in Christ, used by Christ, blessed of Christ, they have in fact what is available to every person who wants it—inner peace.

18

The Way to Inner Peace

■ ■ ■

When I was a young minister, newly ordained, I was so nervous about Sunday mornings that my stomach would become upset. And when I made mistakes—well, I still remember my first Easter sermon. When I saw the size of that congregation, people whom I had never seen in church before, I was even more nervous than usual. I tried to remember the instructions of my seminary homiletics professor: "Memorize your first words; the rest will follow." So, while the choir was singing the Easter anthem, I kept repeating to myself the opening sentence of my sermon, the words of the angel: "He is not here; he is risen." Over and over again, under my breath, I repeated that statement, "He is not here; he is risen." The choir stopped singing. I stood to my feet, strode to the pulpit, and in my loudest voice announced to the congregation, "He is not risen; he is here!" Then I simply stopped and stood there because I didn't know what to do next. Somehow, sputtering and stumbling, I got through the rest of the sermon.

I wanted to hide. But still, God used it. The congregation seemed to be listening even more intently, probably to hear what other blunders I was going to make, not wanting to miss any of the mistakes. They enjoyed it, and that night many more people than usual turned out for the evening service, perhaps still chuckling. Yet it was an opportunity, so I took it, discarding the planned evening message and preaching on the text, "If he is not risen, we are without hope," using the morning mistake as my introduction.

Did I learn to relax from that? No! For the next two years I was still so nervous that I had to take stomach medication before preaching. I wanted to preach so well that I was getting in my own way. I was not learning how to trust the One who had called me to preach; I was trusting myself. I could preach about the gifts of God, including his peace, but inner peace escaped me. I had to learn to seek it.

It wasn't until several years later, when a returned missionary saw my problem and prayed for me and my emotions, that I was helped to see that the One whom I was trusting for eternal peace was also the One who offered daily peace. Jesus said, "Peace I leave with you; my peace I give you. I do not give to you as the world gives" (John 14:27). And he keeps that promise. This didn't eliminate my mistakes, but I began to see that I could make mistakes and still have his peace.

I've Learned Slowly, but I've Learned

Seeking peace sent me to the Scriptures. I've had to do that because given any difficult situation I too readily run back to depending upon myself. I need the promises of God.

It is the appropriation of God's promises that has helped me to have inner peace. For the One who bought me for eternity certainly holds me now. I don't have to find peace in what others think; I don't have to impress people. I've learned that I can't impress them anyway. I can't impress people with my talents or my skills or my wisdom or my repartee or my put-on *savoir faire*. I've learned that slowly, but I've learned.

One morning, shortly after I joined the Billy Graham Team, Andrea and I were having breakfast in a hotel when Ruth Graham joined us at our table. We had not met before and I certainly wanted to make a good impression. After a while I could see that I was doing very well because she was gracious and warm, and by the time breakfast was over I was glowing. At least I was glowing until I got back to our room and glanced in the mirror. Stuck to the side of my nose was a piece of scrambled egg.

There is a way to inner peace but it isn't through our own sophistication, abilities, talents, or internal make-up; it is through God. Knowing that, I have to make an all-out determination to seek him, to obey him, and to appropriate all that he is and gives.

G. Steinberger says:

> We find peace in the same degree that we follow Him. And we retain it as long as we are one with Him. This peace is not something we must strive or pray for; it is given to us as soon as we take His yoke upon us and follow Him (Matthew 11:29). [1]

I have to follow him. I have to wait on him. I have to come to him and want him and trust him and then move on in his strength. Then, and only then, can I have the peace and assurance that all is well. And, having found that peace, I can delight in it.

Some people delight in personal progress, social gains, accumulation of things, the pleasure of accomplishment. I've learned that my delight comes from him or it doesn't come at all.

God wants to give his peace. He is the Peacegiver. It is his nature to give it. Inner peace comes to me not because I merit it but because he wants me to have it. That's not something that I have to hope is true or somehow convince myself is true. It is something that he is trying to convince me is true and so, being convinced by him, I take it. It's because of the peace he gives that I can move around in this world and function and take risks and take responsibility and make decisions and make mistakes.

Hannah Whitall Smith, who wrote *The Christian's Secret of a Happy Life*, said:

> I believe God has made me a pioneer, so that I do not expect much sympathy or understanding as I go along; and the breaking through of hedges, and fences, and stone walls is not a very pleasant path. . . . But it is my nature, I cannot help it. [2]

No wonder she could talk about the happy life.

And Thomas Kelly, the Quaker, expressed the way I feel:

> The basic response of the soul to the Light is internal adoration and joy, thanksgiving and worship, self-surrender and listening. The secret places of the heart cease to be our noisy workshop. They become a holy sanctuary of adoration and of self-oblation, where we are kept in perfect peace, if our minds be stayed on Him who has found us in the inward springs of our life. And in brief intervals of over-powering visitation we are able to carry the sanctuary frame of mind out into the world, into its turmoil and its fitfulness, and in a hyperaesthesia of the soul, we see all mankind tinged with deeper shadows, and touched with Galilean

glories. Powerfully are the springs of our will moved to an abandon of singing love toward God; powerfully are we moved to a new and overcoming love toward time-blinded men and all creation. In this Center of Creation all things are ours, and we are Christ's and Christ is God's. We are owned men, ready to run and not be weary and to walk and not faint. [3]

I have found that the true sanctuary of the soul comes not only in the quietness of my sanctuaries but even in the raucous marketplaces of life. The peace is his. It is in him, and he gives it.

It Is God's Enjoyment to Hold Me

I need to give my early mornings to prayer to have this peace. This is not a ritual—it's an absolute necessity. I would miss breakfast before I would miss my time of prayer. I cannot go into the world each day without having first enjoyed the sanctuary of the quiet time with God. If my day begins at 6:00, my inner clock says I have to be up at 5:00 or 5:15 at the latest. If I'm up all night on a long flight, I will spend part of it in prayer even if I am too sleepy to read Scripture. I run in fear—not a crippling fear but a healthy fear, a fear of not wanting to live apart from him and his guidance. And what comes from that is a deep peace, not because I have generated that peace through my activity but because he is God and he meets me. In any rough moment I can go back to him and say, "Lord, this morning I committed all of this to you. You promised to be with me." That helps, especially when difficult situations come.

There is no failure in the Lord. My mistakes might be just that—my mistakes. But there are no failures in him. He can and does correct my life's errors as long as I practice obedience, commitment, and trust.

And I have learned that there is peace even when things happen that are not of my doing, events or circumstances that come because I am a part of this decaying world. There is peace in the pain of illness, separation, loss, and failure. In my disappointments and frustrations, he is still God. He is my Rock, and I know he is there regardless of whether or not I sense him. Thomas Kelly said:

Don't be fooled by your sunny skies. When the rains descend and

the floods come and the winds blow and beat upon *your* house,
your private dwelling, your own family, your own fair hopes,
your own strong muscles, your own body, your own soul itself,
then it is well-nigh too late to build a house. You can only go
inside what house you have and pray that it is founded upon the
Rock. Be not deceived by distance in time or space, or the false
security of a bank account and an automobile and good health
and willing hands to work. [4]

None of our ways or gathered things is going to guarantee
peace. When all is gone, the peace is either there or it is not. It can't
be manufactured. The house is either on the Rock or it is not. We
either flee to the house we have or we get washed away.

There is comfort in knowing that it is God's enjoyment to give
me his peace. It is God's enjoyment to hold me close to himself. It is
God's pleasure to satisfy me and walk with me. It is his intention
not to leave me or forsake me. That is not a realization we all come
to quickly, but come to it we must. In his book *The Legacy of Bunyan*,
the Reverend W. Y. Fullerton said:

Rabbi Duncan, that modest but eccentric saint of Edinburgh, in
one of the melancholy moods which occasionally overtook him,
thinking himself unworthy of God's salvation, began to croon a
lullaby of scripture texts in the original language, which was as
familiar as his own; and all of the texts he murmured to himself
contained the word "grace." Suddenly it struck him; "Why the
word 'grace' means 'joy'.... Shall I deny God His joy in refusing
the joy He gives me by His grace?" [5]

Will we do that? Will we deny God his joy in giving to us?
Look at what is ours on the whole broad avenue called inner peace.
Look at the blessings and then learn to revel in them. Don't settle
for your accomplishments or else that's all you will have. Don't be
satisfied with your salary or else that's all you will have. Don't
glory in your prestige or else that's all there will be. All of that is
empty. Let God have his joy. Allow him the opportunity to enjoy
giving himself and his gifts to you.

A Passionate Need

Look what comes from walking the road with him. Look at his
promises! They are "beatitudes." They are his "blesseds" offered

to us.

"Blessed are the poor in spirit," he said. Not the poor in money; they can be spiritually wealthy. Not the rich; they can be spiritually poor. But the poor in spirit. We are poor; we need to admit it. We need spiritual "handouts" from God. Those who are not spiritually wanting are the ones who will not be spiritually receiving. It is the poor in spirit that Jesus is talking about. The promise follows: "Theirs is the kingdom of heaven." This is not a someday-you-had-better-hope-it-will-be-yours kind of promise. It is a straight-out statement of fact—theirs is the kingdom of heaven. The poor in spirit are the kingdom receivers. They are God's kingdom dwellers. And in that kingdom, spiritual food comes not in snacks but in banquets.

"Blessed are those who mourn, for they will be comforted" (Matthew 5:4). Just as the poor are not necessarily only the physically poor, neither are the mourners only those who lament the loss of a loved one. It is a deeper kind of mourning than that, just as poor in spirit is a deeper kind of poverty. It is a lament over sin. It is a lament over personal wickedness.

When we mourn like that we have God's assurance that we shall be comforted. We have his Word: "Your sins are forgiven." Jesus does that. Scripture promises: "If we confess our sins, he is faithful and just and will forgive us our sins and purify us from all unrighteousness" (1 John 1:9). Some people feel a little sorry for the consequences of their sin, the trouble it has caused them, but more than that is required for forgiveness. Forgiveness can come only when we confess our sins and turn from them. When we come to him as mourners, in deep sorrow over our spiritual condition, we shall be comforted. That is the gateway to peace. For, "he is able to save completely those who come to God through him" (Hebrews 7:25).

"Blessed are the meek." He doesn't say weak, but meek. Often the strongest people are the meekest. It takes a strong person to be meek, to be like Jesus, to be kissed by a traitor, to turn the other cheek. Believers who walk with Jesus can be strong like that—waiting, enduring, putting up with something. "Perseverance must finish its work so that you may be mature and complete, not lacking anything" (James 1:4). The blessed meek person is the humble one, the one who bows to God. The ungodly, the ones "too strong" to need God, will soon be swept away. When the end comes, they will be gone. God remains, and so do the meek who by God's act inherit the earth.

"Blessed are those who hunger and thirst for righteousness." Be careful with this one. It is the hungering and thirsting for righteousness that Jesus calls "blessed"—it isn't eating or drinking. We usually call a person "blessed" when he or she has plenty to eat or drink or wear or use. But that's not what Jesus is saying.

We have all been hungry and thirsty, and when we are that's all that we can think about. Hunger and thirst overrule every other human desire. We don't want to do anything or go anywhere or have anything until that hunger and thirst is satisfied. It is a passionate need—it controls us. It drives us.

What do you hunger for? Listen to the talk in a locker room, at an investors' meeting, or at your club. You can tell what people hunger and thirst for by the things they talk about. Their conversations reveal the appetites that drive them.

The psalmist said, "As the deer pants for streams of water, so my soul pants for you, O God" (Psalm 42:1). When we crave God and his righteousness more than we crave anything else, when to savor and delight in the righteousness of God is the only thing that will satisfy us, then that is what Jesus calls "blessed."

When we receive his righteousness and have the satisfaction of it, we will want that righteousness every day just as we want food and drink every day. And when we want Jesus Christ and his righteousness day after day, we will be satisfied. We won't be complacent, but we will be satisfied. For we will come to Christ craving his satisfying food and drink; he is himself that food and drink, and he does satisfy.

"Blessed are the merciful." God is a God of mercy; he proved that in giving his Son Jesus Christ on the cross. He proved it on Easter morning when he raised his Son from the dead. His followers, those who are really his, are merciful too. They can be no less nor do no less than the Master they call their own. The Christian will not say, "I'll get him!" or "Just wait; my turn will come!" We can't, we won't, because God is merciful. What God is, the Christian is. Being in him is the description of a believer. If people hear me claim his name, they have every right to expect me to be an example of what he is like.

And lest we forget, the model prayer that Jesus gave us includes the words, "And forgive us our debts [trespasses] as we also have forgiven. . . ." In other words, we pray to be forgiven and we receive forgiveness to the same degree that we forgive others. We are asking for God's mercy in the same amount that we offer mercy to others. Some of us wouldn't pray that way if we knew what we were really asking of God. Some of us don't show much mercy. If God showed mercy to us only to the same degree that we show mercy to others, what would become of us?

Is God's mercy free? Then ours must be too. Does God first expect me to become better to receive mercy? Not at all. "While we were still sinners, Christ died for us" (Romans 5:8). So there is to be no qualification to our mercy-giving either. We are to be as merciful as the Mercy Giver is merciful. "They will be shown mercy" is not a trade-off policy, a tit-for-tat policy; it's a love policy.

"Blessed are the pure in heart." There is only One who is truly pure in heart—God. A pure heart is not ours by our own nature. Jeremiah said, "The heart is deceitful above all things and beyond cure. Who can understand it?" (Jeremiah 17:9). We need what God alone can give: "I will give you a new heart and put a new spirit in you; I will remove from you your heart of stone and give you a heart of flesh" (Ezekiel 36:26).

In order to be pure like him, we have to be washed by him. That's why Jesus said, "Unless I wash you, you have no part with me" (John 13:8). That's a promise. "They will see God" (Matthew 5:8). And not only later, in heaven, but now—every day. We will see God: We will see him now in the events of our lives, and we will see him someday face to face for all eternity.

The cleansing Savior is the fellowshipping Savior—we will be made clean and we will be with him; and the more intimate we are with him, the cleaner we will be. He makes us pure by virtue of his purity.

That Wonderful Personal Word

"Blessed are the peacemakers, for they shall be called the children of God." Only a child of God can be a peacemaker, for two reasons. A peacemaker is one who knows what peace is. A person cannot work for real peace if he or she doesn't understand real peace. Peace with God is the ultimate, final peace. It is more than a cessation of hostilities. It is more than a cease-fire. It is a coming into harmonious relationship. That's what the followers of Jesus Christ have, a harmonious relationship made possible for them by the One called the "Prince of Peace." Christians can be peacemakers because they know real peace.

The other reason is that peacemakers are in the reconciling business. The followers of Jesus have been reconciled. They have been brought back into fellowship with God and are therefore able to be an extender of that reconciliation to all who are around them, to their whole world. Where they are, there is peace. How sad when a Christian is the sower of discord or dissension, causing strife instead of bringing warring parties together. God ended the war between us and brought us to himself in peace. We can be no less than bearers of that peace to others who are still at war with God and with their fellow humans.

As children of God who are able to use that wonderful personal word, "Abba" (Father), we are justified. "Therefore, since we have been justified through faith, we have peace with God through our Lord Jesus Christ" (Romans 5:1). And since that's what we have, we cannot give less than what we have to others.

The last beatitude (or "blessed") is, "Blessed are those who are persecuted because of righteousness, for theirs is the kingdom of heaven." That doesn't mean we will always be persecuted as part of our discipleship or that it is a necessary part of being blessed. It does mean that when "people insult you, persecute you and falsely say all kinds of evil against you because of me" (Matthew 5:11), there will still be reason to rejoice and be glad because we know that our reward in heaven is great.

Jesus is not giving an invitation for persecution; he is giving his word of comfort, a promise for when we are persecuted. The faithful follower of Jesus doesn't look for persecution, but we can expect it when our honesty, our moral character, our obedience to God run counter to what Satan's people practice. Faithful believers also know that the reward from God is great. A person can bear anything knowing that.

We can expect suffering as God's people—not seek it or cause it, but expect it. It has always been that way: "For in the same way they persecuted the prophets who were before you" (Matthew 5:12). We are not exempt. We should not expect to be. The prophets spoke what God told them to speak, and it was enough to infuriate people. Jesus came loving people and preaching the kingdom, and it was enough to send him to the cross. The disciples then and the disciples now are no different than their Master.

Will you be called "blessed"? When soldiers die on the battlefield, we may call them heroes. When statesmen die for a cause, we may call them patriots. When people die in old age, we may call them venerable. When people die for others, we may call them martyrs. But there is a term that only God can use, a label only he can give: "Blessed"! It is a term or label ascribed to people who are his. The bestowal of that title is not dependent upon our opinion of ourselves; it is God's statement about us.

"Blessed" is not a casual term. It is a special term for a special people, a people obedient to their Savior and Lord and blessed because of it throughout all eternity. And the blessed ones have peace.

The "Blesseds" Make All the Difference

God had something so important to say about this blessing that when he gave his message to John he said emphatically, "Write it down." "Then I heard a voice from heaven say, 'Write: Blessed are the dead who die in the Lord from now on'" (Revelation 14:13). Blessed! Happy! The blessed are happy as they live in the Lord and happy when they die in the Lord—they have his inner peace.

The emphasis is on the word "in." We die in the Lord because we have lived in the Lord. For some that is for a blessed lifetime, for others a blessed last breath; for those who refuse him, even to the end of life, it is never. If we are in him, abiding in him, living as new creatures in him, then we will also die in him. "Blessed are the dead who die in the Lord from now on.... They will rest from their labor, for their deeds will follow them." Our works don't go ahead of us; they follow. Jesus is ahead of us. God sees Jesus, then us, and our works follow after.

The "blesseds" make all the difference in how we live. Inner peace and stability come to us as a result of being his. I know a man who has been suffering with extreme pain for years. In all this time he has let the "blesseds" in his own life flow out to other people. He is a man at peace because he is a man with the blesseds of God—and he offers what he has.

Watch people when they face death or financial reverses or any critical change. The people who suffer the most are the ones who don't know how to live without their social, financial, or physical crutches. But watch the followers of Jesus. The difference is dramatic; they have peace. They are the blessed ones.

Not only is the difference obvious in the physical and the material realm, but in the psychological too. Who would believe that people can face insults, persecution and all kinds of evil being said falsely and not be personally destroyed? But they can, just as Jesus promised in the Beatitudes.

It is painful to be victimized when you are trying to do what is right. It hurts deeply to be criticized, or, even worse, to be persecuted when you are trying to give your best. But the deep peace of Jesus is a blanket of love that covers and soothes the one suffering persecution. The outward happiness may be gone for a while, but not the deep inner peace and joy.

Following Jesus may seem foolish to those who don't know him, but when people can come to the end of their days contented, knowing what it is to be blessed and happy, they will say with certainty that it was the only adventure worth taking.

God's blessing—his peace—is for us. God doesn't leave us comfortless. He knows what he is calling us to and knows why he is calling us to it. He has peace for those who follow him such as no person or situation can provide. Following him is an adventure with blessings.

Pray about your life, every part of it. Present your life to him. See what he will do with it. Join the band of God's friends—the others around you who are following Jesus. It is the "peace-full" life, the blessed life, now and forever. It is the gateway to happiness; not excitement always, or bubbling joy constantly, but happiness—real, deep happiness.

19

In the Joy of
Ascending Moments

■ ■ ■

Ascending moments with God—what are they? The ever-rising approach to God in worship, in growth, in commitment. Is it difficult? Can I have such moments too?

Growth in worship is not like standing on an escalator or riding in a chair lift or being carried to a pinnacle by helicopter. Oh, no! It is movement that is sometimes as imperceptible as an inch-by-inch struggle to move with chained feet.

Friedrich Von Hugel spoke of the advice about spiritual growth given to him by an older man. He said it is like climbing a mountain. Each step is slowly taken with pauses to find the next handhold, the next level, the next rock on which to place a foot. There may be long periods between steps, longer times of encampment on rough ledges, sometimes whole days waiting for better conditions. Sometimes we wait in the clouds, sometimes in the dark, sometimes we huddle down in the rain or sleet or snow. We don't scale great mountains unless we are willing to go slowly, waiting sometimes, thinking through each step, and then planting our feet firmly on what we know is safe and solid ground. In the same way, those who think great spiritual heights are gained speedily do not understand Christian growth.

The *Twentieth Century Encyclopedia of Religious Knowledge* lists three forms of worship. There is the spectacular in worship when we think about those who are leading us, the subjective worship when we think about ourselves and what is happening to us, and the objective worship when we think about God.

The spectacular is soon finished. At best, we say of those who lead us: "My, weren't they good." It is much like going to a good concert or play. I remember being in a church where the choir anthem was a hymn of great adoration and praise. It contained the lines, "Not unto us be glory, O Lord, but unto thee...." I was led by the words to focus on God—his sovereignty, his right to be praised. The sense of his wonder overwhelmed me. But evidently others in the congregation did not hear those words because as the anthem was concluded, after the choir sang those emphatic words pointing to the Lord himself, the people applauded the singers; the choir director smiled and bowed.

Later, in another worship service, a man was reading a Scripture text that spoke of God, his power and his might. The person in charge looked over the shoulder of the man who was reading and saw that he was reading from the Greek text. No one else knew it, but he saw it and it was too much for him. His own insecurity or desire for praise apparently made him think that people would applaud the reader for his knowledge of Greek. So, though no one knew that the man was reading from the Greek text, as soon as he finished, the worship leader, without any reference to the fact that God's Word had been read, immediately turned the attention of the people from the Bible to himself. He stepped to the pulpit and said, "Oh, you're reading from the Greek," and then proceeded to repeat from memory a few Greek words that he had learned as a youth—words that had nothing to do with worship, nothing to do with the text read, but recited boastfully to show off. He was trying to impress us. He might just as well have said, "See what I can do!"

It was as if a bucket of cold water had been thrown on that warm experience of worship. God's Word was pushed aside for one man's own ego need. He hadn't really been listening to the Word in the first place, being occupied instead with the concern that people might praise the reader—and he wanted that praise for himself. A. Kuyper reminds us:

> Just as the anthem of the Seraphim around the throne is one uninterrupted cry of "Holy,—Holy,—Holy," so also the religion of man upon this earth should consist in one echoing of God's glory, as our Creator and Inspirer. The starting point of every motive in religion is God and not man. Man is the instrument and means, God alone is here the goal, the point of departure and the point of arrival, the fountain, from which the waters flow, and at the same time, the ocean into which they finally return. [1]

A Feeling of Failure

Subjective worship, thinking about ourselves, puts us on the pedestal as gods. Eventually it leaves us with a feeling of failure because the more we think of ourselves the more we know that we are not God. But, reacting against subjective worship to have a true focus on God does not mean that we ignore ourselves or our sins. We can't take ourselves out of worship; that is impossible. On the contrary, we know our sins, and our failure is always with us. We know it because we compare ourselves to One who never fails. When we love God, our own shortcomings are obvious. And even our seeking to please God reminds us how much we, in fact, do not please God. But that involvement of self in worship of God is different from purely focusing on ourselves.

If we don't care what God thinks, only what we think or feel, it is because we don't love God. But even outright hatred of God, as bad as that is, is not so bad as ignoring God or putting ourselves ahead of God or trying to use God. To be lukewarm to God is worse than being cold or hot. "I know your deeds, that you are neither cold nor hot. I wish you were either one or the other! So, because you are lukewarm—neither hot nor cold—I am about to spit you out of my mouth" (Revelation 3:15-16).

Lukewarm means we don't care. We have written God off; he doesn't matter even enough for us to consider him with any degree of emotion, be it love or hate. Subjective worship is as bad as spectacular worship; worse, actually, for we have turned from gods outside ourselves to the god within ourselves.

But in objective worship, looking to him and praising him, we discover true splendor—the spectacular of God. As we discover him we also discover ourselves, for we know best who we are to the degree that we recognize who he is. Isaiah knew that:

In the year that King Uzziah died, I saw the Lord seated on a throne, high and exalted, and the train of his robe filled the temple. Above him were seraphs, each with six wings: With two wings they covered their faces, with two they covered their feet, and with two they were flying. And they were calling to one another: "Holy, holy, holy is the Lord Almighty; the whole earth is full of his glory" (Isaiah 6:1-3).

Want God in His Way

J. Oswald Sanders noted in *Prayer Power Unlimited*:

"I have known men," said Thomas Goodwin, "who came to God for nothing else but just to come to Him, they so loved Him. They scorned to soil Him and themselves with any other errand than just purely to be alone with Him in His presence." [2]

And he further explained:

Dr. R. A. Torrey, who was God's instrument to bring revival to many parts of the world, testified that an utter transformation came into his experience when he learned not only to pray and return thanks, but to worship—asking nothing from God, seeking nothing from Him, occupied with Himself, and satisfied with Himself. [3]

Himself! God only. The joy of ascending moments for us is as it was for Sanders and Torrey, and most of all as it was for our Lord Jesus who knew those moments with the Father.

But how do we come to the joy of ascending moments? How do we turn from spectacular worship and subjective worship to the objective worship of God? Should we seek the sensations of the emotions—an ecstatic experience? Satan can counterfeit those. God is more than that, even though sometimes we mistake experiences in ourselves as experiences with God. How then shall we worship in the ascending moments that place him before us and place us where we can know more of him?

It takes desire, decision, and discipline.

First, we have to desire God. We have to want God in his way, on his terms, more than we want anything else. We have to desire the joy of the presence of God and then go beyond that desire, past the joy itself, to the presence of God. Is this mysticism? No, though mystics seek to capture it. Rather it is faith: a trust, a quieting down before God, a centering on him. It is the expression of our genuine desire for him, an expression made to him when we are alone with him wherever others can't make us less than sincere.

Second, we have to decide that we will seek God. Some people have the desire for God but they don't act on that desire. They wish for all that God is but do not decide to seek all that God is. We have to make up our minds and exercise our wills as surely as athletes make up their minds to train or business tycoons decide they will be a financial success. The mind is given over to it as of first importance. The will is brought into positive action. Oh, that the mind of every person would focus on God by a willful decision to do so. What could God do with such persons?

Third, it takes discipline—working at it. It is something we desire. It is something we decide to do. We all discipline ourselves in some way. We do it all the time. One year I sought to bring my weight into line by shedding one pound a week. Emotionally I would have liked "instantly" to be fifteen pounds lighter, but it was going to take fifteen weeks. I made up my mind to that, and day by day, with that weight loss in mind, I ate less and exercised more. The weight would not just disappear by wishful thinking. My mind had to be made up; the discipline had to be applied.

In the same way I know that if I am going to meet certain writing commitments I must write so many hours each day. That is a discipline. I "will" write. The same is true for what is really important—the worship of God. The joy of ascending moments, like the climbing of a mountain, is an inch by inch process; it takes one day at a time. But the beauty of all this is that God meets us in our discipline. We find joy in these ascending moments even as we do what seems to be hard work in the self-discipline of seeking God. My daily morning time of worshiping God offers joy—now. But it wasn't as "joy full" before I disciplined myself to a daily meeting with God in the morning. I didn't do it then for good feelings it gave me (in the first weeks the only feelings I had were sleepy feelings), but for the anticipation of meeting God and wanting him desperately enough to discipline myself to seek him. It is what we all must desire, decide upon, and discipline ourselves to do.

But I Hadn't Worshiped

In *Doors into Life*, Douglas Steere says:

Devotion requires continual nurturing, continual cultivation, continual renewal, continual beginning again, if it is to prepare us for the tasks this generation ahead requires. If this is true, then it is the task of the Christian religion not only to hold constantly before its members the necessity of their yielding themselves continually in acts of devotion to God, but also in encouraging them in the cultivation of these acts. [4]

Why isn't it a part of our faith then to experience automatically the joy of ascending moments? It should just happen if we know God, shouldn't it? Why don't we just take to it, as a newborn colt when it is nudged by its mother stands up? Why isn't it automatic when God nudges us? It should just happen if we know God, shouldn't it?

This discipline of worship, of ascending the holy mountain of God, like tithing or honesty or faithfulness, has to be taught. And to be taught we need teachers who are themselves experiencing the joy of ascending moments with God. Unfortunately, many of our teachers are not.

It is difficult to teach worship. Even when we train men and women for the ministry of the church and the conduct of formal worship, there is little instruction in real worship. We teach homiletics and hermeneutics. We teach theology. We teach liturgy and the treatment of worship, but very little is done for those in training for the ministry of souls to help them experience firsthand something special for their own souls. What they don't know they can't teach.

The joy of having one's soul brought up close to heaven must be taught by showing it, doing it, and experiencing it. For only when they have experienced it can Christian leaders help others to do the same. I recall once saying to someone, "I haven't known worship in this church." He didn't know what I was talking about. The reason he didn't understand is that we were in the worship service together every Sunday. We went through a printed order of service, we sang hymns, we prayed prayers, we listened to a sermon, and we took an offering. But I hadn't worshiped God.

"Isn't that your responsibility?" he asked. Then he repeated the well-worn, "You only get out of it what you put into it." That's true, of course, but I also need to be led in worship. And in contrary fashion, I can be led away from worship. I need to be helped to see the Lord high and lifted up—the splendor filling the temple as Isaiah saw it. Those who thrive in worship, who are sensitive to the Holy Spirit, can help me do that.

When I realized that the man to whom I was speaking had no concept of what I was talking about, all I could say was, "If you ever worship, you will know what I mean." Then I quickly added, "That's offensive, I know. It sounds like a put-down but it isn't. It's like explaining the touch of a loved one's hand—you have to experience it."

My friend didn't understand what I was talking about; neither did the minister. He thought listening to his sermons was the same as worshiping God. He had no idea what worship was. I know he didn't because he would follow a great hymn of faith with an announcement about the church softball league.

But that's not really his fault. He never learned for himself the joy of ascending moments with God because he was never taught it. And he was never taught because he didn't have anyone to teach him.

When Can God Talk With You?

In the training of Christian leaders, if we do not give them experiences in Christian worship how will they then lead others to worship God? At best, we urge ministerial students to attend chapel, and that is usually optional. As I recall my days in seminary, a number of students preferred to use chapel time to read the morning newspaper or play a game of ping pong. After all, they said, why go to hear another talk? They had no idea of worship; it was to them another talk, another lecture, a sermon, more preaching just like the classroom. They knew nothing of meeting God. And unless they have since learned, they probably can't lead their parishioners to meet God either.

I remember at my ordination service in Detroit a clergyman in that city spoke about worshiping God. He told the story of a minister showing his appointment calendar to the women in a Bible class. Every day and most hours of the day were filled with appointments. And all the people in that class were duly impressed. All, that is, except one little elderly lady who raised her hand and asked, "May I ask you a question? When do you do your thinking? When do you do your praying?"

We need to ask that of ministers who lead in worship and ask it of people who attend worship. When can God talk with you? When do you honor and praise him? When, if not in the congregation when there should be openness and responsiveness to him, can God speak?

In the average church service people visit with each other during the organ prelude. They aren't worshiping God. A few come late "after the preliminaries" to hear the important part, the minister's sermon. During a hymn which is meant to lead us to think about God, people look around to see who else is there. During the offertory prayer they fill out a check or search their wallets rather than present themselves to God, which is the first and most important act of an offering. Some think about their afternoon appointments, others muse about dinner or sleep off their breakfast. One Sunday a man in front of me brought his morning cup of coffee into the pew with him and sipped it during the service. At least he stayed awake.

Norman Paullin, who for many years taught pastoral ministries at Eastern Baptist Theological Seminary, used to tell about a church organist who found a solution for morning talkers. Dr. Paullin explained to his class:

> Every church has two people, one who can't hear and one who can't whisper, and they always sit next to each other. One Sunday morning during the prelude two women were busily engaged in conversation, oblivious to those around them whom they were disturbing. The organist, noticing them, gradually increased the volume of the hymn she was playing until the music was resounding through the sanctuary. The women, to compensate, increased their own volume until they were shouting into each other's ears. Then at the height of the crescendo the organist paused, changed the stops, and in the sudden silence the entire church body heard one woman shouting to the other, "I fry mine in butter."

Worship is not just being together; true fellowship, as the Anglo-Saxon word means it, is a "grazing together," a feeding in a common pasture. We are together, yes, but for a reason greater than just being together.

Into the Flames Again

Worship is not just personal introspection, or we would worship our feelings. Worship is not even a warm glow, or we would worship that. We worship One outside ourselves. We concentrate on him, we praise him, we adore him, we hear his Word for he is announcing it to us. We listen in holy awe to the Word of God, for it is a part of that "all" of Scripture which is given by the out-breathing of God and is personally necessary for "my" correction and "my" instruction in righteousness.

How do we find the joy of ascending moments? We find it long before we go through the church doors; we find it upon our waking in the morning, we find it as we bow down before him in our own adoration and personal praise.

We are to be quiet before God. That is not an easy attitude, for most of the time we are so active that we are unable to relate to the still small voice. As activists, we are more interested in picking the fruit of the Spirit than in going to the root of the Christian faith. We mistake acting out the commands of the Lord in our lives (which, of course, we must do) with first knowing the One who commands. For if we do not first seek him, no amount of knowledge about him will substitute. For then what we are acting out are not his commands at all but our whims, our fancies, and sometimes Satan's subtle beguilings.

The joy of ascending moments comes not just because we are quiet, however, or we would seek only quiet and still not have God. In the quiet we would have wandering minds that could lead us into even greater trouble. Ours is to be a conscious focusing on God. When we do that, there come the ascending moments of the joy of God.

In *The Imitation of Christ*, Thomas à Kempis writes about rust-covered iron. He saw that rust will come away when the iron is put into the flames. To be clean, the iron had to be made red-hot again. Those of us who are rusted, who are coated with the weakening agents of all sorts of encrustation, need to be put back into the flames of God again. Once more we need to be red-hot for God. When iron becomes clean, so much can be done with it; it is the same for each of us.

In worship we come to see not ourselves as the focal point, but God. It is not our talking at him that is important, it is our listening to him. It is what he says more than what we say that counts in the prayer that leads to worship. Our inner groanings are often more adequate for our approach to him than all of our polished speaking. his heart wants to beat with our heart. His desire is to draw us close enough to himself for us to sense that beating heart of God.

This is a quickening, these ascending moments of worship. God is interested in us. He wants to have our lives. He wants us to come into the inner place with him, to seek his direction, to find his purpose, to know his joy and experience his smile.

Should we not want that too? Should we not worship God rather than conduct worship services? Is he not worth more to the people he calls to worship than our attempted innovations in our worship services—some new angle, a new trick to please and draw crowds?

Let our affection be for him, the unchanging One. Adore him. Know that you need him for life, all of life. We do need God—right to the end of our days. In God's great heart is the longing to meet us, speak to us, and quietly raise us up to where he is, to those greater heights where we can see more of him and love him.

In that will come the great joy that he wants for us, the joy of meeting God himself in great ascending moments.

20

Growing When I Am All Alone

■ ■ ■

It was raining in Osaka, Japan, that October morning, and my mood was as gray as the sky. Work kept me busy most of the hours, and some days I was in my hotel room only to sleep. But this rainy morning I felt alone. I was trying to write and I couldn't. I was feeling sorry for myself. I was homesick.

Then, as I sat looking out the window, I began to think of the other people alone in that city of millions. So many were like me, only they were lonely all the time. There are plenty of interesting things to see and do in that city: There are the shops, the restaurants, the parks, the canals, for this city is called "the Venice of Japan." And yet people who are lonely like me really have no interest in doing anything; we let the hours go by, just sitting—feeling depressed, dull.

My head ached, too, maybe from the weather, maybe from anger at my situation or myself or God. I reached for the New Testament that was on the table in front of me and started thumbing through it, not looking for anything in particular. I'd had my morning devotions earlier, though my time with God that day had not been particularly profitable—just a custom not to be broken.

But as I thumbed through the Scripture, I glanced at Matthew 14 and stopped. I started to read about those disciples in the boat. They too were feeling alone when the waves were about to swamp them. They thought that Jesus was off in the hills somewhere conversing with his Father in prayer, certainly not thinking about them.

And it was true. Jesus was off praying. But the Scripture indicates that he saw them, he saw their need, and he came to them walking on the sea. In a few minutes a calm had come, and the disciples worshiped him. I realized that in all of their fear, in their feeling of being alone, though they didn't realize it then, Jesus knew exactly where they were and what was happening to them.

Then it hit me! Jesus knows where I am too. He understands my loneliness. He knows all about my depression. He understands how my emotions go up and down depending on my thoughts or my situation or the weather. He knows when I am far from my family and miss them. And this same Jesus who could calm the wild sea and give peace to those fishermen can handle my problems too.

A New Expectancy

I began to look at my situation with a new expectancy. How will he help me? How will he support me? My mind went back to the many times and situations when he had met me before. The waves had come before, and in those times when I thought that he didn't see me he had seen me and known of my loneliness.

And I thought: How can I tell that to the newly widowed who feel so alone and deserted by God? How can I tell that to the one in the hospital who has been awake all night thinking about what the doctors told him the day before? How can I convince the lonely student who cannot find a friend? And how can I tell those who have no family left: "Jesus knows where you are; he sees"?

Then, because God sometimes uses what is already in our minds, a passage of Scripture came to me. It was one I intended to preach on a few days later in a Japanese church. I had thought carefully about that passage because I would have an interpreter, and I wanted to be sure that I fully understood the text. Those words came into my mind as a comfort to me: "For the eyes of the Lord range throughout the earth to strengthen those whose hearts are fully committed to him" (2 Chronicles 16:9).

And I knew that God was looking at me. He sees me. He always has; he always will.

God is there even when I feel all alone. And many of us often are alone—sometimes even when we are in a crowd. But we don't have to be victims of loneliness. Harold B. Walker said, "There is no escape from the truth that at the core of our minds we are profoundly alone. We have a choice, therefore, between loneliness and solitude, between melancholy and depression . . ."[1]

God Comes to Our Minds

The ancient philosophers knew the value of the lone mind. For those thinkers, their minds were a laboratory. They worked with thought and often did it walking, perhaps as Plato did, through olive groves. God touches us, often in the deepest part of our being, when we are alone. We can think when we are alone. Indeed that's why those ancient philosophers often found themselves somewhat apart from society—for society then as now preferred the active, the noisy, the aggressive, the busyness that tranquilizes the mind and keeps it from working.

The human mind needs God, and often he comes to our minds with his deepest teaching when we are alone. He is the God of the mind as much as the will. We are instructed to be transformed by the renewing of our minds (Romans 12:2). Alone we ponder, alone we can be creative, alone we can learn to express on paper or in art our inner discoveries. People need to be alone. For out of solitude comes clear thinking that helps us, and through loneliness can come growth.

Not everyone wants to be alone. Many grow into themselves when they are alone, almost narcotized by the sameness of their self-imposed confinement.

Walker said:

The recluse is a sad and lonely man whose attitudes and feelings are distorted by his lack of companionship. His opinions have no source for correction and modification. His feelings fester without the healing grace of sharing. His ways are never challenged by the company of others. Lonely and depressed, he has no surcease from the self-pity that engulfs his life. His aloneness is no virtue if there is nothing in it beyond aloneness. [2]

The empty mind turns inward and is bounded by the self. It is haunted by remembered hurts and anxious fear, swamped in the end by towering waves of self-pity. Its inscape is bleak and its horizons zero. The full mind turns outward to embrace the things of beauty that are a joy forever. [3]

> We cannot sweep our minds clear of self-pity, fear, anxiety, and loneliness unless we fill the vacuum with ideas and knowledge that crowd out the unwanted and the hurtful. [4]

This One Who Is Other

Except for this danger of growing inward, of listening only to self and not to God, being alone gives opportunity to do more, give more, expand more, think deeper, grow stronger, and this is missed by those who will not accept lonely times.

We need in our world the people, especially Christians, who grow when they are all alone. Those who know how to utilize the gifts of Christ in the alone times can be the innovators, the thinkers, and the teachers for the vast portion of society who resist being alone to think. For example, I know college graduates who haven't read a book (of any kind) since graduation twenty or thirty years before. Some don't even read a newspaper. They don't want to stretch or think. What if our world were left to them?

People who won't think must be cared for. They must be helped to think, to understand, to grasp both themselves and their world. Why? The answer is admittedly a Christian one: so that in understanding themselves and their world they will know how much they need God's wholeness. Only when they think will people turn to the Savior and come to live in the enjoyment of God. The nonthinkers, filling their lives with noise and pulsing sensations, won't do it; neither will the nonactivists who go inward with only themselves as a resource.

Humanity must be shown God—the omnipotent yet all-present God. They must be shown the Incarnate Son, the Emmanuel, the God with us. And only as they stop, think, and question will they be open to this One who is other than themselves.

Counsel for Us

Alone, we have time to pray and opportunity to receive God's biblical counsel. There is an example of this in Scripture: In 1 Chronicles 28:9 David spoke to his son Solomon on the occasion of the building of the temple. What he said teaches anyone who seeks the wisdom of God as Solomon did. This is God's counsel; it is given through David, yes, and it is given to Solomon, but it is God's counsel without limit for all time. It is given to us:

> Solomon, my son, get to know the God of your fathers. Worship and serve him with a clean heart and a willing mind, for the Lord sees every heart and understands and knows every thought. If you seek him, you will find him; but if you forsake him, he will permanently throw you aside. So, be very careful, for the Lord has chosen you to build his holy temple. Be strong and do as he commands (1 Chronicles 28:9-10, TLB).

If you have a lot of time alone, God knows and will use it. God knows if you are suddenly widowed, or if you lose your children, or if your friends move away or die, or you find yourself living alone for any reason; that is God's potential time—a gift. God isn't closing shop on you. He will lead when you are alone. That is a special time for the personal and majestic touch of God.

My Time With God

When I was a seminary student in Philadelphia, I was working long hours to earn tuition money. I worked weekends in a church in New York and carried a full course load. I was so busy that I couldn't even get enough sleep. I certainly couldn't be alone with my thoughts and God. But one week I was sick. My parents telephoned me the day before I was to leave for my weekend in New York, and they could tell that I was sick. My dad offered to send me the wages I would have earned had I gone to my student ministry that weekend. Having that gift of money, I was able to telephone the church, tell them I was too sick to come, and stay in my room. It was my time with God—a retreat.

The building was quiet that weekend as other students were out on their ministry assignments. I slept, recuperated, studied, and I did a lot of thinking. It was then, in the quiet time—a luxury I hadn't had in several years—that I was able to think about my life and get a sense of direction.

I also found myself thinking about and then writing a letter to a young woman in Chicago—a letter I hadn't had time to think about before. But I remember saying later to a friend, "I wrote a letter after a lot of prayer, and I feel such peace about it. I believe that she is the woman I'm going to marry." And the next year I did marry her.

God didn't cause me to be sick. But he used the quiet time to reach me as he hadn't been able to before. That isn't rationalization after the fact; I sensed him near me then. I knew I was having a special weekend with God. I had time with him. There is rest and healing in the quiet of being alone with God. Those are discerning times, influencing everything that we do.

A Time to Stand Still

In the Book of Numbers, a book of Scripture that is not often read, is a passage that tells a lot about life as God wants us to live it. "So it was that they camped or traveled at the commandment of the Lord; and whatever the Lord told Moses they should do, they did" (Numbers 9:23, TLB).

At the command of the Lord they camped; at the command of the Lord they set out. Whether they stayed still or moved forward, they responded to the word of God. There is just as much obedience in standing still, in not acting, as there is in movement and action. We often forget that. We want to be moving out and going ahead all the time. But there is a time to stop and regroup, a time to stand still, a time to rest, to get organized and wait for God's next order. It is important for progress.

Christine Wood, an English writer, in her article in *Decision* magazine, July 1981, observed that the tide cannot keep coming in; it has to go back before it can come in again. There is as much progress in retreat as there is in advance. No one can advance all of the time. We have to stand still, even go back, to gain a momentum for the next advance. We have to encamp if there is to be the strength to go on. We need our times alone; we need perspective, a withdrawal time, to get a better view of all that so often gives anxiety when we are in its midst.

Maybe that's why God gave one day a week for special rest. I like Sundays; I like the quiet time to think. Worship, Sunday school, and evening service feed me. They bless me and bring me into a supportive prayer fellowship. Those hours in church focus my attention on God, who he is and what he does. But that still leaves quiet times on Sunday.

I don't work on Sunday, so I'm free to be quiet. It is a "down" time but a rich time. I wouldn't work on Sundays for anything if I could get out of it, or if I did have to work, I would have another day with no work just because I have the need for quiet time with God. I need a day when my mind isn't working on some project or anticipating the next assignment. Even if I doze off for a nap or turn on the television or read a book, I'm at rest. Because none of what I'm doing is "required," my mind is free, and in this freedom I have had some great times with God. He has taught me, led me, and encouraged me.

God wants us to encamp as the children of Israel did, to listen to him, to get our orders, to renew our strength. Then we can move out again. There is a blessed rest, a quiet, in the presence of the One who gives us our orders. There is satisfaction in knowing that we are doing the right thing even when at the moment we are not doing anything, just sitting by the door of our tent.

I know a woman who is happy only when she is partying. She has to be with a crowd, she has to be going. She thinks being active, being involved, mixing it up all the time, is wonderful. But it's wearing her out, and it's a mark of her own insecurity. She doesn't know the Lord; she doesn't know the place of peace and rest; she can't enjoy her own company. She's too busy trying to escape her own company. She does not know the great satisfaction that God offers: "Be still, and know that I am God" (Psalm 46:10).

We who are God's people, coming under his orders, advance when he commands and stay still when he commands. In quiet, alone, we hear the orders. We can think, we can put together the complicated parts of life, and then we can act and help others to act.

Being alone is not bad; it can be good—if our company is God's company. With God, we aren't really alone at all.

21

With Family Love
Around Me

■ ■ ■

By the time our son was four years old, he was asking to go fishing. "Go fishing with me, Dad," Grant would say. But except for a few times, I wouldn't take him.

We lived in Highland Park, New Jersey, where I pastored a church, and although a park bordering the Raritan River was close to the house and had places along the shore where we could drop a line, I knew that there were only a few scavenger fish in the river. To me there was no point in fishing. It certainly wasn't worth my time. I was busy; I had a congregation to look after.

"Go fishing with me, Dad," Grant would say. And my response was almost always the same: "Not today."

So the weeks went by. Grant didn't beg, he just asked. And most of the time I had too much to do, or so I said. Being four years old and trusting, he believed me. He didn't know, nor did I, that God was getting ready to teach me a lesson.

Wanting to be a good minister, wanting to help people, I enrolled in the Master of Theology degree program at Princeton Seminary, majoring in counseling. One day a week I took classes learning how to be a better counselor. Now, having added the Princeton studies to my work load, I was really busy.

"Go fishing with me, Dad."

"Not today, Son. Daddy's too busy."

One of the requirements for the degree was a year of clinical work at a psychiatric hospital. I went to the hospital each Friday and spent the whole day. As students we talked to the patients, analyzed each other's counseling techniques, and spent intensive times in sensitivity training under the direction of a chaplain-supervisor. I didn't need the latter, I thought; I was already a good pastor, just trying to be a better one. Certainly I was sensitive to people. What could that chaplain-supervisor tell me? Besides, he had admitted that he was divorced and didn't believe in the divinity of Jesus. How could he teach anything to a happily married, committed evangelical Christian?

But the chaplain didn't ask me about my theology or my biblical beliefs, he asked about my relationship with my son. And after a few minutes of listening, he laid me bare.

Roughly, our exchange went something like this:

"Don't you even hear your own son?"

"Of course I hear him. He wants to catch fish. But that's a waste of time. There are no fish in that river worth catching."

"Did it ever occur to you that catching fish isn't really the important thing to him? Your son wants to go fishing with you. He wants to be with you. He is asking for your companionship. He wants to be with his dad."

That chaplain—and Grant—had me. And, as I was quickly learning, so did God. My orthodox theology couldn't substitute for my availability to my son. I was cheating Grant of the one thing in life nobody else could give him—me. God had given Grant to me; he was entrusted to me; the gift of father-son togetherness had to come through me.

The only difference between Grant and that chaplain was that the chaplain could state bluntly to me what my trusting four-year-old couldn't express. But I began to realize that Grant could feel, and what he had to be feeling was rejection. I was saying, "Daddy doesn't have time to go fishing." He was hearing, "Daddy doesn't have time to go fishing with you." Grant couldn't put that into words, but the chaplain could and did.

Fortunately, God understands a father's change of heart. He can correct a bad start. He can overrule inept parenting. And he did.

I tried to change my ways with my son. We went fishing together and did some other things. But, I wondered, was I starting too late? Guilt rode me hard. *I've failed,* I thought. *He'll be scarred.*

I didn't have to punish myself, but I didn't know that then. One day, years later, I timidly asked, "Do you remember, as a little boy, how you always wanted to go fishing with me and I said I was too busy?" I steeled myself for the response. Here was his chance; he had probably saved all of his pent-up anger—now it was going to come out.

Grant grinned. "I guess I'd forgotten about whatever times we didn't go fishing. I just remember one time when we did go and you snagged your line on the opposite bank. I thought that was really funny."

And together we laughed at me.

We can all tell stories like that. We know our own weaknesses, we know how we wish we had done some things differently. We want to live with our families under the guidance of God. And God in his goodness wants to help us. He knows if we want faithfully to serve our families and if we do not.

Family Is Ministry Too

No one who has his eyes open needs to be reminded of what is happening to the family. As it goes, so will society. The family is society's basic unit of love, security, learning, and cooperation—a unit blessed by God.

In your circles, who helps Christians when family problems are first getting started? Do people keep silent or simply talk behind each other's backs? Who addresses the temptations and weakness that we all have, and speaks openly and candidly without condemning but without compromising either? Who is saying to believers, "Your family is your ministry too," and saying it before a wayward drift begins?

The sacred vows of marriage and the responsibility of building a Christian home are too often treated in a secondary manner by church members and church leaders. How many of us in our family lives are examples of what Christ wants the home to be? How many of us as parents are able to say with the Apostle Paul, "Follow my example, as I follow the example of Christ" (1 Corinthians 11:1)? Each of us might ask ourselves, "What would be the example set for our world if I could say that too?"

As it is, not only are we not teaching each other (if that were the only problem we would simply be struggling along with no teaching), but we are being taught by everyone else—and we follow their examples very well.

We need clear direction and reinforcement from each other and from the Word of God if we are going to be distinctive examples of what God intends families to be. We need help to stay married, and encouragement to build Christian families. God expects it, and we will answer for our casual, even cavalier treatment of God's order if we ignore him. His teaching and our responsibility to each other are meant to be high priorities.

Why Faithfulness?

Why have a Christian home? Why, in the light of all the divorces, remarriages, and extra-marital relationships, do we even stress God's order? Why faithfulness; why the struggle? Why not do what some other people do—just split and run? No one seems to be less respected for it. Why fight for what may be only our concept of traditionalism in home and marriage?

The answer is this: We have made a vow to God. Each of us has stood before God and said words similar to "in sickness and in health, for richer or poorer, for better or worse, till death do us part." Each of us who is married made that promise to another person in a pledge before God.

Yet when the electricity seems to be gone or someone else seems more attractive, some are willing to break that vow. That cannot be done! God speaks clearly about promises (Deuteronomy 23:21-23, Ecclesiastes 5:2-6).

I have to be aware that if God cannot trust me to keep a vow no matter what the difficulties, he may never be able to trust me in anything else. In the instructions to husbands to live with their wives in understanding and honor, Peter warns, "so that nothing will hinder your prayers" (1 Peter 3:7). If there is any explanation for the weakness in some churches, can it be, at least in part, due to the hindered prayers of those whom God knows will quickly break a vow made to him?

This sounds harsh, and in one sense it is. But note, it is true that we can make mistakes and God will heal. It is true that the love of God is greater than any of our failures. It is true that if we fall we don't have to stay down. It is true that if we break God's Law, he doesn't push us aside and say, "That's all for you!" God doesn't treat people like that, nor should we. But he doesn't smile at flagrant sin either, especially when he knows that we are more interested in our own pleasure and personal satisfaction than in obedience. Only by being trusted and trustworthy can we build a lasting Christian marriage and family relationship. Because only then can all the strength of God be on our side.

Strength in Commitment

There is strength in total commitment; it is the strength that comes from the success of overcoming. But the undisciplined, the weak, the escapist will never find it—they will never overcome; they will never know what God has for them in the true intimacy of marriage.

One evening, after both our son and daughter had had an early supper in order to be on time for their own planned evening, my wife and I had a quiet dinner together. We didn't go out; we stayed in the kitchen. She didn't cook anything difficult or fancy; it was just a casserole that the children aren't fond of but we are. We ate by candlelight, leisurely talking about everything and anything that was important to us. Then, when dinner was over, we had devotions together, holding hands. It was an intimate evening— just ours—and we both sensed the presence of God and a deep, deep love. That comes from commitment and years of trust.

It takes years to build that kind of relationship, which is the reason that many couples declare that what they have after twenty-five or thirty years of marriage is so much more special than even the excitement of their newly married life. Ephesians 5:28-29 frankly admits that there is self-love in that, and that is quite appropriate: "Husbands ought to love their wives as their own bodies. He who loves his wife loves himself. After all, no one ever hated his own body."

That is why some in the body of believers seem to have trouble getting along with their spouses. They dislike themselves. They are the ones who are looking around for someone else, someone who will give them value, some reason for being, some stature in their own eyes. They need someone who will appeal to them because they are so insecure in themselves that they do not know who they are, they do not know their own self-worth. They do not love themselves, and as a result cannot receive love from the one with whom they live. But the ones who know themselves and their needs, and want to love, can be loved and give love. There are many spouses longing to give love to the mate who is looking elsewhere. And as long as people are looking for another to give the security and value they crave, they will never really open themselves either to their mate or to God. If it is true on any level, it is true on the level of marriage: "For anyone who does not love . . . [one] whom he has seen, cannot love God, whom he has not seen" (1 John 4:20).

A Legacy of Love

Think of the impact on the world if married couples who are Christians would give visible testimony to the love in their marriage because God is love and they love God. Many people do not know that it is possible to have God because they don't see God in overflowing love, especially in marriage.

A strong Christian marriage has an impact which will be felt for generations to come. We offer a heritage to our children in our faithfulness to our spouse; there is a legacy in love that we give them. Their home, the framework in which they try their wings, needs a commitment that is not shifting. They need a solid footing. They have to have models and security in the home to achieve emotional strength and spiritual depth. When they have it, their own security makes them healthy and able to give the same to the next generation. But it's difficult to relay to others what they never get themselves. There is evidence of that in third- and fourth-generation divorces, battered children, and socially destructive adults.

It is in the home that children learn to pray. It is in the home that they learn what love is, how to give and how to receive it. It is through the exchange of love between a father and a mother that children themselves understand how to be a father or a mother. They learn marriage by seeing it in the workshop of the home. And experiencing human love, they have a basis for accepting God's love. If their world is shattered by separating parents, where will they turn? We know all of the excuses made by those who leave their children and their spouses. And we know the heartache in many marriages where couples stay together for appearance's sake or for the children. That's why love, care, and nurture is needed—not condemnation. But duty is connected to joy. When a husband and wife fulfill a duty each to the other, they also fulfill a duty to their children and joy does come.

Satan's Delicious Traps

"But," you say, "Christians too have roving eyes." It is "acceptable." And therein is one of Satan's most delicious traps. Passing fancies are shallow. What can some other person offer? Suppose I pursued someone else because I thought God wanted me to have "more." Suppose I found another woman who to me was special. Suppose I married her. She would never be able to trust me! For as long as I lived, no matter what I promised her, she would always know deep down inside that I have not only already broken a similar promise to another woman, I have broken a promise made to God. My word would be worthless. If I went after her while I was still married, how would she ever be secure in my promise that I would not do the same to her? She could never be secure. She could never relax and be truly herself. She would never be at ease, or comfortable, or secure, or at peace. She would always be uncertain, always wonder, and would never have the true openness that makes a marriage strong.

Who knows me better than the one who has cried with me, prayed with me, and knows my soul? Who can give and take with me better than the one who has shared life with me? The "passing fancies" can never do that. If a person is concerned to obey 1 Corinthians 7:33 about how to please his spouse, that spouse will be the center of all his thoughts and desires. No outsider will ever be able to enter into a fenced enclosure that two have built together.

It is not just simple reasoning that makes us obey the teaching that God wants us to stay married. It is the matter of not willfully being disobedient, of slapping God in the face and saying, "No, I won't." Jesus said in Matthew 19:5, "For this reason a man will leave his father and mother and be united to his wife, and the two will become one flesh." A married couple is one flesh, and one flesh cannot be divided. If we try to cut it asunder, or encourage others to cut it asunder, what will we say to God? Will we say,

"You didn't mean what you said"? Will we tell him, "I thought you were joking"? Will we try to face him down and say, "I thought you were telling a lie"? Will we become theologically verbose and declare, "You don't understand me; I still trust you to save me for eternity but I just can't trust you to save my marriage"? "I will be faithfully yours forever in heaven but not during these years on earth"?

We have a responsibility before God for our families. The Apostle Paul stated, "Believe in the Lord Jesus, and you will be saved—you and your household" (Acts 16:31). Before God, my faith involves my family. I am responsible.

Me and My House

The statement, "As for me and my household, we will serve the Lord" (Joshua 24:15), is one that a Christian needs to make. When Christians refuse to make it, when they determine that their salvation is strictly personal and the salvation of their children is strictly personal too, they are opening the door to fragmented Christian families that carry over into the church and into society. It promotes breakdown of the family; it opens the door to divorce. As a husband and father, if I am responsible only for me, and "my soul is saved," then I can convince myself that I am free to leave my wife and children because I have no responsibility spiritually for her or for the children. I have determined that each of them stands individually before God and I am not obliged to be involved; they are God's business, not mine.

But God has given me my family. He has placed them in my care. Their souls, it is true, are his apart from me, but I am a teacher, the one to pray for them, the one to whom they look for counsel, an example of Christian living. Can I be satisfied with my personal salvation in Christ if there is not also for generations to come a dynasty of Christians following after? Christians must face this.

How can we live this Christian life of obedience? By singleness of eye, by one desire—by obeying.

Life is so vast; it has so many facets and sides that, like a multifaceted diamond reflecting in so many different directions, we can neither grasp it, understand it, nor live in it all at the same time. Our lives are too complex. Temptations and pressures come from many places. We can only focus on one place and call it the focal point of our lives, the center. That center is the place of my praying the place of living out my Christian life, the place of my security. That place is home.

My Reference Point

In my work, I travel a great deal. I am geographically in many places, but there is one focal point in the world, one place that is always my reference point—it is home. No matter where I am, no matter which continent it is, how many miles from home, my traveling is possible only because emotionally I am back home. Nairobi is not so many miles from London or New York; it is so many miles from home. Sydney is a certain distance, a certain time in travel from home. Tokyo is a certain number of hours and plane stops from home.

One night, after being away from home for three weeks, a colleague asked, "What time is your flight in the morning?"

I replied, "The first flight out, 7:40."

"What time do you have to get up to be at the airport on time?"

"I'll be up at five."

"Why don't you take a later flight? Why get up so early?"

"Because I'm going home."

Home is where my heart is. And I think God teaches a lesson through that. He teaches a lesson about the heart's longing for heaven. That is where God is. Someday I'll really be Home. Only a few more years of travel on this earth and then I'll be Home. I'll be secure within the warmth of Home. And in the vastness of life, like the vastness of the globe, there is that focal point—Home. Every distance, every moment of time, is referenced by the word "Home."

God knew that. He gives homes now and he gives a final Home. He puts the temporal and the eternal together in our hearts. Don't shatter your home. It is there that you will experience the love of God. And it is there that you will learn to live out the training in all the dimensions of yourself that you will take with you when you don't have to journey anymore and are truly "Home."

Live with family love around you now. Don't destroy it. Home is your training ground for eternity.

22

If I Should Die
Before I Wake

■ ■ ■

The Christian faith is the answer to death because it is the answer to life.

I have in my files a clipping from *Christianity Today*, February 1, 1963, in which an 82-year-old pastor, the Reverend S. F. Marsh of Leland, Mississippi, talked about his own death. He said he had been getting ready for death for most of his life because fifty-five years earlier he had struggled with tuberculosis. Every year he expected to die. Apparently the fact that he was then eighty-two years of age surprised him. He said, "I have been getting ready for the last impressive hour for many, many years."[1]

That's a delightful thought: "The last impressive hour." Everything Mr. Marsh did was in anticipation of and in preparation for that last impressive hour. Whether he was preaching, teaching, or caring for people, everything was weighed not by its greatness at the moment but by the belief that this might be his last message, his last act of kindness. Always he was getting ready for that last impressive hour.

If we, like the Reverend Mr. Marsh, always had our death before us, it would influence everything we do. We would sit by the bedside of a sick child just as readily as calling on presidents, advising business leaders, or holding high office. Perspectives change and values are measured differently in the light of getting ready for that last impressive hour. Mr. Marsh went on to say:

In all these and a thousand other activities I was getting ready to

die. Let me make a suggestion here. Just go along living a Christian life of usefulness the way a Christian should, and when you
approach eighty-two you'll find yourself thinking, "Why, I've
been getting ready for my last hour on earth for a long
time." [2]

A Wonderful Balance

It is not a morbid thing to think about getting ready for death.
Quite the contrary, it makes every hour before it so much more
meaningful. No wonder the Apostle Paul could say that he was
willing to leave the body and be at home with the Lord (2 Corinthians 5:8). Why not? He had an ongoing work that was measured
in the light of eternity. If it went on another year, then he would
have another year's ministry. If it ended that day, he'd be present
with the Lord. It didn't matter. What a wonderful balance for
thinking about life.

Most people, even Christians, fear death; at least they fear the
dying process. Then there are other Christians who make death
sound like such a delightful thing that they doubt the Christian
faith of any who fear it. They become spiritually superior—looking down their noses at those who tremble at the unknown, the
passage into heaven. We may fear the pain of death, the sickness
that brings on the deterioration of the body, the anxiety. We do
fear what we have never experienced before. We don't know what
dying will be like. There is nothing un-Christian in being concerned about the process of dying.

We Christians are entitled to depression. We are weak—that's
why we need the strong One. We are finite—that's why we need
the Infinite. When a Christian talks about being free from the fear
of death, he or she is really talking about not being afraid of meeting God.

The Christian is God's child through adoption. The Bible says,
"And so we should not be like cringing, fearful slaves, but we
should behave like God's very own children, adopted into the
bosom of his family, and calling to him, 'Father, Father'" (Romans
8:15, TLB).

But being human, we still have instincts for self-preservation. I
don't want to be run over by a car. I don't want to be burned in a

nuclear blast. I don't want to have a hideous cancer or go blind. I don't want that.

But I know God and I know that some day I "shall be like him, for [I] shall see him as he is" (1 John 3:2). Therefore, as I prepare for death I am both happy and sad. Fortunately the desire for liberation from all the pain of this earth grows as that last day on earth approaches so that even the deterioration and pain that may lead to death does not seem as frightening.

Don't Be Afraid to Walk Out of It

If our life here has been good because we have drawn on the gifts, the promises, the love, the wisdom of God, and have lived in him, how much more then is waiting for us when we move out beyond the limitations of this world? Don't be afraid to say goodbye to this world and walk out of it with him.

What do you think death is? Do you realize that you have no idea at all what death is? You have not experienced it, nor have you talked with one who has. We read books about those returning from a death state. We are eager to know what they were feeling, to record what they tell. We want to know.

Some say they were happy and experienced a sense of light and peace. Others were frightened, terror-stricken. But these reports are only that—reports. We don't know where these "dead" people were, or even if they were dead at all—we still don't know the meaning of death. The Christian does know, on the authority of God's Word, that "Blessed [happy] are the dead who die in the Lord" (Revelation 14:13).

Look Forward to the Journey

The fear of annihilation, the end of us, is not a legitimate fear for one who is alive in Christ. For the Christian has already been through real death. We now face only physical death; that is not annihilation, it is liberation. Even the process, the journey, can be an experience with God. We can look forward to the journey for even if it is through a valley, he is with us in that journey (Psalm 23:4).

And when the journey is over, when we are "gone," will that produce sorrow in those around us? Of course it will. Jesus felt sorrow for Lazarus (John 11:33-35). Our friends, our relatives, are bound to be hurt by our cessation of life. They will miss us. That's normal, that's healthy; but it also makes the anticipation of reunion with one another much sweeter.

One of the important things about anticipating our own death is that we likewise anticipate the deaths of others, and this influences the way we behave toward them. Don't leave yourself open to remorse and regret when you stand by a grave: "I should have treated him better." "Why didn't I do more?" "I should have shown more love." "We should have taken that trip together." "I should have listened to her." Know on the basis of your own mortality the mortality of others, and leave people in a way that will deposit for you and them good memories no matter who goes first.

In Christ, death and hell have been judged. In Christ there is new birth, a beginning. We move not toward the end of life. We are moving toward life in all of its completion and fulfillment. We work and act not to become something—we already *are* something. It is already clear where we are going, and we move toward the excitement of that. The progression we enjoy is our own further growing in him. This is not life after life, this is life itself. This is not a great cyclical development leading to the Hindu idea of liberation. It is a moving from the very point where human religions will never be—new birth. We are going from new birth in Christ—a post-grave life—into life developing in Christ.

The Unbeliever Only Exists

Ludwig Wittgenstein said, "Death is not an event in life. Death is not lived through."[3]

But Christians do live through it. Because we are already in the One who lived through it. For the unbeliever it is not so. Unbelievers only exist, they don't live. They don't live through death because they aren't even alive on this side of death. They go on as they are now—existing as created beings but not as living souls. They exist first on this side of death, then on the other, but apart from God. That is their choice. They aren't the victims of fate or of some cruel cosmic roll of the dice; they have looked at the One who said, "I have come that they may have life" (John 10:10), and they have said no!

But, people ask, "How can one be moving and acting in this world and not be alive?" Doctors in a hospital decide when someone is brain-dead even though his or her body is functioning. Is that person alive? Likewise, if people eat and work and sleep but their souls are so hardened that they are not responding to the stimulus of God, are they alive? Activity is not the same as life. Commenting on Wittgenstein's quote, I wrote in *Decision* magazine:

> Ludwig Wittgenstein in his "Tractatus Logico-Philosophicus" told his readers that death is not an event in life because it is not lived through. Now, that is something to think about. For the unsure person, that statement is frightening. For the Christian, that statement is erroneous.
>
> Jesus Christ is Victor over sin and death. In him, being redeemed, given new life, I have already been through death. Eternal life began for me the moment that I was born into that new life. My body will someday physically die, to be sure, and it will be buried. But let there be no mourning. Because I had eternal life from the moment of my new birth, I will keep right on going into an even fuller life, one without the encumbrances of the physical. I will go on with the eternal Christ. That is a surety for the Christian, because it isn't built on fantasy but on true hope, and that true hope, unlike wishful thinking, is certain.
>
> To the unsure person, Wittgenstein's statement is frightening because all that is beyond the body's cessation of function is unknown. Yet he has a sense that there is more; he has an innate awareness of the tripartite aspect of the human—the body, the mind, the spirit. What happens to that, he wonders. He can't be sure and assumes that no one else can be sure either.
>
> God, in Christ, acted upon the separation and death that mankind brought upon himself by his own volition. Because God has acted, man doesn't have to have eternal death; he chooses to die by refusing God's gift of new life in Jesus Christ. He can choose that life, he doesn't have to go cursing and screaming into death as so many do when the reality of death hits them. He doesn't have to be always unsure, trying to forget what his mind won't let him forget. He doesn't have to pretend that all is well by gathering like-minded people around him who by unspoken agreement keep each other busy lest they face a moment of doubt about what will happen when their self-generated party is over.
>
> With the believers of the ages, we can and do rejoice in the risen Christ. Raised with him, we shout our Hallelujahs! Jesus

Christ lives. We can say with the apostle, "Death is swallowed up in victory. O death, where is thy sting? O grave, where is thy victory?" (1 Corinthians 15:54-55, KJV).

We can live right past Easter into the fullest life, whether it is here in time or there in eternity. Death and its root of sin are conquered; it is settled for us; we are alive forever—and it is life as it was intended to be.

For it is always true of the one who has responded to the proffered gift of life: "I am crucified with Christ: nevertheless I live; yet not I, but Christ liveth in me: and the life which I now live in the flesh I live by the faith of the Son of God, who loved me, and gave himself for me" (Galatians 2:20, KJV).

If there ever is a nonevent for the Christian, it is his own death. He has already been through real death—with the Conqueror. 4

Toward Greater Life

How sad that we talk of growing old in the same way as the world does. We are not moving toward death but from death toward greater and greater life. For we are dead in Christ now and alive in Christ now. The life that has already been to the grave and hell is our life, and in him we have come out on the other side with heaven before us. Life in its fullness is the life within us, to be even so much richer when the encumbrances of the dead world that hold us drop away. How good, then, to be reaching toward next year or the next decade! How we can rejoice in each passing year and dedicate the years remaining to using every moment faithfully for the One who takes us by the hand and leads us and calls us his own. How good to "offer [our] bodies as living sacrifices, holy and pleasing to God—this is [our] spiritual worship" (Romans 12:1). How good, then, not to be conformed to the pattern of this world but to be "transformed by the renewing of [our] mind[s]. Then [we] will be able to test and approve what God's will is—his good, pleasing and perfect will" (Romans 12:2). We are in the process of living, and someday we will be more alive than we are now.

And so we enter into rest. A holy rest. It is not a rest of sitting around bored, neither here now nor in heaven later. It is a rest of completion, a rest of accomplishment. For we have all of that in him who is complete even as we continue to move along on this earth, serving, loving, giving, and obeying. We rest in the security of knowing to whom we belong, where we have come from and where we are going. We have the rest of knowing that even our work is not our accomplishment, whether or not it is completed by our definition of complete. Ours is the rest of knowing that he is Lord, he is the One in control—the God of history, the Master of our lives. Ours is the rest of knowing that we belong to the eternal God who is in all yet above all and beyond all. He is our rest, our true security.

We belong now in the physical creation as God's created ones, and we belong outside creation as the redeemed children of our heavenly Father. We are citizens of both time and eternity. We are not finishing our lives, we are just beginning our lives—for we have him, his very gift of life, and we will have that for all eternity. This security is God's love gift to us, his great heart gift—and it is intended for all. Some will miss it. That is the saddest of all realities. But others will find it, and in that we continually rejoice.

People tease: "You're not getting older, you're getting better." They may only be joking about it, but for the Christian that is true. And because it is true and we know it, we can handle whatever comes to us on this journey we call life. And we can handle our death.

Manage Your Death

Who is going to manage your death? Think about that now before you are incapacitated. Do you want heroic methods used to prolong your life? I've known cancer patients who, although given no hope, still allowed their lives to be prolonged with great pain and sickness. It isn't that the treatments might have worked; the doctors and the patients knew that they wouldn't because of the nature of the disease. This isn't an argument for euthanasia, terminating everyone who "ceases to be useful"—not at all. Life is too precious. It is a gift from God. But it is a question of the dignity of personal choice—especially for the Christian who is going Home.

Arrange with your family now about who is going to make decisions when you are dying. Personally, I don't want to undo a lifetime of trying to be an encouragement and help to others by becoming a financial and emotional strain on everyone during my last weeks. I'd like the dignity of loving and giving even in my death.

But I don't say that out of fear of prolonged personal suffering. Suffering personally is different from inflicting suffering on others. We can suffer and endure it, even teach the dignity and the strength of suffering as we go through it. But allowing ourselves to die may be the better gift to those left behind. Each of us needs to think that through.

If you are killed accidently, have you already arranged your will to take care of your family? Have you already arranged for useful body parts to be given to somebody else so that person can live? As a Christian, if you would work day and night for the salvation of a soul, won't you also donate what you can no longer use for the benefit of someone else's life? If someone is starving, would you give food? If that person needs an eye or a kidney, will you provide it?

As you think about death, not morbidly, not in a ghoulish fashion but as an inevitable part of the experience of living, see it as an adventure. It is the next step, the graduation, the translation, the moving out of here and into there. To anticipate death makes all of life fall into perspective. What you do now counts. The time you waste now counts too. And the mistakes you make now, in the long run, don't really matter. Nor do the successes.

Use Pain—Let It Teach You

Is there value in suffering? Obviously there is. It can make us and those around us rethink our human frailty, our dependence upon family, our need for God. God is not sadistic when he allows us to suffer. There is teaching in suffering, for us and for others.

There is always another side to suffering, especially for the Christian. I've been thinking about the story of Margaret of Molokai:

Forty-seven years ago a twelve-year-old girl was taken from a hula recital in the city hall to exile on the island of Molokai. Over those years, she lost three husbands to leprosy. Her four children were taken from her at birth and delivered to adoptive families on the mainland. Over the years, the disease mangled her feet and hands. 5

What did she say about this? "I no blame God for disease. I blame germs. . . . If my pain no get better, I become one better person from my pain."[6]

Don't be afraid of suffering; it is an enemy, but it is not greater than God's grace. Use pain—let it teach you about yourself, your strengths, your resolves, your commitment. You can grow too, through the value of your pain-free minutes and the gift of yourself to others.

Years ago I read *The Man Who Lived Twice*. I never forgot that book. Edward Sheldon, a Broadway actor, was crippled by arthritis. He spent his remaining years blind and unable to move. Yet from his bed he touched the lives of great numbers of people with his encouragement and help. He was a giving man.

There may be great pain ahead for some of us in this life, or there may not be. But there will be death. Don't be afraid to think about death while you are still strong and in the full bloom of life. You needn't fear it. Be ready for it.

Someday I'll Be in God's Mansion

One Sunday afternoon when Jimmy Carter was President of the United States, Andrea and I were invited to the White House for an afternoon with the Carters and other guests, mostly people related to Christian media. It was an informal time in the "backyard" of the White House. At breakfast that morning I thought, "This afternoon I'll picnic at the White House with the President." And later we did, enjoying the music and informal conversation with President and Mrs. Carter under the warm summer sun.

That made me think past that particular afternoon to a future event. There will come a day, whether I'm in a hospital bed or at home, when I'll be able to say, "This evening I'll banquet with the Lord in his House."

That thought went through my mind again three years later, this time at lunch with President Reagan. Only something else was added. I looked around and thought, "The White House is the same, but the Presidents change." Someday I'll be in God's mansion where there is a room prepared for me, and the Host will never move out. He who invites us to heaven will always be there. No matter what changes now, God does not change ever—nor does my place with him. "But you remain the same, and your years will never end" (Psalm 102:27). I'm going to live with God!

I want to be ready, so that when I arrive and circulate among friends and visit with God and listen to the music and enjoy the warm sunshine, I'll be able to say, "I'm glad I was invited. I'm glad I'm here."

Death Is Total Gain

Death is total gain; we must never forget that. "For to me, living means opportunities for Christ, and dying—well, that's better yet!" (Philippians 1:21, TLB).

The death of a Christian is precious to God. "His loved ones are very precious to him and he does not lightly let them die" (Psalm 116:15, TLB).

Don't worry about the suffering of those who have gone on before you. Or even about all that happened leading to their deaths. Whether it was torture or other pain, they are past it now; God is already wiping away their tears. "He will wipe every tear from their eyes" (Revelation 21:4).

No death is a surprise to God. He is prepared for our death even if it surprises us. He knows exactly when it will occur, and he is ready. It will come right on time. He is there at your death, beside you.

The Psalmist expressed, "You are with me; your rod and your staff, they comfort me" (Psalm 23:4).

Death is both a final act and a prelude, for we are living sacrifices. Death is part of our worship. Death—that final sacrifice—is the last drop of this libation given in our worship. Then the fight here will have been fought, the last gift to God complete. Now there is nothing more to offer. Now for us is face-to-face enjoyment—forever.

Thomas à Kempis said, "For he that loveth God with all his heart dreadeth neither death nor punishment, nor judgment, nor Hell; for perfect love giveth sure access to God."[7]

We will at last be the perfection that God intended. Think of having a nature that is no longer rebellious but which responds to God easily and naturally. "We shall be like him, for we shall see him as he is" (1 John 3:2).

Like him! What a holy wonder that will be!

And, of course, the last word on the matter of death is God's Word. "There will be no more death" (Revelation 21:4). "Death has been swallowed up in victory" (1 Corinthians 15:54).

Victory! It is ours, in the risen Christ now; it is ours in the risen Christ then. He is our proof that truly we live, and live, and live forever.

23

Come, Live a
Happy Life

■ ■ ■

God designed me to be happy. Knowing this is not some form of
self-hypnosis or an attempt to convince myself against all reality.
Happiness is not an act I perform or a mask that I put on. It is a
truth. It is based on the assurance that God himself holds my life. It
is an awakening to who I am in him. It is knowing that I don't have
to wait to become or have something; I can start to live fully,
totally, obediently where I am. This is a happy life now

"But that's unrealistic."

"You are in the real world."

At least that's what some people say when they listen to an
explanation of this happy adventure called following Jesus Christ.
But that's not really a conviction they hold, it's a wish—a very sad
wish. It is a wish built on a fearful hope that discipleship won't
work, because if it does, and they are not practicing it or experiencing it, they will be unhappy now and forever.

There are always going to be people around who tell us why
obedience to the teachings of Jesus isn't realistic, even when deep
down inside those same people suspect that obedience to him and
his teachings *is* realistic. Those who speak the loudest against the
disciplines of obedience are usually the ones who are most certain
deep down inside that theirs would be a different life if they ever
did obey him. They want "happiness," but they don't understand
what it is. Certainly they can't imagine that it comes from following Jesus. They don't have friendship with God; they aren't disciples. They don't know what this dimension of life is.

But we know.

"The disciple is not above his master: but every one that is perfect shall be as his master" (Luke 6:40, KJV). We will be like Jesus.

"Any of you who does not give up everything he has cannot be my disciple" (Luke 14:33). If we follow him, we may end up poorer than even the foxes who "have holes and birds of the air [who] have nests" (Matthew 8:20), but we will follow him anyway.

Such a life sounds undesirable to pursue and impossible to live, and in our own strength it is. But Jesus calls us to it because he calls us to himself. In him everything else becomes relative. If we have property, it is his, whether we are called to give it up or keep it. Our money is his and our families are his. That's not a frightening thought: If we do what he asks, he takes care of his own.

The ones who are surrendered in obedience to Jesus Christ can relax and live and enjoy themselves whether they have much or very little—because logically, sensibly, through good counsel and with prayer, they are doing what they know God has asked them to do. To those who won't trust God, such an act seems foolish. To those who do trust God, anything else is foolish.

Unrealistic?

Who is going to stand before Jesus Christ and tell him that what he teaches is unrealistic?

Just "holy" talk?

Who is going to go to God the Father and tell him that Jesus is just making noises, strange "holy" word-sounds?

Who is going to tell God that his Son doesn't mean what he says or tell him, "I think you are mistaken," or say, "I looked at what Jesus said, but then I looked at my own logic, and frankly, God, my own logic makes a lot more sense"? Who is going to say those things?

Following Jesus Is Never a Burden

God has given his Word for us to build upon. Ignore that, or substitute our own fragile words for it, and we have crumbling stones or sand. Dietrich Bonhoeffer, who followed Jesus, returned to Hitler's Germany and died for his faithfulness to Christ. Bonhoeffer explained what obedience and faithfulness means:

The word which we fail to do is no rock to build a house on. There can then be no union with Jesus. He has never known us. That is why as soon as the hurricane begins we lose the word, and find that we have never really believed it. The word we had was not Christ's, but a word we had wrested from Him and made our own by reflecting on it instead of doing it. So our house crashes in ruins, because it is not founded on the word of Jesus Christ. [1]

Following Jesus is not a burden. Following church dogma can be a burden. Following certain theological pronouncements can be a burden. Trying to be good can be a burden. Trying to be obedient by our own "logic" can be a burden. But following Jesus is never a burden.

"His commands are not burdensome" (1 John 5:3), we are told, and they're not. Where did the idea ever start that they were? It probably started with people who never tried to follow Christ or, worse, tried to follow the Master without first surrendering their lives to him. His commands, without his indwelling Spirit, cannot be kept.

Following him is not determined by our own feelings about following him. We do not obey our concept of his commands. Following him means following what he teaches, being prayerfully aware that Scripture is not to be filtered through our own method of determining what is important for us and what is not.

Following Jesus is not provisional. We do not follow him on our terms, we follow him on his. If there were conditions, those conditions would monopolize our thinking and our time. We are to be monopolized by him. One man who approached Jesus tried to put conditions on his obedience. He said, "Lord, first let me go and bury my father" (Matthew 8:21). Jesus wouldn't accept that.

The man was putting up his own condition. It came between him and Jesus. Anything can become a condition. Even following him for what he may do for me spiritually or emotionally or physically is a condition. I do not follow him because it feels good. I do not follow him because he provides bread or water or escape, but because he asks me to follow him. It must be that way. We sign the bottom of the contract. He fills in the top.

It is a famous saying now, though it was new when Bonhoeffer said it: "When Christ calls a man, he bids him come and die." [2]

That's true! We are no longer our own; we are crucified with

Christ, yet we are alive because we are born again to new life in him. And the life we once had (though it was in reality no life at all) is gone. We are alive in him because we have already died, and what we have in Christ now is "eternal" life. Everything is changed. The values we had while we were dead are no longer the values we have in our new life in Christ. We have died! One cannot live in Christ until he or she passes from death into life.

It is interesting that new Christians seem to know that this is true and start their new life building on the Rock. Then, too often, they are turned away after some exposure to the compromising lives of older Christians. New Christians, having the fresh experience of trusting Jesus as Savior and being prepared to trust him as Lord, approach discipleship with the belief: "It is right and it will work, because Jesus taught it." They believe Romans 8:28 and believe that "all" things mean both the negative and the positive, not just the events in life that are pleasing.

But there are senior Christians who become jaded about life, so they compromise and teach compromise (or what they call "realistic Christianity"). They become the sadly troubled ones who, looking back on their lives, wonder, "Could obedience have worked? What if I had stuck to my earlier convictions about taking Jesus at his word? What would have happened; what would my life have been if I had followed Jesus as he asked me to do? What would it have been like to have been truly a friend of God?"

Can I Be Happy?

And at the end of life, preparing to meet him, many Christians carry guilt because the corruptive things of "moth and rust" had more importance to them while God's friendship had little value. There are Christians who late in life become aware that the life "worked out for myself" was not a fulfilling one and wonder what "he might have worked out for me." And they don't know; they can only guess. They never really lived. They have never been truly happy.

The happy life doesn't mean that we are complete, for completion would mean we would no longer strive. Yet we are fulfilled. For all that he is, is fulfilling us. In that sense, the redeemed sense, the spiritual sense, we can be complete even now, for we belong to the One who is completeness.

God is complete, and in his completion is himself our fulfillment and happiness. Nothing more needs to be added. Someday all that I have in hope will be mine in fact. But even now all that he gives is mine, mine to the extent that I allow him to fill me. God can make me happy now and someday even happier. He is happiness. He offers the happy life, the perfect life—because he offers himself.

C. S. Lewis, writing in *Mere Christianity*, said of God:

> He meant what He said. Those who put themselves in His hands will become perfect, as He is perfect—perfect in love, wisdom, joy, beauty, and immortality. The change will not be completed in this life, for death is an important part of the treatment. How far the change will have gone before death in any particular Christian is uncertain. 3

But though the degree is uncertain, the fact is not. We can begin to enjoy to the fullest what we have in him now, to indulge ourselves now in who he is and what he gives. We are brought into wholeness in him through his rescuing and his claiming. We know the fact of "Christ in me." We have been made alive through resurrection life, and everything we are and have—growth, expansion, discipline, enjoyment, happiness, holiness—comes from this. None of this can come to the dead who are decaying, but it does come to the living, the alive in Christ. It is all there for the man or woman of God.

Can I be happy? Of course I can, for I have his life and he is the source and essence of happiness. The question for me is not, "Can I?" but "Will I?" Will I allow that happiness to have its full work in me? Having been made by God and redeemed by God, it is impossible for me to say, "But I cannot be like him," for that would be a contradiction. He has made my being in him possible. John Haggai said, "No one but God stills the mind. No one but God steels the spirit. No one but God thrills the soul."4

What is this happiness? Can I explain it? Probably not. Can I measure it? No! Can I experience it? Yes! One cannot measure what happiness is any more than he can measure the holiness that produces it. For we would have to stand still to measure, and we cannot do that. We are growing when we have his life. We are not dead anymore. Tomorrow will be richer for me, and fuller and deeper than today. Certainly next year, building as it does on this year, will give an even larger dimension of God's fulfillment.

We often look at a child and say, "What a happy child," and we suppose he is. But he can be even happier when he is forty or seventy. Why? Because his capacity for happiness increases with growth and experience. We tend to mistake simplicity for happiness; we think of not knowing as innocence and mistake absence of problems for peace. But real happiness is knowing and understanding and still having genuine happiness with deep peace. That's what God offers.

Then do holiness and happiness go together? Yes, the one comes from the other. The Apostle Paul speaks of putting off the old self which is being corrupted by deceitful desires and putting on the new self created to be like God in true righteousness and holiness (Ephesians 4:22-23).

Holiness is like putting on a new suit of clothes—not a patched suit but a new suit. Jesus made it clear that we can't put new cloth on old garments; it won't hold. There are no halfway measures with God, not in obedience, discipleship, happiness, or holiness. It has been said that a moderately good Christian is as unsatisfactory as a moderately good egg. Both are useless.

There are people who are always looking, always trying to get a sensation or a feeling or an experience, trying to add happiness to what is dead and decaying and rotting—and it can't be done. Jesus Christ is life. "I am the way and the truth and the life. No one comes to the Father except through me" (John 14:6). Coming into his life, finding his fulfillment, yielding to him, letting him be all that is holy in us—that's the way to happiness.

A Different Perspective

In *Mere Christianity* C. S. Lewis wrote:

If you decide to make thrills your regular diet and try to prolong them artificially, they will all get weaker and weaker, and fewer and fewer, and you will be a bored, disillusioned old man for the rest of your life.... It is much better fun to learn to swim than to go on endlessly (and hopelessly) trying to get back the feeling you had when you first went paddling as a small boy. [5]

Living the happy life is like learning to swim—as you make

progress you enjoy it more because you see that you are going somewhere.

You can be happy in your mind because you can be holy in your mind. There is peace for anyone whose mind is stayed on him. That's perfect peace. The mind—a mind that is proving what is that good, acceptable, and perfect will of God—can be renewed toward that peace.

Everything takes on a new perspective when we seek to know him and understand him, and think through, on the basis of who he is, the meaning of holiness. It has nothing to do with accomplishment or education or success or financial stability or social relationships or health. Richard Baxter understood that. In 1650 he said:

> Take a poor Christian that can scarce speak true English about religion, that hath a weak understanding, a failing memory, a stammering tongue, yet his heart is set on God: he hath chosen him for his portion; his thoughts are on eternity; his desires there, his dwelling there. . . . I had rather die in this man's condition, and have my soul in his soul's case, than in the case of him that hath the most eminent gifts, and is most admired for parts and duty, whose heart is not thus taken up with God. [6]

If my mind is fixed on him, then money, job, prestige, security or the lack of it take on a totally different significance. World affairs, though they be a concern, are seen in a different perspective. Pleasure, self-seeking, and gain are no longer important. Loneliness becomes something that I can handle, whether or not I like it, because God is my source of happiness. He is in my mind, my heart, and my soul, and he will always be there—forever.

Again, it was Richard Baxter who said:

> As we paid nothing for God's eternal love and nothing for the Son of his love, and nothing for his Spirit and our grace and faith, and nothing for our pardon, so shall we pay nothing for our eternal Rest. . . . The broken heart that hath known the desert of sin doth understand and feel what I say. What an astonishing thought it will be to think of the unmeasurable difference between our deservings and our receivings; between the state we should have been in and the state we are in. . . . O, how free was all this love, and how free is this enjoyed glory. [7]

He gives the fullness of his love that we may receive it and enjoy it forever.

We can be happy not only in our feelings but in our wills, for it is the will that determines our steps toward holiness. Christians are people who have declared "I will" when they determine to follow Christ. By our wills we have gathered up all that we are—our strengths, weaknesses, talents, gifts, shortcomings, emotional difficulties—and surrendered everything to the living Christ. It is an intentional act. To be a Christian is a step of faith, one made by a definite act of the will. When Jesus called those fishermen and that tax collector, they had to will to follow him. He told stories about those like the rich young ruler who would not.

Thomas Kelly in his *Testament of Devotion* wrote:

> The crux of religious living lies in the *will*, not in transient and variable states. Utter dedication of will to God is open to *all*. . . . Where the will to will God's will is present, there is a child of God. When there are graciously given to us such glimpses of glory as aid us in softening own-will, then we may be humbly grateful. But glad willing away of self that the will of God, so far as it can be discerned, may become what we will—that is the basic condition. [8]

It is not our will to be happy that makes us happy. It is that we will to be God's person, that we will to be wholly obedient, that we will to seek his completion in us, that brings happiness. Jesus said, "I have come down from heaven not to do my will but to do the will of him who sent me" (John 6:38). His friends do the same.

Is It Well With Your Soul?

Was Jesus happy? I think he was, not because he did what we call "happy" things but because he knew who he was and did what he was sent to Earth to do. The dedication of the will is not just a matter of being better equipped, better educated, better trained, and having better opportunities; but through the Holy Spirit it is determining to live obediently in the perfect will of God.

Happiness goes with holiness. The soul is the God-breathed part of us that distinguishes a human being from all the rest of creation. We are uniquely and purposely created for holiness, happiness, and peace.

People don't ask it very often of each other, but they should because it is the most important question, the only one with eternal dimensions: "Is it well with your soul?" We need to ask that. It is a reminder of what is important.

We ask, "How are you?" "How is business?" "How is the family?" We even ask, "How is your car running?" We need to be asking, "Is it well with your soul?"

Kelly said:

The life that intends to be wholly obedient, wholly submissive, wholly listening, is astonishing in its completeness. Its joys are ravishing, its peace profound, its humility the deepest, its power world-shaking, its love enveloping, its simplicity that of a trusting child. It is the life and power in which the prophets and apostles lived. It is the life and power of Jesus of Nazareth, who knew that "When thine eye is single, thy whole body also is full of light" (Luke 11:34, KJV). [9]

We come into peace and happiness when we give the soul back to him. He alone has right of ownership. Through his redemption the soul is purchased with the price that is higher than any price ever paid for anything—the shed blood of Jesus. The soul comes once more as the prodigal son did—to its proper home—and begins to live "at home" in a secure and expanding life.

The first act of the soul is the act of surrender. But it is not a single act; it is a continuing act. Let it always be that act throughout all of life. For the happy person is the surrendered person, the one who belongs knowingly and intentionally to God.

Because we are not fragmented beings and because we are not just matter or emotion but both and more, the happiness that is ours is a happiness that is central to all that life is. William Law said:

If, therefore, we are to live unto God at any time, or in any place, we are to live unto Him at all times, and in all places. If we are to use any thing as the gift of God, we are to use every thing as His gift. If we are to do any thing by strict rules of reason and piety, we are to do every thing in the same manner. Because reason, and wisdom, and piety, are as much the best things at all times, and in all places, as they are the best things at any time or in any place. [10]

And then he added:

He therefore is the devout man, who lives no longer to his own will, or the way and spirit of the world, but to the sole will of God; who considers God in every thing, who serves God in every thing, who makes all the parts of his common life parts of piety, by doing every thing in the Name of God, and under such rules as are conformable to His glory.[11]

You do not function in parts; you are a whole. Your life encompasses all that you are. Every minute is experienced by the "all" of you. Your difficulties cannot be compartmentalized; neither can your joys. If your situation changes in any way, it changes for your whole person. If you face a responsibility or a task or an adventure, you face it not in segments of yourself but with your whole being. If you fall into failure, it is not just the failure of your mind or your will or your body; it is a failure of you.

We live a life that is new every breathing second. Therefore every second is holy—for every second is his. In knowing that, we can realize the larger dimensions of "happy" because we know it is a product of our total life in him.

Happiness is beyond my understanding of what happiness is, just as God is beyond my understanding of who God is. But if I desire to live with God on his terms and in his way to the best of my understanding, I will have God and I will have his happiness. Enter into this holy life and you will enter into the happy life, for he is the Source of both. Don't settle for anything less. Focus on him. Run the race he sets before you. Look toward eternity and go with Christ.

Philip Doddridge had his eyes focused that way. He said:

ETERNITY! ETERNITY! ETERNITY! Carry the view of it about with you, if it be possible, through every hour of waking life; and be fully persuaded that you have no business, no interest in life, that is inconsistent with it: for whatsoever would be injurious in this view, is not your business, is not your interest.[12]

Come, live a holy life. What is there that keeps you from it? Certainly God doesn't keep you from it. He wants that life for you more than you could ever want it for yourself, for he understands all that it will mean to you. He designed you to have it. He redeemed you to have it. He lives for you to have it.

24

Living Under the Smile of God

■ ■ ■

Alone in a hotel restaurant in Nagoya, Japan, I sat watching the fish swimming in a little stream outside the dining room window. The Japanese, in an artistic, creative way, often surround a hotel with plantings and streams. It gives a pastoral feeling even when the hotel is situated in the midst of factories and commercial buildings.

One hotel in Tokyo has gardens and streams placed in a tiny area, giving a feeling of spaciousness. An Osaka hotel has a waterfall, creating the appearance of a deep forest even though directly behind the waterfall, out of sight, is a factory. The stream from the waterfall flows down through greenery, right into the lounge of the hotel.

But there in Nagoya, I watched the fish. They were all colors. Some were red, some blue, some gold, some green, and some were even mottled, having many colors. They swam leisurely, and as I sat watching them I sensed a calm come over me. They gave a comforting mental change from the worries of a hectic day. They were beautiful fish—but they were carp!

How can scavenger fish like carp be beautiful? These were. I had always thought that if I had to be a fish I would want to be a rainbow trout or something tropical and exotic. But there they were, ordinary carp to whom God had given beautiful colors to make them esthetically pleasing to watch.

Most of us are ordinary too—like carp. Yet just as God can take an ordinary carp and give it the beautiful hues of tropical fish, he can do the same with us.

I may be just a carp, but I can be beautiful to watch. Maybe I'm just a carp, but I can bring something uplifting into drab lives. I may not be an "exotic species," but I can have an influence on people even if all I ever do is "swim" by.

God made me. To many I may seem to be an ordinary piece of creation, but I'm not. There is beauty in me because God put it there.

Christians may be "ordinary" or live in plain or even ugly settings, but by the touch of God they can be beautiful to all who are around. That beauty, even in its silent passing near by, brings peace. It gives people the hope that "maybe God can do something beautiful in me too."

In Nagoya, the fish swam quietly. But their influence gave me a different perspective on my surroundings and my day. If God can do that with a carp for me, what can he do with me for others?

A carp can point to the beauty of God, and give peace. I want to do that too. And I know I can as I live under, and live enjoying, the wonderful smile of God.

Isn't It Time?

God loves you. You know that he does. Let him do what he wants to do in your life; let him express that love for you. Isn't it time you started living every day—with good times and the bad—under the smile of God, being his friend? Isn't it time?

In Exodus 23:20 God said, "See, I am sending an angel ahead of you to guard you along the way and to bring you to the place I have prepared."

Here is a promise that none of us can ignore. This is God's Word to his own people. He will guard us; he will bring us into the place which he has prepared. There is an assurance here of the leadership of God. He will do with us and for us what we cannot do for ourselves. We could never adequately guard ourselves. Not on the streets, not in the world, not in our relationships to other people. But God has sent his angels, his ministering angels, to help us. "For he will command his angels concerning you to guard you in all your ways" (Psalm 91:11).

He provides the protection for us and he has a place for us. We don't have to run around seeking God's protection or agonize if we don't see the angels who are around us. We have one responsibility, to be obedient to the One who sends his angels. God's Word promises that he will guard me and lead me into the place he has prepared for me—even if I am "only" a carp.

In surrender, in the refusal to be rebellious, is the key to the door of God's caring love. In Numbers 1:54 we read: "So all these instructions of the Lord to Moses were put into effect" (TLB). These children of Israel did exactly what God told them to do; they obeyed every order given by God. He could lead them because he knew that they would carry out his orders.

Did they understand every command that God gave? Probably not. Did they know the outcome of every order? They couldn't possibly have known. They had one objective—to obey. God gave them orders; they did what he said.

We have our orders too. God knows what he is doing with us. He knows the thoughts he thinks toward us (Jeremiah 29:11). He has an expected end for us; he loves us with an everlasting love. Our job is to obey him.

Freedom in Obedience

H. C. G. Moule said:

Let my mental habit be so full of "my Master" that I shall be on the watch, always and everywhere, to be used by Him, or to "stand and wait" close to Him, as he pleases; only always knowing myself to be His property, and glad indeed so to be. [1]

There is freedom in that obedience, great freedom. We don't struggle anymore. We walk, we run, we act—on his terms, by his orders, for his sake. And we know as we do it that we are his. Jesus put it in terms that we can all understand: "You are my friends if you do what I command" (John 15:14). We are friends, obedient friends—and more than that, we are heirs of God and joint heirs with Christ. As heirs we are to obey. Let there be for all of us heirs life in fullness, a life as friends of God.

David said:

You love me! You are holding my right hand! You will keep on guiding me all my life with your wisdom and counsel; and afterwards receive me into the glories of heaven! Whom have I in heaven but you? And I desire no one on earth as much as you! My health fails; my spirits droop, yet God remains! He is the strength of my heart; he is mine forever!

But those refusing to worship God will perish, for he destroys those serving other gods.

But as for me, I get as close to him as I can! I have chosen him and I will tell everyone about the wonderful ways he rescues me (Psalm 73:23-28,TLB).

Jesus, by a miracle, provided a large catch of fish for his disciples. But they had to obey his command to draw it in. They even had to obey him when he told them where to cast their net. They did obey, and look what Jesus did! He invited them to haul in and cook their fish, yet he was the one who provided that meal.

Life is that way. When we obey him, he tells us where to cast the net. He gives to us abundantly, often more than we could ever ask. Our nets nearly break with his goodness. And he gives us the meal to share in, too. He does that for all of us. That biblical illustration of the fish tells far more than the story of one miracle; that illustration tells of the great care and concern God provides by helping us to do what we already know how to do. These men were all fishermen—not successful that night, but they were all fishermen. They knew how to cast nets, they knew how to haul in the fish, they knew what to do with the fish they caught. Jesus provided for the fishermen in their circumstances in a way that they understood best—he provided lots of fish.

God does that for us. He provides for us in our circumstances in a way that we understand best. Sometimes we look for the unusual while he provides his miracle in ordinary ways. As he did for those professional fishermen, he gives us our provisions every day; he makes it happen. And, as he did for the disciples on the shore, in the meal that he provides he may give not a banquet but a few fish. The point is, he does it. When we see the substance of life like that under the guidance of his hand, we begin to understand the daily miracle of living with him and we have cause for daily thanksgiving. Martyn Lloyd-Jones said:

It is God Himself who gives us life, and the body in which we live it; and if He has done that we can draw this deduction, that His purpose with respect to us will be fulfilled. God never leaves unfinished any work He will most surely fulfill. And therefore we come back to this, that there is a plan for every life in the mind of God. [2]

Am I a Hypocrite?

As I write this, it is Saturday morning. I woke early. In fact, it is 2:30 A.M. Why I woke now, I don't know. I think about some deadlines that are pushing at me. I can't touch them anyway until I make long distance calls on Monday morning. I think about a lot of other things, as we all do when we can't sleep.

Finally, getting up, I came down here to my basement study to work on this final chapter. The things I had written before haunt me. I wonder, am I a hypocrite to write about living under the smile of God when I wake up at 2:30 A.M.? Am I one who worries just as those who do not have a heavenly Father to trust? I think about failure, frustration, the lack of what I'd like to see accomplished in my life, and I wonder about me, about God, about his smile.

I reread the opening story in this chapter and think about the carp, and me, and the blemishes on what God would like to make beautiful. My mind begins to wander as I think about another event in another Japanese city and what it taught me about myself when one day I unintentionally embarrassed a gentle Japanese floor manager in an Osaka hotel.

Embarrassed by a Dead Leaf

I was standing outside a manager's office on the fourteenth floor of the hotel waiting for an appointment when I noticed a beautiful flowering plant on a desk. So I walked over to admire it and said, "It is very pretty." The manager looked at me, then at the plant, and suddenly his eyes showed alarm for he saw what I had not seen. There was a dead leaf on the stem.

He was embarrassed. Quickly he stripped off the dead leaf and moved the plant behind a lamp. By his words, which I did not understand, and his actions, which I did understand, he was showing that he was ashamed. He was conscious that I had seen less than his best. His plant had a dead leaf on it. And all I could do, as I realized what he was thinking, was to back away and repeat, "It is a very pretty plant."

We bring shame to people in so many ways. Often it is without any intention of ever doing so. Yet their embarrassment is not something that we can control; it is in the other person's mind. The other person is seeing or feeling something that we do not perceive. If only I could have convinced that quiet, gentle man that I was not drawing attention to a fault, that I really did admire his plant.

Sometimes we are ashamed ourselves by something that another person says to us, not because he or she wants to shame us but because the feeling of shame is already harbored inside. If people express what they think is an innocent thought or observation about me, sometimes I am ashamed. For I know that there are "dead leaves" in my life too. Knowing that can mar my attitude, the way I speak, and can even make me avoid others. It can mar my witness too; I hide for shame that someone will see my "dead leaf."

And yet one dead leaf doesn't mar the beauty of a whole plant. Neither does error, real or imagined, destroy the beauty of a believer. It is important that any flaw be taken away, for it is a shameful thing to see the "dead leaves" in our lives and leave them there. But there is no cause for shame if we want to get rid of them and do. When we go to God about "that leaf," he trims the plant and removes the shame. That's the kind of considerate Gardener he is.

God sees the overall beauty of the believer in Christ. If flaws are there, they are not a reason for hiding or withdrawal. The flaws are to be stripped away, but the flower, the beauty of the believer, can still be displayed.

Shame Has Value

Zephaniah the prophet said, "The unrighteous know no shame" (Zephaniah 3:5)—and that's true. But the Christian is not "unrighteous." The Christian is one who has been made righteous in Jesus Christ. That's why Christians feel shame when unbelievers often do not. Because Christians know the beauty of holiness, they know when they have strayed from it. The unjust do not know holiness, do not know that they themselves are marred.

They feel no shame.

Shame has value if it is allowed to have its improving work in the life of believers. It comes not to make them withdraw or feel embarrassed, it comes to remind them of their greater beauty in Christ, a beauty not in themselves but a beauty of holiness that needs to be displayed because "it is no longer I who live, but Christ lives in me" (Galatians 2:20, NASB). That "Christ in me" life is not to be hidden by shame.

This morning, in this quiet house, with the rest of the family asleep, as I pray, there are thoughts I have to put into action. I must as a Christian be quick to strip off the dead leaves, but I can't as a Christian think that dead leaves destroy the beauty of the plant. A beautiful plant is still that, even with an occasional untrimmed, unsightly, and somewhat distracting dead leaf. As a believer I can and must display the true beauty that is placed in me, allowing the Gardener to find and trim what is unsightly and dead.

Beauty in the Work of God

The beauty of believers is never in themselves; it is in the work of God. We show his beauty as he opens up the flower in us. We neither hide our beauty nor assume that we can promote it as our own. It is not ours because we are not our own.

The plant on that man's desk in Osaka should not have been hidden behind a lamp. Once he trimmed the dead leaf he should have pushed that plant forward for me to see. He hid it, but he didn't have to. He was ashamed, but he shouldn't have been.

We don't have to be ashamed either. Just as that floor manager identified the ugly part of his plant and got rid of it, so day by day the same must be true in my life and yours. Why should any dead part mar the beauty of God's plant? God made us and set us out for the world to see. Beautiful and on display, the Christian needs to be seen. God is not ashamed of the beauty he gives us. We are not to be ashamed either. God plants, trims, waters, tenderly encourages and, most of all, provides the warmth of his smile. We can live under that warm, life-giving smile of God. It is the only place where we can provide beauty for the world to see. In a not very pretty world, God has in us something to show.

Be what God made you to be—come, live a happy life. Come,

live a holy, obedient, disciplined life. Come, enjoy the closeness of God. Come, know the pleasure of being his friend.

Notes

Chapter 1   Sand Castles Don't Last

1. *Minneapolis Tribune* , July 21, 1978, 1C.
2. John Bunyan, "Of the Boy and His Butterfly," from Roger C. Palms, *Upon a Penny Loaf* (Minneapolis: Bethany House Publishers, 1978), 33.
3. *Minneapolis Star*, November 19, 1979, 1A.
4. Ibid., 8A.
5. A. H. McNeile, *Discipleship* (London: Society for Promoting Christian Knowledge, 1923), 51.

Chapter 2   Winning

1. C. S. Lewis, *Mere Christianity* (New York: MacMillan Publishing Co., 1952), 124.
2. G. Steinberger, *In the Footprints of the Lamb*, trans. Bernhard Christensen (Minneapolis: Bethany Fellowship, Inc., © 1936, The Lutheran Free Church Publishing Company), 39.
3. Richard Baxter, *The Saints' Everlasting Rest* (London: The Epworth Press, 1962), 85.
4. From *The Dynamics of Spiritual Life: An Evangelical Theology of Renewal* by Richard Lovelace ©1979 by InterVarsity Christian Fellowship of the USA and used by permission of InterVarsity Press, P.O. Box 1400, Downers Grove, IL, 94.
5. Steinberger, *Footprints*, 38–39.
6. Baxter, *Everlasting Rest*, 100.

Chapter 3   Starting Over

1. A. W. Tozer, *The Pursuit of God* (Harrisburg, Pennsylvania: Christian Publications, Inc., 1948), 15–16.
2. From *Celebration of Discipline* by Richard J. Foster. Copyright © 1978 by Richard J. Foster. Reprinted by permission of Harper & Row, Publishers, Inc., 79.
3. McNeile, *Discipleship*, 94.
4. "Robert Runcie: The Mustard Seed Man," *Crusade,* January, 1980.
5. Ibid.
6. *Decision,* June 1980, 13.
7. McNeile, *Discipleship*, 71.
8. Ibid., 84–85.

Chapter 4   Another Way to Live

1. Lewis, *Mere Christianity*, 75.
2. Lovelace, *Dynamics*, 19.
3. James H. McConkey, *The Surrendered Life* (Kalamazoo, Michigan: Master's Press, Inc., 1977), 45.
4. Emile Cailliet, *Journey Into Light* (Grand Rapids, Michigan: Zondervan Publishing House, © 1968), 49. Used by permission.
5. Thomas R. Kelly, *A Testament of Devotion* (New York and London: Harper & Row, Publishers, 1941), 29.

Chapter 5   I Don't See God Smiling

1. Francis A. Schaeffer, *True Spirituality* (Wheaton, Illinois: Tyndale House Publishers, 1971), 43.
2. Ibid., p. 153.

Chapter 6   When I Want to Be Honest With God

1. Harold B. Walker, *To Conquer Loneliness* (New York: Harper & Row, 1966), 24.
2. David A. Redding, *The Couch and the Altar* (New York: J. B. Lippincott Co., 1968), 57.

3. Josiah Royce, *The Problem of Christianity*, vol. 1. (New York: The Macmillan Co., 1913), 399–400.

Chapter 7 Praying When Prayer Doesn't Seem to Work

1. Thomas à Kempis, *The Imitation of Christ* (Great Britain: William Collins Sons & Co., Ltd., 1957), 174.
2. J. Oswald Sanders, *Prayer Power Unlimited* (Chicago: The Moody Press, 1977), 74.

Chapter 8 When I Am Pressured to Do What Is Wrong

1. H. C. G. Moule, *Thoughts on Christian Sanctity* (Chicago: Moody Press, n.d.), 15.
2. Reprinted with permission of Macmillan Publishing Company from *Creation and Fall/Temptation* by Dietrich Bonhoeffer. Copyright © 1966 by SCM Press, Ltd., 99.
3. Ibid., 127.
4. Ibid., 116.

Chapter 9 Becoming Free

1. Abraham Kuyper, *Calvinism* (New York: Fleming H. Revell Co., n.d.), 89.
2. C. Roy Angell, *Iron Shoes* (Nashville: Broadman Press, 1953, Renewal 1981), 59. All rights reserved. Used by permission.
3. *The Watchman–Examiner*, April 12, 1962, 1.
4. Kuyper, *Calvinism*, 57.

Chapter 10 At Last! I Can Say No

1. Linette Martin, *Hans Rookmaaker: A Biography* (Downers Grove, Illinois: InterVarsity Press, 1979), 129.
2. *Western Asceticism, The History of Christian Classics*, vol. 12., comp. Owen Chadwick (Philadelphia: Westminster Press, 1958), 50.
3. Ibid., 62.
4. Ibid., 42.

5. William Law, *A Serious Call to a Devout and Holy Life* (London: Society for Promoting Christian Knowledge, 1910), 148–49.
6. McConkey, *Surrendered Life*, 3.
7. Foster, *Celebration*, 2.
8. *The Sun*, Cambridge, England, February 11, 1980, 7.
9. Thomas Merton, *The Monastic Journey* (Garden City, New York: Image Books, A Division of Doubleday & Company, Inc., 1978), 99.
10. McNeile, *Discipleship*, 17.

Chapter 11 My Life, My Gain

1. McConkey, *Surrendered Life*, 16.
2. Ibid., p. 7
3. Kelly, *Testament of Devotion*, 34.
4. Ibid., p. 42
5. Ibid., p. 43
6. A. W. Tozer, "The Cry of a Man of God." *Challenge Weekly*, October 5, 1979, 24. (Auckland, New Zealand). The article is from his message on the day of his ordination.
7. Martin Luther, "Letters of Spiritual Counsel," *The Library of Christian Classics*, vol. 18, ed. and trans. Theodore G. Tappert (Philadelphia: The Westminster Press, 1955), 92.
8. Kelly, *Testament of Devotion*, 97.
9. Law, *A Serious Call*, 227.
10. Ibid., p. 150

Chapter 12 Regardless

1. Malcolm Smith, *Blood Brothers in Christ* (Old Tappan, New Jersey: Fleming H. Revell Co., 1975), 112.
2. Brian Jones, "Perspective: The Basics of Islam," *Minneapolis Tribune*, February 6, 1980, 7A.
3. Ibid.
4. Reprinted with permission of Macmillan Publishing Company from *The Cost of Discipleship* by Dietrich Bonhoeffer. Copyright © 1959 by SCM Press, Ltd., 32.
5. Cameron V. Thompson, *The Master Secrets of Prayer* (Lincoln, Nebraska: Back to the Bible, © 1959, Good News Broadcasting Association, Inc.), 27.
6. Bonhoeffer, *Cost of Discipleship*, 193.

7. Ibid., p. 137
8. Hudson T. Armerding, *Leadership* (Wheaton, Illinois: Tyndale House Publishers, Inc., 1978), 153.
9. Roger C. Palms, "Holiness: The Good Life." *Decision*, April 1980, 9.
10. McConkey, *Surrendered Life*, 13.
11. Philip Doddridge, *The Rise and Progress of Religion in the Soul* (Philadelphia: Presbyterian Board of Publication, n.d.), 258.
12. Ibid., 172–73.

Chapter 13 When People Don't Like Me

1. Thomas à Kempis, *Imitation of Christ*, 86.

Chapter 15 And God Will

1. Cailliet, *Journey*, 49. Used by permission.
2. McNeile, *Discipleship*, 38.
3. Lewis, *Mere Christianity*, 176.
4. Baxter, *Everlasting Rest*, 79.
5. John Haggai, *How to Win Over Loneliness* (Nashville: Thomas Nelson, Publishers, 1979), 178.
6. Doddridge, *Rise and Progress*, 263.
7. Kelly, *Testament of Devotion*, 39.
8. E. M. Bounds, *Power Through Prayer* (Chicago: Moody Press, 1979), 127.
9. Thompson, *Master Secrets*, 61.

Chapter 16 Able to Be Trusted

1. McNeile, *Discipleship*, 6–7.
2. F. P. Harton, *The Elements of the Spiritual Life: A Study in Ascetical Theology* (London: Society for Promoting Christian Knowledge, 1934), 3.
3. Lewis, *Mere Christianity*, 73.
4. H. A. Ironside, *The Way of Peace* (New York: American Tract Society, 1940), 177.
5. Dr. Ludv. Munthe/HGB/Revised Draft: Reaching Secularists/ 6/21/80. Conference on World Evangelization, Pattaya, Thailand., 20.
6. Baxter, *Everlasting Rest*, 98.

7. Harton, *Elements*, 309–10.

Chapter 17   Love Giver

1. George Laird Hunt, *Rediscovering the Church* (New York: Association Press, 1956), 140.
2. Law, *A Serious Call*, 341.
3. Hunt, *Rediscovering*, 142.
4. Law, *A Serious Call*, 142.
5. Floyd Shacklock, *Man of Two Revolutions: The Story of Justo Gonzales*. (New York: Friendship Press, 1969), 59–60.
6. Thompson, *Master Secrets*, 45–46.
7. Cailliet, *Journey*, 104–105. Used by permission.

Chapter 18   The Way to Inner Peace

1. Steinberger, *Footprints*, 15.
2. Hannah Whitall Smith: *Philadelphia Quaker: The Letters of Hannah Whitall Smith*, ed. Logan Pearsall Smith (New York: Harcourt, Brace and Company, 1950), 13.
3. Kelly, *Testament of Devotion*, 30.
4. Ibid., 69.
5. W. Y. Fullerton, *The Legacy of Bunyan* (London: Ernest Benn Limited, 1928), 84.

Chapter 19   In the Joy of Ascending Moments

1. Kuyper, *Calvinism*, 53.
2. Sanders, *Prayer Power*, 7.
3. Ibid., 6.
4. Douglas V. Steere, *Doors Into Life* (New York: Harper & Brothers, 1948), 19.

Chapter 20   Growing When I Am All Alone

1. Walker, *To Conquer Loneliness*, 148.
2. Ibid., 149.
3. Ibid., 19–20.

4. Ibid., 22.

Chapter 22   If I Should Die Before I Wake

1. S. F. Marsh, "Thoughts About My Death," *Christianity Today*, February 1, 1963, 23.
2. Ibid., 23.
3. Ludwig Wittgenstein, *Tractatus Logico–Philosophicus* (London: Routledge & Keagan Paul LTD, 1922), 185.
4. Roger C. Palms, "Event," *Decision*, April 1982, 13.
5. Mel White, *Margaret of Molokai* (Waco, Texas: Word Books, 1981), 185.
6. Ibid., 183–84.
7. Thomas à Kempis, *Imitation of Christ*, 75.

Chapter 23   Come, Live a Happy Life

1. Bonhoeffer, *Cost of Discipleship*, 169.
2. Ibid., 73.
3. Lewis, *Mere Christianity*, 175.
4. Haggai, *Loneliness*, 93.
5. Lewis: *Mere Christianity*, 100–101.
6. Baxter, *Everlasting Rest*, 109.
7. Ibid., p. 63–64.
8. Kelly, *Testament of Devotion*, 25.
9. Ibid., p. 54
10. Law, *A Serious Call,*, 60.
11. Ibid., p. 1
12. Doddridge, *The Rise and Progress*, 218.

Chapter 24   Living Under the Smile of God

1. Moule, *Christian Sanctity*, 51.
2. D. Martyn Lloyd–Jones, *Studies in the Sermon on the Mount*, vol. 2., (Grand Rapids, Michigan: Wm. B. Eerdmans Publishing Co., 1960), 115.